My Twelve Years with
John F. Kennedy

My Twelve Years wit

by EVELYN LINCO

Personal Secretary
the Presid

ohn F. Kennedy

VID McKAY COMPANY, INC.

York

With Love
To CAROLINE and JOHN

Acknowledgment

I owe the original impetus toward writing this book to my old and trusted friends Jack and Blanche Kelly and the temerity to attempt it to the encouragement and helpful advice of Ray de Member and the late Basile Papdopoulos. I also want to express my appreciation to Marie Smith, Peter Rona, Tim Larkin, and Howard Cady, for their invaluable assistance in reducing and organizing the original manuscript to what I hope are readable portions covering my long and active life with the late President Kennedy. To Ruth Meehan, who patiently assisted in typing the manuscript, I say thanks.

To my husband, Abe, my debt is greatest of all.

EVELYN LINCOLN

Contents

ix

PART I

CHAPTER 1

As I Remember Him

SOMEWHERE a long way off a bell was ringing. It kept ringing and getting closer. Finally it completely shattered my fitful sleep, but the weariness that made my body seem a lump of metal was still there. Automatically I pushed the alarm button on the clock, slowly swung my legs out of bed, and came fully awake as the soles of my feet touched the floor.

Later, as I went to the office, it seemed impossible that nothing had changed. The streets were filled with cars, and people were rushing to work as usual. The faces that came into focus at the bus stops as my car sped along were the same faces I had seen so many times before. I looked at the back of Joe Giordano's neck and it reassured me. Joe had driven me down Sixteenth Street into Pennsylvania Avenue and to my White House office so many times during the last three years.

This morning we arrived, as usual, slightly before eight o'clock, and I was at my desk a few minutes later. But this time it was in a different office in a different building. The old familiar objects were there—the President's padded rocking chair, his leather desk chair, the Presidential flag, the books and pictures—but they were shoved against the wall or stuffed into cartons. It was like seeing all the letters in your name arranged in a different way. You knew they were the same letters, but it wasn't your name.

I caught myself wondering, What would the President think

3

if he should walk in and see all of this? I couldn't stand seeing the things he loved so much in a state of confusion, and I started searching through the boxes, looking for the picture of Caroline sitting solemnly in his Harvard chair. It had been taken on one of her evening visits to his office, and it was one of his favorite pictures. I wanted to bring it out to hide the ugly bareness of the room. I guess I wanted also to reassure myself again that nothing had changed. But I couldn't find the picture.

Searching through one of the cartons, I rubbed my finger against the razor edge of a sheet of stiff White House stationery. As I squeezed a drop of blood from the hairline cut, the sharp pain brought me back to reality. With a sudden rush, for the first time, I fully realized that in that horrible split second four days before in Dallas all my dreams during the last twelve years had been shattered, and those years, like an untended boat, were in danger of drifting away.

I sat down at my desk and looked out the window. Where once I could see the wedding-cake architecture of the old War-Navy-State Department Building, now I was sitting in that very building looking toward the White House, where I had lived so many hours filled with hard work, historic events, and happy times. I thought of the man for whom I had worked, once so alive and eager to accomplish, now lying silent under the sod just two miles away. I had thought there could not be any more tears to shed, but they began to come again.

Yet, as I sat and wept, I felt that he would come dashing through the door any moment to ask me about the mail. He almost seemed to get his energy and inspiration from the letters he received, and he always read the ones that criticized him because he felt it was from those that he learned the most.

A kaleidoscope of memories as I had seen him during the twelve years he was my boss tumbled through my brain as I sat there that morning. I could see his swift grace, his easy smile, his eagerness to crowd as much living as possible into every single hour. I could almost see his proud head held high,

4

his eyes fixed firmly on the goals—sometimes seemingly impossible goals—he set for himself and all those around him.

Those goals became my own and I dedicated my life to helping him attain them. Each day became more exciting and thrilling than the last. Every challenge was more welcome as the days swiftly sped by and scores more who believed as he did joined in the race. It was exciting, satisfying, and fun. But it was not always easy.

Soon after I went to work for John Fitzgerald Kennedy I learned that if he wanted something done, he wanted it done immediately. If he selected you to do it, it was because you were on the job and near him at the time. If you proved up to the task, he called on you again. If you were slow on performance, the next time he asked someone else to do it. If he thought you were taking a little longer than necessary to get the job done, he would ask you about the delay. If you had a logical answer, he was satisfied. But if you said, "I haven't had time to do it," once again he would lose confidence in you.

He always wanted perfection. If I ever said, "I'm sorry, Senator, I couldn't get the reservation for you," he would say, "Why?" It didn't make any difference what the reason might be, he would still say, "Well, call someone else," or, "Let me talk to them." I soon learned that I could not take "No" for an answer when trying to fill his requests.

He liked to have the people around him available at all times. When he called, whether it was ten o'clock in the morning or twelve o'clock at night, he wanted to be able to reach you. If you were at the beach or at a night club and couldn't be reached, he was upset, and once again he would turn to someone else. You had to earn his confidence all over again.

President Kennedy had a practice of giving instructions to two or three people. Each person was unaware that the others were working on the same problem. In this way, he was sure to get an answer. The person who was the most efficient and most interested in doing the task promptly would be given more and more responsibility. When he was beginning to work

5

on a speech, he would ask several people to prepare some remarks for a specific occasion, then he would draw ideas from all their proposals. Yet his speechwriters were rarely aware that he had asked others to prepare material on the same subject.

If someone he relied upon asked for a few days off, he would say, "I would like to take a vacation, too." That was his way of registering his displeasure at not being able to reach them. It was not that he felt they did not merit a vacation, it was only his way of expressing his reliance upon them.

When he was in a mood to talk, he would stop by my desk and question me. If I didn't notice the twinkle in his eye, I might not catch that he was needling me. If I didn't respond to his kidding, he didn't get disturbed, but would either go back into his office or pick up a newspaper and start to read.

He wanted to be friendly with everyone who worked for him, and had a way of putting people at ease with his wit. He was also very careful to introduce anyone near him to the man or woman to whom he was talking. He wanted people around him to feel his comradeship.

In his personal life, the President had a routine he liked to follow without deviation or interruption. Immediately upon awakening he wanted the morning newspapers. When he was in Palm Beach at his father's house, he would come out to the dining room to find the papers neatly arranged at the left side of his table setting. As soon as he told the cook what he wanted for breakfast, he would start reading, and he did not want to talk or be disturbed until he had finished both the papers and his breakfast. When he was in the White House, he followed much the same routine, with breakfast in his bedroom, but he would permit interruptions by his two children, Caroline and John, who were always a joy to him. But their nurse, Maud Shaw, was careful to make certain it was the right time for the children to go bounding into his bedroom, and that time was usually just as he was finishing his papers and breakfast.

There were many other things that I can remember; but most

6

of all I remember his love for the finer things in life, not only for himself but for all mankind.

This was the man I picked in 1952 to be my boss and to be a future President of the United States, although I had neither met nor seen him at the time.

CHAPTER 2

Making the Choice

John Fitzgerald Kennedy was a thirty-five-year-old Democratic Congressman from Massachusetts serving his third term in the United States House of Representatives when I decided I was going to work for him. I often saw his picture in the papers and read stories about his activities as a member of the District of Columbia Committee and the Education and Labor Committee of the House. There were stories also about his independence. He refused to go along with the Democratic leadership if he felt they were wrong, and he voted with the Republicans on issues where he felt they were right. He seemed to be working for the people and that was what I liked about him. But most of all, I was impressed by what he had to say in his speeches and his obvious sincerity.

I was doing double duty on Capitol Hill in those days and had an opportunity to read some of his speeches and press releases. During the daytime I was on the clerical staff of Congressman E. L. Forrester of Georgia. At night I would stop by the print shop run by a long-time family friend, Truman Ward, who had the title of Majority Clerk of the House of Representatives when the Democrats were in power, and Minority Clerk when they were not. Congressmen sent their speeches and newsletters to Mr. Ward's print shop to be reproduced, and I

7

sometimes contributed my services by running the robotypers when he was especially rushed. I also liked to see what the Congressmen were telling their constituents about the problems of the day. Some would bring down almost letter-perfect manuscripts, while other Congressmen expected us to decipher a maze of arrows and spider webs. We could only hope we were doing it right. When we guessed wrong, Mr. Ward would hear from them.

The work in Congressman Forrester's office, where I was the third girl from the top, was not particularly demanding. The heavy responsibilities fell on the two girls ahead of me. I enjoyed helping out in Mr. Ward's office and I considered myself lucky to be working on Capitol Hill.

My husband, Harold (Abe) Lincoln, was also working on the Hill on the staff of one of the House committees, so it was almost as if we were working together. He had been teaching government at New York University, where he was also working on his doctorate, when the offer came to go to Washington. At the time I was very happy in our little Greenwich Village apartment, but Abe's offer was too good to pass up, and it would give us a chance to be near my parents, who were then living in Washington.

My father had served in Congress as a Democrat from Nebraska and had returned to the state to serve in its first unicameral legislature, for which he had written the rules. But it was difficult for a Democrat to win every election in a Republican district in Nebraska, so he had returned to Washington and worked in the Department of Agriculture.

Since he and Abe found working on the Hill so interesting, I decided I would try it. After several days of looking, I found there were no jobs available in the Congressional offices and was about to give up when Mr. Ward offered me a clerical job in his office. I had studied law at the same time Abe was going to law school, but I still had a year to go to get my law degree. While making the rounds, I had learned that a Congressman might approve of my college education, my interest in government, and my knowledge of law, but he would always hire the girl who could type and take shorthand rather than the one who offered Plato and Plutarch. So I taught myself to type and I was soon able to take a fast but rather ragged shorthand that only distantly resembled Gregg.

It was while working in Mr. Ward's office that I heard about the opening in Congressman Forrester's office. As soon as I could get away I rushed to a telephone and called his office to apply for the job. Someone there told me, "Unless you're from Georgia and available to spend time in the district during adjournment, we really can't use you. Sorry." I was sorry too, but I was also persistent. I pleaded for, and got, permission to come up and talk to the Congressman's secretary. She was courteous, but not very helpful. As I saw the door finally closing on any possibility of working in that office, I asked, "If you don't want me, do you know of someone who does?"

Reluctantly she asked me to come back the next morning and speak to the Congressman. I had no sooner been introduced to him the next morning when he started dictating a long letter full of legal jargon. I hurriedly transcribed the letter, worrying meanwhile that Mr. Ward would be looking for me and I, instead of getting a new job, would lose the one I had.

The next morning I received a call from Congressman Forrester's office. They wanted me! At last I had my foot in the door. I was going to get experience in a Congressional office. I had a lot to learn, not only about the routine, but also about Georgia.

My desk was near the door, and, though the constituents coming in stopped at my desk first, I tried to be as inconspicuous as possible because I couldn't really understand their way of speaking and I didn't want them to hear my Nebraska accent. My duties consisted mostly of filing, taking an occasional letter from the Congressman, and reading the birth notices that appeared in the newspapers from his district. When I located a birth announcement, I would send the new parents baby books issued by the Department of Agriculture. Most Congressmen

9

do this to win votes between campaigns, and to build a mailing list.

It was apparent the people of Georgia's third district loved their Congressman, whom they called "Tic" because of his short stature. ("He's no bigger than a tic.") Everything was quiet and peaceful in our office.

As I continued to drop into Truman Ward's office, I became more and more engrossed in some of the ideas that appeared in speeches I was typing.

One evening after reading some of the newsletters of those fighting Congressmen, I went home and immediately announced to my amazed husband, "I'm going to work for the next President of the United States."

He said, "Eisenhower will be mighty pleased to have your support, I'm sure. Have you told him yet?"

"No, silly, not Eisenhower."

Things looked very good for General Eisenhower at that time and I can well understand why Abe was mystified. I explained, "It won't be this President, but the next one, the one who will follow the man elected this fall."

Abe knew a lot more about politics than I did, but he was still curious to know whom I had in mind. He was disappointed when I said, "Well, I really don't know who he is yet. But that is the one I'm going to work for. I've decided there is no use settling for anything less."

I told him I was going to study the question thoroughly and pick someone then in Congress who seemed to have what it takes to be President. A few weeks later, after watching the work coming into Mr. Ward's shop, I went home and told Abe I had almost come to a decision.

"I've decided that it is going to be young Franklin D. Roosevelt, Jr. or the Congressman from Massachusetts, John F. Kennedy."

He agreed that both seemed to have great futures but said, "There are a lot of other able men in Congress. Don't be too hasty."

Several weeks later I announced at dinner that I had made my decision between the two. "The man I'm hoping to work for, and the next President, after the one elected this fall, is John F. Kennedy."

I explained why I picked Kennedy. I had heard that he was planning to run for the Senate against Henry Cabot Lodge. Everyone considered Lodge, who was powerful in national politics as well as in Massachusetts, unbeatable. I told Abe, "If Kennedy takes on Lodge, he has courage. And if he wins, he will be on his way."

The more I thought about Kennedy's challenge of Lodge, the more I wanted to help in some way. I had learned from my work in Ward's shop that Kennedy's office was working on a book analyzing Lodge's voting record. "Maybe I could help on that," I thought.

One night I asked Abe if it would be all right if we didn't eat at home in the evenings for a while because I was determined to work for Congressman Kennedy. He understood and didn't object.

"Are you going to stop working for Tic Forrester?" he asked.

"No, I've arranged to work for Kennedy at night as a volunteer, so I'll just go on working for Tic during the day."

For several weeks after that, Abe and I would meet after work and walk down Independence Avenue to a row of drugstores and restaurants, where we would get a quick bite to eat. Then I'd rush off to work in Congressman Kennedy's office until close to midnight. Abe had work to do at the Library of Congress, so we rode home together.

This went on for two or three weeks, and I had not met Congressman Kennedy. My work was with Ted Reardon, his administrative assistant, who was preparing the book on Lodge. But one night, about six o'clock, I came in, sat at the desk I was using for research on the voting record of Lodge, and noticed that the light was on in the Congressman's office. I heard a rustle and thought perhaps it was Ted or Mary Davis, Kennedy's personal secretary. But when I heard a voice talking over the telephone,

I was sure it wasn't Ted Reardon. The Congressman was there.

All kinds of thoughts raced through my mind. Will he see me? What shall I say to him? My typewriter faced the door of his office; he couldn't help but see me when he came out. Then I heard footsteps coming across the room. I bent over my typewriter and kept working, hoping at the last minute he would not notice me. But I was so curious to see him, I looked up and there he was standing in front of my typewriter.

My first thought was, "He looks so young and thin." His gray suit seemed much too big for his frame and he kept pushing his hair off his forehead. He asked me, "What's your name? Where are you from? What are you typing? How long is it going to take you? Is the light all right? Do you have a comfortable chair?" As he talked he leafed through the papers on the desk.

After he had satisfied his curiosity about me and my work, he said, "Close the door when you leave," and he was gone.

I didn't see him again for several weeks. Then one day I went to his office to see if there might be some way to help a friend of mine from Massachusetts get a job as physical therapist with the Veterans Administration. I made the appointment for ten o'clock, but I got there a little early. While I was waiting for Ted Reardon, the Congressman came out. He saw me right away and called, "Miz Lincoln,* are you waiting to see me?"

I was about to answer when I saw he was leaning heavily on a cane. I was so surprised that I blurted out, "Did you hurt yourself?" I knew immediately that I had said the wrong thing because he stared at me and ignored my question. Embarrassed, I said quickly, "Oh, I don't want to bother you. I just came over to see about one of your constituents."

The next time I saw him, he was getting ready to leave town for Easter vacation. He stood dictating dozens of last-minute instructions to his secretary. As he passed me, he said, "Have a nice Easter." Then he turned to his secretary and said, "Oh, yes, one last thing. Easter Sunday." I could see the poor girl's

* From the first time to the last time it was always "Miz" Lincoln, although it will be written as "Mrs. Lincoln" in the pages that follow.

face fall. She was expecting a chore that would keep her working on Easter Sunday. "Yes, Easter Sunday," he repeated. Then, laughing, "You can take Easter Sunday off." And he was on his way.

The campaign was picking up speed, and the voting-record book was finished. I could have accepted their thanks and gone back to my regular work, but I wanted to continue working for Mr. Kennedy. So I volunteered for the dullest jobs they had, addressing envelopes and filing letters. I soon realized that most of the work on the campaign was being done from the headquarters on Kilby Street in Boston. The Congressman was spending as much time as he could in Massachusetts, traveling around the state speaking to anyone who would hold still.

In Washington they were counting him out. Lodge, people were saying, has had fourteen years in the Senate and has forgotten more than Kennedy will ever know. Why would anyone in his right mind want to vote for Kennedy instead of Lodge, they were asking.

Others figured that Kennedy was a lightweight. "He'll never win," I heard a supposedly friendly Democratic Congressman say. "Why, he's nothing but a playboy." There were whispers, too, about his health. "Did you know that he walks around on crutches most of the time?" "I heard that he has only six months to live." And all the while feelings were strong that Eisenhower would swamp the Democrats. "How could Kennedy possibly beat Lodge, the man who managed Eisenhower's campaign for the nomination?"

These statements made me angry. And I was frustrated, too. All the real work on the campaign was being done in Massachusetts, and there was no way I could be of much help in Washington.

Congress adjourned and Congressman Forrester asked me if I could come down and work in his office in Americus, Georgia, for about six weeks. I had never been to Georgia, and perhaps there would be enough work there to take my mind away from the worry about Congressman Kennedy's campaign. Abe drove

13

me down to Georgia, and I thought it had some of the most beautiful country I had ever seen. When he left me there and returned to Washington, I found myself wondering why I had accepted the invitation.

The people were as nice as they could be and the Congressman and his wife did everything possible to make my stay there pleasant, but I was completely out of touch with what was going on in Massachusetts. Adlai Stevenson, the Democratic Candidate for President, was giving Eisenhower a good fight, and I was hoping this would be of some help in Massachusetts. I thought Stevenson's speeches were masterful, and I never missed any of his television appearances, but I realized that Eisenhower seemed certain to win.

Several times I called Kennedy's Boston headquarters, but there was so much confusion I never could get a satisfactory explanation of how things were developing. After my return from Georgia, I persuaded Abe we should take our vacation in New England. We drove up through New York, stopping at Hyde Park to see Franklin Roosevelt's grave, and then up through Massachusetts where we could see the "battle of the billboards." Kennedy had taken billboard space all over the state, promising "More for Massachusetts," and Lodge replied, "Lodge will do most for Massachusetts." It seemed that Lodge had the last word, on billboards anyway.

Election day was fast approaching, and I sent Kennedy a wire congratulating him on being elected to the Senate. I was told later that it was the first such wire he received, which didn't surprise me too much since I sent it the day before the election.

On election night we stayed with the television reports all night. It became obvious very early that Eisenhower would continue to stay far ahead of Stevenson. The reports started to move across the country, as the count came in from the Atlantic Coast, then the Middle West, and finally the Rocky Mountain States. Only occasionally did we get a report from Massachusetts.

Then the electrifying news: "There is an upset developing

14

in Massachusetts. Young Congressman Kennedy is gradually moving up on Lodge." Later on that morning we heard the news that Lodge had conceded to Kennedy. "See, I told you he's going to be President," I sang out to Abe.

One of my prayers was answered, but what about the other one? I still hoped to find some little niche in Kennedy's office, and I kept hounding Ted Reardon. But everyone there was taking it easy. After all, they had won and it would be six years before they would have to face the same problems again. The Senator was exhausted from his campaign, so he took a vacation in Europe. After his return he went to Florida to spend Christmas with his family.

I considered whether I should quit my job on the Hill and perhaps go back to law school. Then one afternoon, I was sitting at my desk ruffling through some Georgia newspapers when the phone rang at the next desk. "Evelyn," the girl said, "it's for you. Kennedy's office."

I snatched the telephone and heard the words I'd been waiting for: "Would you like to work for the Senator?" I could hardly believe Ted Reardon. It must be one of his jokes. But, he explained, the Senator's secretary, Mary Davis, preferred to work for someone in the House of Representatives. Many secretaries who have worked on the House side prefer to stay there rather than move over to the Senate Office Building. I couldn't imagine what she was thinking of, but I would have been the last one in the world to try to change her mind.

At last I was going to work for him.

CHAPTER 3

His Personal Secretary

The next morning another call came from Kennedy's office telling me he would like me to attend his swearing-in ceremony in the Senate the following day. I shall never forget that day—January 3, 1953.

When I arrived at his office, I found several other girls also waiting to go to the swearing-in. These girls were from Massachusetts and had worked in his campaign there. Looking them over I thought, he certainly knows the practical side of politics; they represented every influential group in Massachusetts. All spoke with the New England flat "a," saying "caar" and "Baaston."

The girls were friendly and looked upon me as something of an expert because I knew Washington and had worked on the Hill. They were all a little apprehensive, too, about whether they would be able to learn fast enough to suit the Senator. I was fascinated by their stories of the campaign, how the Kennedy family swarmed over the state meeting people at tea parties and how the Senator one day shook hands with so many factory workers his hand became numb.

As we were getting acquainted that first morning, Ted Reardon called out from the Senator's office, "Where is his blue shirt?"

"Why does he want a blue shirt?" I asked.

"In case he might be on television."

We went over to the Senate chamber for the swearing-in and watched him come down the Senate aisle escorted, as is the custom, by the senior Senator from Massachusetts, Leverett Saltonstall. He seemed a little self-conscious standing with all those gray-haired politicians who were so much older and more experienced, and I noticed him trying to button his coat to hide his necktie, which was hanging down far below his belt. Someone must have found the blue shirt because he had it on.

After the ceremony we all went to the Senate dining room for lunch. Ted Reardon had not told me what my job would be. He had asked me at one time if I thought I could supervise girls who might be working in the office. When I learned at lunch that I was to be the Senator's personal secretary, I could not believe it at first.

It was a wonderful day, full of lighthearted talk and laughter. Everyone joined in, celebrating the victory of the man for whom they were now working.

Ted Reardon, a pleasant Massachusetts Irishman, had been a Harvard roommate of the Senator's eldest brother, Joseph P. Kennedy, Jr., who was killed during World War II. Ted had helped the Senator in his first campaign for Congress, and I learned that he was well liked on Capitol Hill. Because of his many friendships, he was a tremendous asset to the Senator, who relied on him concerning Massachusetts problems.

Mary Barelli Gallagher, a happy-go-lucky girl of Italian descent, was extremely neat and efficient and was given the assignment of handling the immigration cases that came to the office. And there were many. During the years at the White House she served as Mrs. Kennedy's personal secretary.

Lois Strode, whose ready wit kept the office in good humor, handled the military service cases and did an extremely good job that won her compliments from the Senator as well as from the people she worked with in the Army, Navy, Air Force, and Marine Corps. In the process she found herself a husband. After working in the Senator's office for a couple of years, she married an Army colonel.

Jean McGonigle Mannix, a sweet Irish girl from Massachusetts, had worked hard in the campaign and knew all the political leaders in the state, especially the Kennedy supporters. She was selected to be the receptionist so that these leaders would be recognized immediately when they came to call on the Senator. She was also Ted Reardon's secretary. Two years later, she married a young lawyer from Pennsylvania.

Lucy Torres from New Bedford, Massachusetts, a friend of Basil Brewer, who played a big part in swinging the Republican votes for Kennedy, was a pleasant, efficient girl who proudly said she was a Republican but a staunch Kennedy supporter. Lucy helped with the legislative mail.

Ted Sorensen, a quiet, reserved, quizzical intellectual from Nebraska, did not join the staff until two weeks later. From the very first he was like the Rock of Gibraltar. He was devoted, loyal, and dedicated to the Senator in every way possible. Time meant nothing to him—he gave it all to the Senator. The Senator found himself relying on Ted Sorensen more and more for ideas, speeches, and political strategy. And Ted was always there to help him.

During the luncheon someone said that when the Senator first came to Washington as a Congressman he brought only one suit and two shirts; soneone had asked him, "Don't you expect to stay very long?"

There were other anecdotes told that day, many about how he was sometimes embarrassed by his youthful appearance. It was the first time I heard the old story of the Senator's experience during his early days in the House when a Congressman, thinking he was a page, called him over and asked him to get a newspaper. On another occasion, when he was serving on the House Labor Committee, an older man who was testifying kept referring to the young Congressman as "Laddie."

We were still getting acquainted with each other when the Senator came over to our table and asked how we were getting along. After talking with me for a while, he said, without directing his request to anyone, "Let's make sure that tomorrow we get lists of all those who worked in the campaign. I want to send each of them a letter of thanks. And I'll sign each one."

That afternoon in his office, it was impossible to work. Seven of us were crowded in one room while we waited for his files and equipment to be moved from the House Office Building on one side of Capitol Hill to the Senate Office Building on the other side. As a result the mail piled up—unanswered. When the Senator walked in and saw the piles of mail, he began to worry. "Surely," he said, "some of the letters can be answered."

He picked up one of the letters and tore it open. "Here's a family that would like for me to help them get into one of the housing projects. They have ten children."

The next day we moved into Room 362, Senate Office Building; it was as bare as Mother Hubbard's cupboard. But we soon got desks, typewriters, and telephones and began to attack the mountain of mail. My desk was right outside his office door.

The Senator never stopped to think that I did not know what his secretary had done for him on the House side. He started right out as though there had been no change at all. It was, "Mrs. Lincoln, get me this ... get me that ... where is this ... where is that ... ?" Things were whirling around in my head the way bugs whirled around the lights on our back porch during the summer evenings. I'd write things down and check them off as I finished them, and before the list was half completed there would be more.

He was not just an ordinary Senator; he was a celebrity, too. He had done something unusual: he had defeated a leading, previously unbeaten Republican with impressive vote-gathering ability at the same time that the Republicans had won the Presidency by a lopsided margin.

The newspapers, magazines, radio, and television people were interested in him. He was news. Interviewers were constantly underfoot, always asking for his time.

"Should I try to discourage them so you won't be interrupted so much?" I asked.

"By no means, Mrs. Lincoln. If I know one thing, it is that a politician can kill himself faster by playing hard-to-get with the press than he can by jumping off the Capitol dome. And besides, I used to be a newspaperman myself. As long as they want to talk to me, I want to talk to them. Maybe longer."

The interviews continued. I could see that he was building

bonds of understanding between himself and the press but it was not a cold, calculated thing. He actually enjoyed talking to newspapermen. Arthur Krock of *The New York Times* was a long-time family friend who years before had helped him turn a Harvard honors thesis into a bestselling book, *Why England Slept*. He was very close to Charley Bartlett, Washington correspondent for the Chattanooga *Times*. He subscribed to a newspaper clipping service, and all of us on his Senate staff were asked to look through Massachusetts papers and bring interesting items to his attention.

Despite his warm feeling for newspapermen, he was not always happy about what they wrote. "Get Sorensen," he would call after reading an unfriendly piece. "Ted, look at what this fellow has said about me. Let's give him the facts and blast him." For the next hour, draft answers would fly from office to office until, finally, a version was agreed upon and prepared for his signature. Often I would have such a letter all ready to mail when he would call over from the floor of the Senate with a new idea to add, and we would go through the whole process again.

If a newspaperman ignored his rebuttal and kept on attacking, he wouldn't repeat the exercise. "His mind's made up and facts won't change it," he would say with resignation.

Senator Kennedy evidently woke up each morning bursting with new ideas. Many mornings, as soon as he opened the door, he would begin, "I have several things for you to do. First . . . second . . . third . . ." and so on, all while he was taking off his overcoat. Then he would say enthusiastically, "Now bring me my mail." He would race through the letters, chuckling as he read a letter from a friend. "Nice letter," he would say, and then dictate a long answer. He couldn't sit still while dictating. He would pace back and forth in his office, or move out into the reception room. Sometimes he would stare out the window, and sometimes pick up a golf club and swing at an imaginary ball, without in the least slowing down the stream of words and ideas.

Since he encouraged people to write to him, he received all sorts of letters. Once a Boston lady of Irish descent wrote a pitiful letter saying she was a shut-in and a television set would make her life seem less dreary. Touched, the Senator wrote Frank Morrissey, who worked for him in Boston. "Buy her a good used television set and send it over to her. She's a poor shut-in."

A few weeks later a blistering letter arrived from the lady. "Never so insulted in my life," she claimed. "Imagine a *used* television set with a ten-inch screen from a man with your wealth." She sent it right back and said next time she wanted a new one with a twenty-one-inch screen. If it were not so far to Washington, she wrote, she would get down there and give him a piece of her mind. He really laughed when he read that one. "She's not a shut-in. Somebody probably locked her in."

As with any new job, there was the problem of secretary and boss becoming adjusted to each other. He had some habits I didn't care for, and I am sure he didn't like some of my country-bred ways. For example, he was careless in keeping track of things. He had a habit of writing a telephone number on any stray slip of paper and then stuffing the paper in his wallet or pocket. Later, when he needed the number, he would dump dozens of such wrinkled slips out of his wallet, add still others from his various pockets, and scratch around in the pile. If he couldn't find the one he was seeking, he would call, "Mrs. Lincoln, what's Tom's telephone number?" More often than not, I didn't even know who Tom was, much less where I might find his number.

The Senator's handwriting caused me endless difficulty and heartache during my first year in his office. After I had seemingly overlooked some item, he would say, "But Mrs. Lincoln, I wrote it all out for you." And he had, too, except that no one but he could understand his handwriting. Gradually I learned, and found that I was the only one who had cracked the code. Once I saw a copy of a report card he received when he was in the sixth grade at the Riverdale Country School in Bronxville,

21

New York. It seemed impossible that one of his best grades had been in penmanship.

Possibly because my family has the Swedish need to be neat, the Senator's carefree housekeeping habits were like an exposed nerve to me. He was always forgetting things, and I was continually tracking down some item, such as his overcoat or his briefcase. "Where did I leave it this time?" he would ask.

"In the closet of the hotel," I would reply.

I really didn't mind checking hotels and planes to locate his forgotten effects; that was something of a challenge. But the condition of his desk was maddening. It seemed as if someone had taken a waste paper basket and turned it upside down on top of the desk. I tried to ignore it, but just couldn't. So, each time he left the office I would rush in, straighten up his desk, and file the papers that had accumulated there. When he came back from the Senate chamber, I would soon hear the buzzer being pressed angrily. "How can you ever expect me to find anything? Why don't you leave my desk alone?"

"I'm sorry you're angry. I'm just trying to be helpful. And I know where everything is."

Actually, I didn't want to be difficult, and most of the adjusting was mine. But sometimes I wondered if I could ever adjust fast or far enough. I was sure that he was wondering whether he had made a mistake in picking me for his secretary. Once, when things were somewhat more confused than usual, he looked at me and said, "I don't believe you and I understand each other." He saw how my face fell, and quickly added, "See if you can't do a little better."

I fully agreed with him. My shorthand was not the best, I didn't always know whom he wanted to talk to when he said, "Get Charley on the phone," I didn't know the names of the towns in Massachusetts, and I didn't know his family and many of the things that were so much a part of him.

Working for him made me want to do my best, and I decided to work harder than ever, to practice my shorthand at home and to make sure that I did everything I could to help him

22

It was a trial by fire, but I was determined to withstand the heat, and I came to regard each trial as a challenge.

Slowly I began to improve a little. I got a slight boost one afternoon when he burst out of his office and wanted to dictate something to me. I was talking on the telephone at the time. Generally, I would hang up immediately if he wished to dictate something because he paid no attention to the fact that I was listening to someone on the other end of the line. But this time I couldn't hang up—I was talking to his father. I motioned frantically to him that I couldn't come, and he asked one of the other girls to take the dictation. A few minutes later she emerged from his office as though she had just been sitting in a steam bath. She began to transcribe, typing and pausing to look off into space, typing a few more words and then pausing again. After a while he came out and said, "How are you coming along?"

"It will be just a second," she replied.

Now she started typing hurriedly like a person racing for time. He appeared again and asked to see what she had written. She reluctantly took the paper out of the typewriter and handed it to him. "Well," he said, "what in the world is this? It doesn't make sense."

"To tell you the truth, Senator," she confessed, "you went so fast I didn't get a word you said."

He sighed and looked at me. I wondered if he was thinking, "Maybe you're not so bad after all."

CHAPTER 4

End of a Gay Young Bachelor

Not long after Senator Kennedy got settled in his new office, writers began to refer to him as the Senate's gay young bachelor. It was a title he didn't exactly relish, but he took it in good humor. It did fit, at least half way. He was young—only thirty-five—and he was a bachelor. But he was very serious about his duties in the Senate, and there was little time left after work for the life of a gay blade. When he walked through the quiet marble corridors from his office to the Senate chamber, I am sure many young secretaries from all over the country gave him wistful glances. The *Saturday Evening Post* did a complete article on the Senator to run with his picture on the cover, and they spent days taking pictures of him and his staff and interviewing him. I don't know what he told the interviewers about his love life, but I thought I could tell them that one of my most unusual secretarial duties was calling his girl friends to ask if they would like to go to the movies.

For example, one evening after a busy day, he sauntered by my desk and said in a low undertone, "See if Ellen can go to the movies tonight." Fortunately, I knew who Ellen was.

As it turned out, however, she had left her office and was on her way home. I called and called and finally after half an hour she answered, a little breathless from having rushed up the stairs to get to the ringing telephone. As soon as I said, "This is Evelyn Lincoln," she knew why I was calling and there was no need for me to say another word. I heard her excited answer: "Of course I can go. What time should I be ready?" I told her, and I could imagine what was going through her mind: "Why didn't I go to the hairdresser on my lunch hour as I had planned?" Or, "Why didn't I take that blue dress to the cleaner's? Well, next time I'll really be ready."

24

But as Ellen, Susan, Jane, and so many others eventually discovered, often there was no next time. I never discovered why. I guess he was an impulsive dater. The mood seemed to strike him suddenly. We would go through the entire operation, sometimes spending an hour or more of constant telephoning to locate the girl. He always seemed very anxious to see her that evening and no one else would do. Then, as often as not, I would never hear her name mentioned again.

When I told him that evening I had located Ellen, he said, "Fine." But now it seemed that his enthusiasm had died. He was not in the slightest hurry to leave the office. He started to read, and then picked up the telephone and talked with one of his newspaper friends. While he hung around, I was closing drawers, stacking up mail, and making other signs that I was getting ready to go; if he didn't move soon, he and his date, by now a very puzzled girl, wouldn't even get to see the last full showing of the movie. And besides, I was getting hungry and wanted to get home.

Finally he strolled out, late as usual, and I quickly left the office.

He really loved the movies and sometimes would see the same one two or three times. One afternoon he saw an advertisement about a movie showing at one of the downtown theaters. He buzzed for me and said, "Check and see what they are doing over on the floor, and if they expect a quorum call or a roll call in the next two hours." I told him nothing important was coming up.

"Ask Ted Reardon if he would like to go to the movies with me."

I asked Ted and he said, "Sure." A few minutes later they dashed out of the office, shouting to me that they would sit close to the door just in case I needed to get in touch with them.

In about thirty minutes things started to pop over on the Senate floor, and a Senate aide called me from the Democratic cloakroom to say they needed the Senator on the floor. I telephoned the message to the theater and the Senator and Ted left

25

immediately. But they got tied up in traffic and the Senator almost missed a roll call. He was upset about the whole affair. "I won't try that again," he said. Then turning to me he said jokingly, "Besides, you made me miss the most exciting part of the movie."

For a bachelor, Senator Kennedy had a pretty comfortable life in Washington. He had leased a house in Georgetown, and his housekeeper was his childhood nurse, Margaret Ambrose, who babied him like a mother hen with her brood. For his errands, taking care of his car, driving it home from the airport, and meeting his plane when he returned there was good old Muggsie O'Leary. Muggsie was a policeman under Kennedy patronage on the Capitol police force and there was never a more loyal appointee. Muggsie's family and Ted Reardon's family lived close together in Massachusetts, and it was Ted who recommended him for the job. But Muggsie quickly became an indispensable aide to the Senator, who took him along with him to the White House years later.

I often wondered if Margaret Ambrose had as much difficulty picking up after the Senator at home as I did at the office, or if she had him trained. Sometimes the situations at the office became almost hilarious.

One evening the Senator said, "You know what I need in this office? I need a couch." Then he walked around a bit and repeated, "I need a couch. That's exactly what I need. Get the Mart on the phone, Mrs. Lincoln."

I immediately put in a call to the Chicago Merchandise Mart, owned by his father, and after I handed the telephone to him, I heard the Senator saying, "Send me some pictures. I want to see what I'm getting." The next morning an air mail, special delivery envelope from Chicago arrived with pictures of all kinds of couches.

A few minutes later he walked into the office and began his usual rapid-fire dictation of the two dozen things he wanted "right away." I waited for a pause and then silently handed him the brochures and pictures I had just opened.

"Hmm," he said after studying them a few minutes, "here's one that looks pretty good." He buzzed Ted Reardon, whom he always liked to consult in making a decision about the office.

"What do you think of this one?"

"I think it looks fine, boss."

Then one by one he asked each of us in the office what we thought of the couch. Finally, he said, "Okay, send this along and tell them to make sure it is tan."

A few weeks later a truck arrived with a tan leather couch with a hide-away bed. As soon as the Senator stepped into his office he spied it. "I don't like the color," he said. "And why did they stick it in the middle of the room? It should be over there in a corner."

"Are you going to send it back?" I asked.

"Well, let's keep it a few days anyway," he said, and we put it in the corner, where it remained.

Next there was the problem of having linens and pillows available in case he wanted to get some sleep. I asked Muggsie to get in touch with Margaret Ambrose for these things, and, when they arrived, I made the bed. I folded the pillow, an extra blanket, and his pajamas in on top of the blanket and sheets and tried to push the couch closed. But it wouldn't close. I finally called the other girls in the office for reinforcements. The three of us finally closed it, after a considerable struggle. We marched out feeling a little proud when . . . bang! I didn't need to look. It had popped open again. I went in, removed the pillow, extra blanket, and pajamas, and presto, it closed with just a slight nudge. I had to find another place for his sleeping things. At last I figured where they should go: in the bookcase. I made some curtains and covered the glass door so that no one would see the kind of "books" we were keeping on that shelf.

Now he could get some rest. It was an arrangement many Senators had in their offices, although most of them stretched out on top of the couch without having it converted into a bed.

Senator Kennedy decided to try it out right after lunch one

27

day: "Make up the bed and wake me in forty-five minutes, unless there is a roll call. Then call me right away."

He had the wonderful faculty of being able to fall asleep immediately so that he got the full benefit from his short nap. Perhaps five minutes after working at the highest pitch, making long distance calls, or thrashing out a serious decision, he was able to relax completely, close his eyes, and drop off into a sound sleep.

I kept my eye on the clock, and when the time was up I went into his office and slowly raised the venetian blinds. When the clatter of the blinds and the daylight streaming in didn't wake him, I shook his shoulder a little and said, "Time, Senator." He came to slowly, stretched, and then was wide awake.

"What are they doing over on the floor? Did I have any calls?"

I gave him the answers and went back to my desk, but before I got seated the buzzer began screaming. I rushed back and there he was on the edge of the bed with one sock on and the other foot bare.

"I can't find my other sock. Do you think it is under the bed?"

After I got down on my hands and knees and tried to find the missing sock he got so engrossed in a newspaper that when I did come up with the sock, he didn't even hear me say, "I found it. Here it is." I laid it on the bed and went back to my work. But again the buzzer. Meanwhile, a visitor was walking in the door so I didn't get back into his office in a split second. I'm afraid the visitor was a bit shocked when the Senator shouted, "What did you leave for? Where is my sock?"

As I dashed into the Senator's office, I wondered what the visitor would think was going on in this office. I hoped he thought that the Senator had said, "Where is my clock?" But from the dubious look on his face, I think he heard correctly.

I remember another afternoon we were searching for a shoe that was not to be found under the bed or desk, or anywhere on the floor. I finally discovered it on the window sill. How it got there I'll never know, unless he undressed all over the room while reading a book and put the shoe there on the way by.

After we located his shoe, he came out of his office and noticed Tom Rice waiting to see him. Tom was interested in the New England fish industry and had a problem he thought the Senator could solve. "I'll be with you in a minute, Tom," he called as he walked through the reception room and into Ted Reardon's office on the other side. He began ruffling through some news clippings on Ted's desk.

"What's this?" he asked. "Looks like they're having some trouble at the Navy shipyards again. Get on this right away, Ted. See what you can find out about this."

"Yes, boss."

The Senator then sauntered into Ted Sorensen's office. As usual Ted, the intellectual with an unquenchable thirst for knowledge, had his nose in a book, but he was glad to be interrupted by the Senator. Senator Kennedy sat down in a chair, leaned back comfortably, and they began discussing the current national or international problems. I hated to disturb them but the Senator had a telephone call. "Senator Symington is calling you," I said. "Shall I transfer it in here?"

"No, I'll take it in my office," he said. With that he got up, stopped for a moment to ask Ted Reardon how he was getting along with the shipyards, and then came back out into the reception room. Tom Rice was still waiting. "Be with you as soon as I've answered this call, Tom," he called back over his shoulder.

Then he said, "Send Tom in," and Tom finally got to talk to him about fish.

At last I felt I was getting to know and understand the Senator and felt that I had my job under complete control. I was even feeling a little satisfied with myself one spring morning as I blithely stepped into the office balancing a container of hot coffee in one hand. Before I had time to remove the lid from the container, the telephone rang. It was the Senator.

"Tell Sorensen to get that quotation from Dooley. He knows what I mean. And would you get some books from the library on John Quincy Adams. I want these by the time I get to the office."

I called the Library of Congress, but it was too early, no one was there. I got the message to Sorensen and finally managed to get the books just before the Senator arrived.

When he came in I noticed that he had a draft of a speech he was scheduled to deliver that evening stuffed into the pocket of his coat. He pulled it out, took off his coat, threw it on a chair, and rushed in to talk with Sorensen. After twenty minutes or so they came out with Ted clutching a number of papers in his hand. They went right into the Senator's office.

I kept wondering when they were going to agree on a final draft of that speech because I had to type it. The first time I typed a speech for him he had difficulty reading it because the type was too small. I typed the next one all in capital letters. He complained, "I could hardly read that speech last Friday, Mrs. Lincoln. All the letters looked alike. Why did you type it all in capital letters?" I wondered how he wanted it this time.

An hour before he was to leave for the plane he came in with the idea that I should use a speech typewriter. That meant I had to go downstairs to the main typewriter room and type on a machine I had never used before. That turned out to be an experience, particularly since the speech draft was a mess: the pages mixed up and renumbered and filled with arrows and incomprehensible lines with little notes in both his handwriting and Ted Sorensen's.

Despite the necessary decoding I started out well enough, somewhat startled at the size of the type. But soon things were not going very smoothly. It seemed I was at the end of the line before I was barely started, and I was at the end of the page before I had typed two sentences. I was making six copies and getting about seventy words to a page. The minutes were ticking by and I felt that all I was doing was feeding paper into the typewriter and watching for the end of the line.

First one staff member and then another from my office came down to bring me messages. "The Senator wants to know why it is going so slowly. Don't you know he is catching a plane?" I was ready to throw up my hands. I suppose every secretary gets to the point sometimes when she feels her boss has no idea what she is going through and what's more couldn't care less. I had reached that point, and as far as I was concerned, he could fly to the moon and take this old typewriter with him.

He left for the airport the way he usually did—a typical Dagwood Bumstead departure except, so far anyway, he hadn't smashed into the postman. He usually sat in his office signing mail or talking to some constituent until I gave him our standard warning signal: "Twenty minutes till takeoff, Senator." I was never sure he heard me because he went right on talking as if I had said two hours instead of twenty minutes. Then all of a sudden he would bounce out of his office and ask, "Where's my car?" Muggsie O'Leary meanwhile had brought the car around to the side entrance and was waiting for him. As I told him this he would say, "Let me see now, what do I want to take with me? Oh, yes, this book, this magazine, those letters." I would start stuffing everything in his black briefcase. Then he would grab the briefcase and head for the door. As he went by, he waved and smiled at everyone as though he were going to be away for months.

Then, just as I fell into my chair with a relaxed sigh, there he was, back again. "That was a short trip," I mumbled. Then he would ask me to call the airport and tell them he was on his way. And to call Hyannis and say that he wanted clam chowder for supper, and tell them what time he would arrive. Then he was gone.

I am told, for thank God I never experienced it myself, that their trips to the airport were like riding in a police car on a chase. The Senator liked to take the wheel and race through the streets, barely missing red lights. Cops would whistle, cars would honk, but he ignored everything other than his objective. When Muggsie came back to the office he would invariably report that they pulled away the steps to the plane as soon as the Senator climbed on. I was always glad when that ride was

31

over, for I fully expected to get a call someday with the news that they had failed to make one of those curves on their way to National Airport.

The next weekend, because of exceptionally light traffic, Muggsie got him to the airport five minutes early. The Senator darted to the telephone. I had just stepped across the hall to return some soft drinks I had borrowed when one of the girls came after me and shouted frantically, "It's the telephone. It's the telephone." I knew it. I just knew it. They've had an accident. I rushed back, grabbed the telephone, and to my relief it was the Senator. I had forgotten that the girls in the office got panic stricken when he came on the phone and I was away from my desk. They were not afraid of him. They were just afraid he would ask them a question they could not answer.

As soon as he gave me some more instructions on things he wanted done before his return, Muggsie related, he rushed over to the newsstand to pick up some reading matter. Muggsie followed him because he knew the Senator, as usual, didn't have a dime with him and he would have to pick up the tab. The last Muggsie saw of him, the Senator was walking toward the plane with his nose buried in a magazine. "He must have a sixth sense, Mrs. Lincoln. I watched him walk down a flight of stairs, pass through groups of people waiting around, miss some sailors walking abreast, and then reach the gate. And he did it without looking up. I swear he never took his eyes off that magazine."

That's the way he always was. It seemed sometimes that he was trying to cram as much as he could into every hour and minute.

He spent his first Easter as a Senator at Palm Beach. A few days in the sun, swimming and resting, always brought him back eager to plunge into his work. This time he really had his work cut out for him. He had asked for time to make a series of major speeches on the Senate floor.

The next few weeks were busy ones. Ted Sorensen and he had been working very hard on the speeches and now, the

32

middle of May, they were all typed up. He was ready to go. Some of the older Senators were skeptical when they heard he was going to speak for three days. "Who does he think he is?" some asked. "Doesn't he know that freshmen Senators should be seen and not heard?" "What can a young upstart like that have to say?" Well, he had plenty to say. It was all about the economy in Massachusetts and what he wanted to do about it. He wanted the people to know that he was anxious to carry out his campaign promises to do more for Massachusetts.

Those of us in his office took turns slipping over to the Senate gallery to hear him speak. His deep voice rang clear in the Senate chamber, and he had a forceful way of chopping the air with his right hand when he wanted to make a point.

The Senator completed his series of speeches just in time to attend his sister Eunice's wedding to Sargent Shriver, in New York. Possibly the occasion inspired the Senator to think of girls again, and one name kept popping up with increasing frequency: Jacqueline Bouvier.

One day Ted Reardon said to me, "If the boss ever gets married, I'll bet it will be Jackie."

"Who is this Jackie? Has she ever been here? What is she like?"

The Senator had never mentioned her to me and had never asked me to call her. I thought she must be someone special he wanted to call himself. I learned they had met in 1951 at a dinner party given by his old friend, Charley Bartlett, that she had been in Massachusetts during part of his campaign for the Senate, and that he had taken her to the Inaugural Ball in January.

As talk continued, I learned more about her, but not from the Senator. I never asked him about his personal life. She was an "inquiring photographer" for the Washington *Times-Herald* and wrote a lively, interesting column. Once she even interviewed the Senator for it. Years later, telling about their courtship during his senatorial campaign in Massachusetts, I am told she said, "He'd call me from some oyster bar up there, with a great clanking of coins, and ask me out to the movies the following Wednesday in Washington."

I was told that Jackie was a beautiful girl with an inquisitive and independent mind, who had been brought up in New York and Washington society. She had been educated at the best girls' schools, at Vassar, at the Sorbonne, and was recently graduated from George Washington University. I was looking forward to meeting her, but the Senator had not mentioned her, so I said nothing.

Finally, the article about the Senator appeared in the *Saturday Evening Post*. I thought it was wonderful and so did the girls in the Senate Office Building, particularly those he had taken to the movies who were still waiting for one of those late evening telephone calls that never again came. I was kept busy getting him to autograph copies for them. But he seemed reluctant to autograph those magazines and I wondered why. Usually he was very obliging about autographs. Finally he said, "I like the article, but I don't like the title. I wish you would not encourage the girls to bring copies for me to autograph." I was shocked because I had just invested in twenty copies. What could I do with them? I stuck them in the bookcase with the pillow and pajamas. The title of the article was "The Senate's Gay Young Bachelor."

There wasn't much he could do about the title, but he did do something about being a bachelor. On June 25th, shortly after the article appeared, Mr. and Mrs. Hugh D. Auchincloss of Newport, Rhode Island, and McLean, Virginia, announced the engagement of Mrs. Auchincloss' daughter, Jacqueline Lee Bouvier, to Senator John Fitzgerald Kennedy of Massachusetts, son of the former Ambassador to Great Britain and Mrs. Joseph P. Kennedy of Hyannis Port, Massachusetts.

They were going to be married on September 12th. He would no longer be a gay young bachelor.

CHAPTER 5

Here Comes the Bride

On the evening of June 25th, the Senator dashed through the door to start another of his breakneck rides to the airport. This time he was going to Hyannis for his engagement party. As he left, he called back to me: "Remind me first thing Monday morning to start working on the guest list for the wedding. I'm going to invite close friends only."

"See," said one of the girls in the office as soon as he left, "I told you he'll never make a good husband. Any man who has to be reminded about the guest list for his own wedding isn't really too interested in getting married."

Another girl said, "Oh, he's too old for her. It will never work. Just think, he will be an old man before his child is old enough to vote." At the time the Senator was thirty-six and his bride-to-be was twenty-four.

I thought they sounded a little jealous. From the way he beat it out of there, he must have been pretty anxious to get to her. And that business about his being too old was quite a switch. Ever since he came to Congress people had been saying he's too young or looks too young. And now he was already too old.

On Monday morning I didn't have to remind him about the wedding guest list. As he came in the door he started giving me instructions. "All right. Here are some names. Get their addresses and send them up to Kay Donovan in the New York office." He was referring to the Lt. Joseph P. Kennedy, Jr. Foundation office.

Now getting the list was one thing, but trying to figure out his writing was another. I had learned to decipher his notes but figuring out proper names is a lot more difficult. Typing up that list was a nightmare, particularly since he kept coming out and saying, "I've thought of some more." And he kept on thinking of more. That list of "a few friends" was getting bigger and bigger.

Finally his well of names appeared to run dry and he said, "I'll take the list up to the Cape this weekend and go over it with Jackie." I could only hope I had figured out those names correctly.

The Senate adjourned early on Friday, July 3, and so the Senator decided to play a game of golf. He told Jackie that he would meet her at the airport. He got to the airport with less than a minute to spare, as usual, but there was no Jackie in sight. He called and asked, "Where's Jackie?"

"I don't know," I truthfully said, "I thought she was going to meet you at the airport."

"So did I," he answered, "but she's not here. Find her and then call me back."

I called every place I thought she might be, but no one had seen her that afternoon. But before I could call him back the telephone rang. It was the Senator again, and this time he was quite irritated.

"She's not here yet, and the plane just took off. Why were you so slow in finding her?"

I had to confess that I had not found her. Just then, who should saunter gaily through the door but Jackie. I told the Senator, "She just walked in. I'll put her on."

I don't know what he said to her, but she seemed to become progressively less comfortable, and it wasn't long before she wanted to know if someone could take her to the airport in a rush. "I was looking at linens and glassware and I guess I completely forgot the time," she said, as if rehearsing her lines for the Senator. I could have told her that you didn't forget about time around the Senator. He looked at time the way one of our Nebraska irrigation farmers looked at water. It was a crime to waste any of it.

While Jackie talked with the Senator I realized I was seeing her in person for the first time. Of course, I had seen photographs of her and I recognized her voice because I had talked

36

to her a number of times over the telephone when she called him. I was immediately impressed with her beauty. She was tall and slender with the sort of easy grace that comes from being a good horsewoman. Her hair was dark, short, and curly and framed her face in a manner that seemed to accent the large expressive eyes that were almost amber in color. And her skin was fresh and glowing with an almost luminous quality about it.

Monday morning he was back again with a still longer list of wedding guests. Now he wanted to invite the staff and perhaps some Senators and Congressmen. When I returned with the list of these additional names he said, "Oh, yes. I have some others in my briefcase." There they were, jammed down in the corner on little wads of paper. Now these I couldn't make out at all, and I had to ask for help. "This one," he said, "lives in New York City. No, wait a minute, I think they're in France at this time of year. But they said they might be moving to Connecticut. Well," he added, dismissing the problem from *his* mind, "wherever they are, be sure they get an invitation." I sent this list to the girl in the New York office, who wrote back saying, "Jackie thinks the list is getting too long. Can we take some names off?" I told the Senator about this, but instead of taking any off, he went right on adding more names.

The wedding invitations were lovely and my husband and I were delighted to receive one. This was like a command performance and none of us in the office even considered the idea of not going. The main conversation around the office for days was, "What are you going to wear?" "Do you think it will be warm in Newport in September?" As for me, I bought a brown and pink ensemble and looked at it admiringly every time I went by the closet.

One day the Senator said to me, "I'm expecting a package from Tiffany's. A registered package. Bring it to me as soon as it comes in." I wondered if this was his gift to the bride. The package soon arrived, and when he came into the office I rushed in with it. Later, when I went in again to tell him his brother

37

Bob was on the phone, there he was, sitting at his desk with six beautiful bracelets all set with jewels before him. As he picked up the phone he motioned for me to put them back into the box. When he finished talking on the phone he called out to me, "Let me see those bracelets again. I'll keep those three and you send the other three back. I'm going to give one to Jackie for her birthday, but I've decided to let her pick the one she likes from those three."

I sent the three pieces back and put the others away in the safe. As he started to leave the office on July 28th to take Jackie out on her birthday he said, "Oh yes, Mrs. Lincoln, please get me the jewelry from the safe."

The next morning the Senator arrived at the office at his usual time. I waited for him to say something about which one she had chosen and to ask me to put the other two back in the safe until we could return them to Tiffany's. But he didn't even mention it. I thought maybe he had given all three of them to her, and dismissed it from my mind.

Just then Muggsie came into the office and said, "Look what I found in the glove compartment when I was cleaning the car. Do you think they are worth anything?"

Little did Muggsie know the two missing bracelets were worth as much as the car. My hair almost stood on end at the thought of it. I put them right in the safe and later in the morning asked the Senator, "Do you want me to return those two pieces of jewelry?"

"Yes, yes, of course."

He must have wondered how I got them back.

Wedding gifts were beginning to pour into the office. Many people didn't have Jackie's home address and mailed their gift to the Senator with the words "please forward" on the package. Then I had to readdress them to the New York office. It got to be such a problem in New York that they appealed to me to open each gift and make a record in case the card was separated from the gift. Every day began to seem like Christmas in the office.

As in previous years, the Senator went abroad right after Congress adjourned. Despite the closeness of the wedding day, he and his Harvard roommate, Torbert Macdonald, later to become a Congressman from Massachusetts, decided to charter a yacht and go sailing off the coast of France. On their way home they visited in Sweden and they stopped off in England to see some old friends.

I knew the minute he landed, for he immediately called the office. The first question he asked was, "Are all my friends coming to the wedding?" Then he added, "I can't find my reading glasses. Call the man who made them last time and ask him if he can make me another pair. Then bring them along to the wedding—you are coming to the wedding, aren't you?" I assured him I would be there, and that I would go to work at once on getting the glasses.

This was on Thursday, and Abe and I were leaving the next day to drive up to Providence, where we would stay Friday night, driving over to Newport on Saturday for the wedding.

The oculist did a fantastic job; I tucked the new pair of glasses into my purse just before we left for Rhode Island.

By the time we got to Providence we sensed a certain air of expectancy, and when we arrived in Newport the town was alive with excitement. Restaurants were jammed and traffic was backed up at every corner. It was early and we stopped at a restaurant for a second breakfast. All around us people were talking about the big event. "I understand that Jackie will have twelve bridesmaids," or "Oh, how I wish I was getting married to Jack Kennedy." The girls at the next table kept repeating, "Imagine, five hundred cars. . . they need five hundred cars to take all the guests out to the reception."

Even at some distance from the church, we realized that a sizable percentage of Newport's 36,000 people had decided to see the wedding. We had to park the car several blocks away, then walk single file through the masses of people. At last, after showing our invitation to the police holding back the crowds, we reached the front steps of the church. Inside we were

39

ushered to very choice seats. I nudged Abe and said, "Look who's in front of us. Marion Davies and her husband."

All around us the array of wealth, power, and beauty in this little church was dazzling. The guests included leaders of the American political and business world. Archbishop Richard J. Cushing, a long-time family friend, was to perform the ceremony. There were fifteen ushers, including Florida Senator George Smathers and Senator Kennedy's newspaper friend who had introduced him to Jackie, Charley Bartlett. The twelve bridal attendants were dressed in pink, and all around were lovely gowns of various hues.

The music began to swell, and there was a feeling of anticipation as we waited for the bride to appear. Then the Senator appeared. Next the bridesmaids. And then the most exquisite of all, Jackie on her father's arm. Her wedding gown was gorgeous. Below the tight bodice, it flared out dramatically into a full skirt made of what must have been at least fifty yards of ivory tissue silk taffeta. There were a dozen or more rows of ruffles running up from the hem. Her classic features, so serious now, were softly shadowed by an antique rosepoint veil. Beneath it her skin glowed like warm ivory.

They met at the altar while a rich tenor voice sang "Ave Maria." Throughout the beautiful and impressive ceremony, I was worrying about the ring. Suppose the Senator had forgotten it. Archbishop Cushing read a special blessing from the Pope, and then—I knew it—they began to fumble for the ring. "Abe," I whispered, "his brother is as forgetful as he is. He's lost the ring. They should have given it to the Senator after all." But it was just the usual nervousness of men at weddings, and after Bob had dug around in his pocket for a while, the ring appeared and then the Archbishop's powerful voice rang out, "I now pronounce you man and wife." The Senator kissed his bride and as the joyful notes of Mendelssohn burst through the silence, John Fitzgerald and Jacqueline Kennedy, now forever united, walked slowly down the aisle, trying desperately to conceal their happiness.

As they neared the door of the church I saw them steal a quick look at each other. As soon as they reached the door and stepped into the sunlight, there was a tremendous roar from the crowd, and newsmen and photographers almost engulfed the couple. In a few minutes hundreds had broken through the police lines and were pressing forward to catch a closer look. The Senator was used to crowds, but Jackie backed away, looking apprehensively at the mass of people.

Finally they pushed through the crowd and reached their car. As they sped away, caravans of cars followed through the weblike streets of Newport and out to Hammersmith Farm on Narragansett Bay. It was the summer home of Jackie's mother and stepfather.

Following the crowd, we wound in and out of the grounds, finally reaching the beautiful house built like a castle. The setting was magnificent. From the lawn the seventeen hundred guests were able to look out across the Bay and hear the slow rumble of waves, and every now and then there was a taste of sea spray on the wind. We could hear an orchestra playing and the hum of hundreds of voices. Out in front of the house a long line of people waited to be received. As we joined the line, we learned that the ones ahead of us had already waited at least half an hour. We were told that the Senator and Jackie were right inside the door waiting to greet us.

As I came through the door I saw the Senator. How happy he seemed! Jackie was peeping out the window, no doubt hoping that she could see the end of the line. The Senator saw me then, and as I pumped his hand and wished him happiness, he turned to Jackie and said, "Jackie, here is Mrs. Lincoln." In her deep, slow voice she said, "Mrs. Lincoln. How nice of you to come."

I didn't have time to tell him about his reading glasses because I was being pushed along, and the rest of the receiving line was all confusion. Bridesmaids were coming and going, Jamie and Janet, Jackie's stepbrother and stepsister, were bowing and curtsying. Janet rushed up to the Senator, whispered something in his ear, and he laughed and gave her a pat on the head.

We went out to the back of the house where the orchestra was playing. Soon the Senator and Jackie, then Jackie and her father-in-law, and then the Senator and his mother, were dancing. As I watched the Senator dancing with his mother I was struck with her beauty and charm. She looked like an older sister of the bride, instead of the mother of the groom. Photographers were underfoot everywhere, snapping pictures as the men cut in on each other to dance with the beautiful bride.

Finally I saw the Senator at the edge of the dance floor and rushed over to tell him, "I brought your glasses." He looked puzzled for a moment, then said, "Oh yes, please go upstairs and put them in my suitcase." I climbed the stairs and went through endless bedrooms until I found one crowded with "JFK" monogrammed suitcases. Then I opened one full of carefully packed clothes. Remembering those stories of how little he packed when he first came to Congress I laughed to myself, "He must plan on staying longer on his honeymoon than he did in Congress." I dropped the glasses in one of the bags and started downstairs, my mission completed.

On the way down the bride rushed past me with her bouquet. I had scarcely got to the bottom before she turned on the landing and tossed the bouquet to the bridesmaids waiting below. I narrowly missed getting caught in the crush.

Now the rest of the guests were gathering at the foot of the stairs waiting for the bride and groom to come down. When they appeared there was loud applause and shouts of "Bon voyage," "Happy landings," and "I wish I were going with you." As they threaded their way through the little groups of guests, they passed his mother. He stopped, left Jackie, walked back to his mother, and slowly bent down and kissed her. And then they were off.

The Senator and his bride flew to New York on the first lap of a honeymoon that would take them to Acapulco and California. While in New York they stayed in Suite 31-B of the

Waldorf-Astoria. My husband and I drove back to Washington right after the wedding reception so that I could be at my desk the following Monday morning. Among the first letters to arrive that morning was one from the Senator, which, the stationery indicated, must have been written that first night while they were still at the Waldorf.

I opened it quickly, full of anticipation. It read: "Would you tell Eddie Boland (Congressman from Massachusetts) that while I cannot come to the Tuesday Club in October because I must speak in Boston that night, I would be glad to speak there in November." It was signed, "Best, Jack." I sighed, remembering his concern about his reading glasses. He must have found a use for them after all.

Shortly after I finished reading the letter, the phone rang. "Long distance for Mrs. Evelyn Lincoln." It was the Senator calling me from Acapulco. "Can he possibly be that anxious to get this Eddie Boland matter settled?" I thought, "and here I haven't even tried to call him yet." As soon as I heard his voice, I braced myself. He was very, very annoyed, particularly since the connection was poor, and every now and then, as he was really winding up, his voice faded away and I would have to ask, "Please repeat that, Senator, I can't hear you."

"Why didn't you let me know that we had to have our birth certificates?" he demanded. "And why didn't we have them with us?"

I told him I was sorry and I would have them sent air mail special delivery immediately.

"It's okay now, the Embassy arranged things, and convinced them we're not spies." About that time his voice faded away again, and I thought he had said something about his eyes. I asked, "What's wrong with your eyes?" Up until that point he was calming down, but my question started him off again.

"There's nothing wrong with my eyes, but there's certainly something wrong with your ears!"

And then he told me that it was things like this that a good

43

secretary was supposed to take care of and that he hoped it wouldn't happen again.

"It certainly won't, Senator," I assured him. I don't remember much more of the conversation, except that he had me so flustered that I ended by saying, "Enjoy yourself."

Later I learned that he and Jackie were held up at the airport for almost three hours while our Embassy in Mexico City tried to reach the right people—no easy task on a Sunday in Mexico. His annoyance may have stemmed from Jackie's amusement at the inability of such a well-known Senator to get them into a friendly country like Mexico. I really felt dreadful about it, because there is nothing worse than a sour note on a honeymoon, and I hoped that my oversight hadn't marred their trip.

We received several little notes from the Senator while they were in Acapulco, and everything seemed serene. He mentioned something about sailing, and I am sure that he enjoyed that because he loved the water.

While he was gone we kept up with the routine office business. One of the last things he said before he left on his honeymoon was, "Don't forget about Bartlett's." Two people he knew slightly were getting married and he was giving *Bartlett's Quotations* as a wedding gift. He probably chose Bartlett's for wedding gifts because he himself enjoyed reading the quotations.

He had a routine set of gifts for special occasions. For acquaintances, *Bartlett's Quotations.* For special friends, an inscribed silver bowl. And for benefits, bazaars, and similar events, a copy of the *Congressional Cook Book* filled with the favorite recipes of the wives of Congressmen and Senators.

Ten days after the call from Acapulco, I got another long distance call from the Senator. This time he was in California. I wondered what I had done wrong this time. But he wasn't angry about anything. While I talked with him, I sensed that he missed being at the center of things in Washington. "What's going on back there?" he asked. I told him about the hundreds of wires of congratulations and letters wishing them well and the calls of his many, many friends asking how they were getting along. "How about sending some of those wires and letters to me out here?" he said. "And perhaps some other mail you think I might like to see." I sent some that afternoon. The following week he and Jackie moved around so much on the West Coast that mail never did catch up with them. Eventually it was all returned.

The second week in October they were back in Hyannis Port. The honeymoon was over, and the Senator was beginning to pick up some of the problems he had left behind on September 12th.

Earlier in the year he had made several commitments for speaking engagements, and he came to Washington to check on his schedule and get his speeches started.

First of all the Senator and Jackie were going househunting. They were staying temporarily at Merrywood in McLean, Virginia, with her mother and stepfather, but like so many other new brides Jackie spent her days looking at houses and riding around with enthusiastic real estate agents. Whenever she found something she liked, she called, and the Senator would rush out of the office to see it. One morning he came in and said, "Mrs. Lincoln, we're going to sign a lease to rent the Blair Childs house at 3321 Dent Place, N.W., starting December 15th. I would like to have you send the lease to the New York office."

CHAPTER 6

Facing an Old Problem

Keeping up with the growing and gregarious Kennedy family could be a time-consuming and difficult job, so the Senator handed me the task of helping him to remember their birthdays, anniversaries, and special family occasions. I kept a little card index on my desk with all the vital information, and as a birthday or anniversary rolled around or a new baby was born, I reminded him and he would either dictate a telegram, telephone, or send a gift.

In this way I got to know the various members of the Kennedy family and I soon came to recognize them by voice through their telephone calls to the office. The former Ambassador was very interested in his Senator son and called fairly frequently to ask about his schedule or activities or just to visit with him over the telephone.

I did not meet his mother until the wedding in Newport. The more I have known her through the years, the more I have learned to respect her unusual qualities. Talking to her and the Senator's father gave me an insight into the strength of their characters; it was easy to understand from where the Senator received his determination and drive.

The Senator was very close to every member of his family, but I never saw him play favorites with any of them, not even Bob. They were a very happy family and they had some lively, good-natured discussions.

The first family member I met was Eunice, his oldest sister. Shortly after I went to work for the Senator, she telephoned asking for copies of a speech he had made. She has his direct manner of speaking, and asked me to put her name on his mailing list for any articles, speeches, or releases that he sent out. It was obvious she was very interested in what he was doing, not only because he was her brother but because she was interested in the same subjects and issues.

His brother Bob was the next one I met. He seemed very quiet and reserved, always deep in thought, and had very little to say when he came into the office. He stopped by frequently with his vivacious wife, Ethel, who was particularly friendly with the girls in the office. Bob and the Senator were very close and enjoyed discussing topics of the day. However, in those early years in the Senate, both brothers looked to their father for advice and suggestions.

Pat, his second sister, who later married Peter Lawford, came into the office with Eunice one day, and I knew immediately they were sisters and sisters of the Senator because of their strong resemblance to him. They had even white teeth like his and a shock of brown hair that sometimes seemed unruly.

I met Ted and Jean at the wedding. Jean was a very sweet girl and a little shy. Ted, who was still in college at the time, was extremely handsome.

None of the family stayed very long when they visited the Senator in his office. They obviously did not want to interrupt his busy life.

For years the Kennedy family customarily spent Thanksgiving together at Hyannis Port, and now the clan was swelled by two new members: Jackie and Sargent Shriver, who had married the Senator's sister on May 23rd. I don't know how Sarge Shriver reacted to his first Thanksgiving with the Kennedys, but I am sure that Jackie found it somewhat overwhelming. The Kennedys were noted for being very competitive, and that long Thanksgiving weekend was one continuous close-quarter battle of wits.

Soon after Thanksgiving the older Kennedys closed their house at the Cape and headed south to spend the winter at their home in Palm Beach, Florida. I continued to send mail to the Senator whenever he was out of Washington, and he called the office nearly every day. Now he was beginning to think about Christmas. "Make up a list of everyone working in my office and where they will spend Christmas, and send the list to the New York office," he said one day. I wondered what it was all about. He also said, "Get a list of all those who have been nice to us during the year." I asked Ted Reardon why he wanted the list and Ted answered, "Oh, he generally gives out some Christmas cheer."

A few days later the Christmas cheer arrived, cases of it. Muggsie was elected to make the deliveries, and for days, back and forth, back and forth he went until almost all of the cheer

47

was dispensed, losing much of his enthusiasm for Christmas in the process.

When I received a package from the Senator, I put it under the tree with the rest of my gifts, though I was curious to see what he had sent me. It turned out to be a bright red purse. When the other girls came back from Massachusetts, where they had spent the holiday, each one had a gift from the Senator tucked under her arm. He had ordered the same thing for each of us, in different colors.

The Senator and Jackie spent the holidays with his family at Palm Beach. Among her gifts to him was a box of paints. Word came back to us from Florida that he was very enthusiastic about it and spent quite a bit of his time out by the pool painting. I gathered that he thought his paintings didn't look too bad, although someone said all he did was to paint rows and rows of little houses.

The Second Session of the 83rd Congress convened on January 6, 1954. It didn't seem possible that only a year had passed since I had joined Senator Kennedy's staff and watched him take the oath of office. I had learned a great many things during that year.

This time, at the opening session, instead of a lot of awe-struck girls watching him, there would be his new bride. He called me and said, "Jackie will come down for the opening session. Be sure that she gets my ticket." I am sure he was proud to have such a beautiful wife up in the gallery where all the Senators could see her.

Shortly after the session got under way and he began working long hours on his committee assignments, Jackie called.

"Mrs. Lincoln, please try to get Jack to come home early at night. I don't think those long hours are good for him."

I promised I would try. And I did. I would say, "Senator, Jackie would like to have you try to get home earlier. She thinks you are working too long hours." At first it worked, and then he would say, "Yes, just a few more minutes." The minutes stretched on and on, and in a few weeks he was back to his old schedule, leaving between seven and eight every night. Jackie soon realized that getting him home early every night was a lost cause, so we worked out an arrangement whereby she called me in the morning if there was an important dinner or other event they were going to attend. Then I would go to work on him, trying to get him to leave a little earlier.

One morning in the middle of January I received a call from a trucking firm in Baltimore.

"We've got an order to deliver a fish over there. How late will you be at the office?"

I remembered seeing some pictures of Jackie cooking for the Senator, and said, "I'm sure there's some mistake. They want the fish delivered to their home." I was sure it was something unusual for one of her recipes. When I gave him the home address, he argued a bit, but I held my ground.

That night while I was telling my husband about the numbskull who wanted to deliver a fish to our office, the phone rang. It was the Senator.

"Please, Mrs. Lincoln, tell me what that fish is doing in my garage."

I couldn't imagine what had happened. But when he said, "That fish is sticking way out of the garage into the alley," I began to understand that this was no ordinary fish.

The next morning I called the trucking firm. The driver snarled, "Why don't you know what you're doing? Do you get paid for making mistakes?"

I swallowed hard and said, "I was wrong, just deliver it to the office."

It arrived that afternoon, a nine-foot stuffed and mounted sailfish. The Senator had caught it during his honeymoon in Acapulco and Jackie had it stuffed and sent to his office as a surprise. He told me later that it really was a surprise to drive up to his garage and see two beady eyes and the wicked-looking sword pointing out at him.

By that time it all seemed pretty funny, and I could see that he was touched by his wife's thoughtfulness. After a struggle

49

we managed to get the monster up on the wall, and a few days later Jackie brought an engraved plate telling where and when it was caught.

We got to know Jackie in the office more through her telephone calls than by her rare visits. One day she had a surprise for us. She was going back to school. Her adjustment to the Senator had already included catching planes on time and coping with hordes of Kennedys at close quarters. Now she was going to learn to keep up with the political shop talk—she was going to study political science and history at Georgetown University.

Now they will be studying together, I thought. For he, too, was going to school. He was taking a Tuesday night course in speed reading in Baltimore in an effort to keep up with the vast amount of reading material his mind was eager to devour.

At the same time he was plunging into his Senate work and related matters with new zest and energy, and he was accepting more speaking engagements. The weekend of January 22-24, 1954, was a forecast of what was to come. He was scheduled to speak at the Cathedral Club in Brooklyn, New York, after which he had an appointment with Dr. Philip D. Wilson at the New York Hospital for Special Surgery to see about his back. It was the first I had heard about his back in some time, although I could see at times that he seemed to favor it. I never asked him about it, nor did he mention it. But I had learned that when he was at Harvard he had injured a spinal disc in football scrimmage and had never completely recovered. And then when his PT boat was struck by a Japanese destroyer during the war his back was injured seriously once again.

After undergoing X-rays of his back in New York that weekend, he went to Boston to cut a ribbon to open a bank, then on to a luncheon to plan ways to raise funds for the Truman Library, then to his Bowdoin Street apartment, which he maintained as his legal residence. There he talked with several groups of constituents before winding up the day with a speech at a Jefferson-Jackson Day dinner. I wondered how long a man whose back was already weak could keep up with the demands of such a routine.

On Monday morning he plunged into work at the office again, starting on the fund-raising for the Truman Library. He put Ted Reardon to work on the project. I was surprised at his interest in the Library; I knew that while still in the House of Representatives he had fought against some of President Truman's policies. But here he was working as hard as he could to raise money for the Truman Library.

Ted and the Senator were in the office for about forty-five minutes, and I began to wonder how they could be taking so long to hammer out the details of a fund-raising list. I peeked in and there was the Senator standing at one end of the room and Ted at the other. They were playing catch, but not with a ball; they were throwing a little rubber man that usually stood on the Senator's desk. Ted once told me that when the Senator was still in the House of Representatives they would cause a lot of head-wagging among the older members by tossing a tennis ball around in the hall outside his office.

Just as the Senator was inundated with requests to make speeches, so were he and Jackie swamped with social invitations in Washington at this time. One Saturday night they went to a dinner given by Mrs. Truxton Beale at historic Decatur House across Lafayette Park from the White House. Since Decatur House was famous for its antiques and Mrs. Beale was noted for the way she entertained, I asked him on Monday how he enjoyed the dinner.

"I guess it was all right," he answered. "But it was awfully dark in the rooms. All she had were candles and I had a hard time seeing what I was eating."

Jackie was finding also that his popularity and the publicity of their marriage resulted in an overwhelming volume of mail for her. One morning the Senator brought me a large envelope from Jackie. It contained a note from her that read: "It would be heaven if you could answer these. I feel so guilty about giving you all these extra things, when just looking after Jack gives

51

you enough work for ten people. Next winter I am going to be much more organized, maybe get someone to come to the house once a week and cope with the correspondence. I never dreamed there would be so much and I think it is so mean to pile it all on you. . . ."

The Senator was constantly broadening the horizon of his work and interests beyond the Bay State and the New England region, which demanded his first attention. He was a member of the Senate Labor Committee, and, having opposed the Taft-Hartley Labor Act in the House, was highly interested in drafting a new labor reform bill. He was working on this with some of his colleagues, and was eager to attend every session of the Senate Labor Committee.

His popularity in the Senate was increasing. More and more Senators came to him for consultation and cooperation. And he in turn was learning whom to consult on topics in which he was interested.

Vice President Richard M. Nixon's office was directly across the hall, and he often dropped in for informal chats with the Senator that both seemed to enjoy highly. Friendly Senator George Aiken of Vermont, whose office was down the hall, stopped in frequently to discuss a New England matter or just to be neighborly. Senator Kennedy very much liked scholarly, Shakespeare-quoting Illinois' Senator Everett Dirksen, whom he had known in the House, and intellectual, hard-working Illinois' Senator Paul Douglas. There were frequent office visits, later between him and Kentucky's Senator John Sherman Cooper, whom he liked to consult on international affairs, especially matters concerning India, where Senator Cooper had served as American Ambassador. The Coopers lived in Georgetown not far from the Kennedys and the wives knew each other; the two couples were often guests of each other at dinner. But perhaps his closest personal friend in the Senate was Florida's Senator George Smathers, who had served as an usher at his wedding.

Despite his warm friendships with many of the other Senators of both parties, Senator Kennedy was a "loner" and did not belong to any of the so-called cliques within the Senate.

During the spring of 1954, when his social life and his work in the Senate was increasingly complex and demanding, I began to notice that he was having more and more trouble with his back. If he dropped something on the floor he would ask me to pick it up for him. He stopped going to Baltimore for his speed reading course because he thought the trip would be too much. Then one day he said, "Maybe getting out in the sun will help me. Would you get reservations for Jackie and me to Palm Beach?"

He always enjoyed trips to Palm Beach but this time he couldn't stay long. He had a commitment to speak at a Cook County Democratic Central Committee meeting in Chicago, so after a few days in the sun, he was on his way to Chicago. Then on April 24 he went to New York to attend the wedding of his sister Pat to Peter Lawford, so he came back to Washington no better than when he left.

I never asked him how he felt, and I noticed he ignored the conventional greeting, "How are you?" A true reply would have been, "Not so good," and he didn't want sympathy. Most of all he didn't want the people of Massachusetts to think he was ill. Many times, when he was using crutches, he would hide them before a visitor entered his office.

Eventually the Senator tried to get a room near the Senate floor so he would not have to walk all the way through the halls to the elevators to answer a quorum or roll call. But the old seniority rule prevailed; those rooms were already taken by members who had served in the Senate much longer than he.

Soon his efforts to disguise the agony he suffered, together with his demanding schedule, became a heavy drain on his nervous energy. He became increasingly irritable, and, because I could not please him, I found myself wondering if perhaps I should try to find a job in another office. But he was making such an effort to carry on, I felt it my duty to stay as long as I could stand it.

When the back pains became too intense, instead of returning to his office between roll calls, he remained at his seat in the Senate chamber and left from there in the evening. Finally, one day he went directly to the floor in the morning and told one of the pages to tell me he was going to stay over there all day. He had some appointments that day, so I took my book and the mail over to the Senate floor to discuss it with him.

"Let's keep the appointments down to a minimum," he said. "Cancel everyone you possibly can."

Around the end of May he began using crutches all the time, and I spent many an afternoon on the Senate floor sitting next to him in the back row taking dictation while another Senator talked on and on. After practically filling a notebook with dictation, I would hurry back to the office to type up the letters. I would send them by page to the Senator to sign, and as soon as the Senate adjourned for the evening the page would return the signed letters. There were also instructions jotted down by the Senator: "Please call the Vice President's office and tell them that we will not be able to come to their dinner. Tell them I am having a little trouble with my back."

Senator Kennedy didn't travel very much during this period. He had a commitment to receive an honorary degree at Tufts College, and he went to that. His old Harvard roommate, Torbert Macdonald, was running for Congress in a solidly Republican district just outside of Boston and needed all the help he could get. The Senator went to Malden, Massachusetts, on the evening of May 14th to speak at a dinner in Torby's honor. Several other Senators and Congressmen asked him to come to their states to campaign, but he always told them he might be laid up most of the fall with an operation on his back. Finally, he told me to make a reservation for him to go to Hyannis, in the hope that he might get some relief there.

The Senate finally decided to recess on August 20 and return the first part of November. That last day was hectic; everyone on the staff wanted to take up matters that had been accumulating and get instructions on matters that might come up during his absence. When I went over to the Democratic cloakroom, just off the Senate chamber, to get his signature on a letter he had requested, he asked me somewhat curtly, "Now, what do you have?" I was so upset by his unusual attitude that my hands shook as I held the letter for him to sign.

I gave him his airline ticket and said, "Muggsie is waiting for you at the bottom of the steps." As I turned to go I mumbled, "I hope everything goes well." But he didn't seem to hear me, and barely said goodbye. As I walked out of the cloakroom, I wondered if he would ever be well again.

He remained at the Cape during the month of September, and then one day early in October we got word that the Senator was definitely going into the hospital. The next morning the front page of all the New York papers had pictures of the Senator on crutches, with Jackie at his side, entering the New York Hospital. At first there were tests and X-rays, and he kept in close touch with us at the office, calling me at least once a day. He sounded cheerful and always ended with the same request: "Don't forget to send me the mail." I did, but it didn't come back quite as fast as when he was at the Cape. We sent cards and flowers and tried to think of things to do to help him in his pain, but there was little we could do except pray.

Cards, wires, and letters were beginning to pour in from everywhere. At first I sent them to the hospital, but I soon learned they were getting their share up there, too, so I made up for him a list of the people who had sent messages. He drafted a letter and asked me to send it to each of the well-wishers. We had to use a facsimile signature because it would have been impossible for him to sign every letter.

The operation was scheduled for Monday, October 11th, and the tension in the office began to rise. There wasn't much work done that day; mostly we waited for a telephone call, even though we realized it was too soon to know the outcome.

Toward evening we learned that he had survived the operation and was back in his hospital room. Then the waiting began. Days passed slowly. His condition changed, sometimes from hour to hour. One day he would be better, the next much worse and sinking. Once I was called at home: the doctors did not expect him to live until morning. The next morning I called the hospital and was told, "The doctors don't understand where he gets his strength—he rallied again during the night." As soon as I heard that I forgot how tired I was. Now I could hope again.

All during those weeks I wrote little notes to Jackie, telling her that everything was coming along fine at the office. I'm sure she read them to him and that he was pleased to know he didn't need to worry about things in the office. Jackie stayed by his side every day, and those who saw her with him said she was marvelous in the way she held his spirits up and kept him informed.

Gradually we were getting more of the details of his operation. It was a double fusion of spinal discs. The doctors had recommended that it be done in two separate operations, but he had insisted on having both operations at one time and thereby increased immeasurably the risk involved. It was a long and difficult operation.

The weeks passed; election day came and went. He was still in the hospital in critical condition. I knew he was cheered, however, to learn that his old friend Torbert Macdonald had been elected to Congress.

Meanwhile, the speculation about Senator Kennedy's health grew. It became the favorite subject of Capitol Hill rumors, particularly since his death would give Massachusetts Governor Christian Herter, a Republican, the opportunity to appoint a Republican to take his place, and thereby give the Republican Party control of the Senate.

December arrived. The family decided it would do the Senator good to bring him to Palm Beach where he could sit in the sun. So they bundled him up, put him on a stretcher, and he was on his way. He was out of the hospital and he was alive! We were very happy in Senate Office 362.

56

CHAPTER 7

Darkness and Dawn

All during the fall of 1954 I found it increasingly difficult to concentrate and to carry on with the office routine. Some mornings I had to force myself to get up and leave for work. I thought that the tension we felt in the office was responsible for my lack of energy, and that I would soon snap back. My back was aching, too, and I half believed one of the girls in the office who said, "Know what's wrong with you? You've got sympathy pains."

My husband suggested a change of scenery, and so we went to Nebraska for a wonderful old-fashioned Christmas with his parents in Lexington. It was good to be back in the state I loved, and my in-laws could not have been nicer, but somehow I didn't feel much better. I thought I must have some kind of deficiency and started taking vitamin pills, but that didn't change the leaden feeling that held me down. Just before the New Year, Abe and I flew to Omaha from Lexington to catch the plane back to Washington.

It was the time of year when Nebraska is really gripped by winter, and by the time we got to Omaha the weather bureau was predicting a storm. The snow began to fall as we were waiting for our plane, but we took off anyway, hoping to get ahead of the eastward-moving storm front, but it was snowing in Chicago, too, and the plane couldn't land. It flew directly to New York and by now we were in the middle of the storm. In the rough air the plane began bouncing like a motorboat skimming over the water. Finally, I sighed as I felt the thumping of the wheels on the ground in New York. Since planes were also grounded there, we took the train to Washington just before dawn. After that four-hour ride, I was ready to fall into bed when we got to our apartment. I could barely summon enough strength to call the office and tell them I would not be in until after New Year's Day.

January 1, 1955, dawned and with it my hope that it would be a better year than its predecessor. Almost immediately it gave signs of being just that, for just before Congress convened my husband learned that Congressman-elect Torby Macdonald wanted him to join his staff. Some things were looking up, but now the ache in my back started again.

I tried to forget my difficulties by taking an interest in what Abe was doing in Torby's office. Every evening he'd come home full of enthusiasm about a pet idea of Torby's to deepen the Mystic River in the Congressman's district, helping industry expand and providing more jobs. Abe was meeting with engineers about the feasibility of the project and writing press releases so that Torby's constituents would know how he was working for their benefit.

I was very happy that Abe was doing the work he loved, and that, together with the fact that the Senator was getting better, should have made me feel better. But I began to feel even worse.

To cheer me up, Abe would get the car and pick me up at noontime so we could have lunch together. February 9th was one of those windy Washington days that remind one unpleasantly that the nation's capital is built on swampland.

"Let's take a little extra time and go to a really good restaurant today," I said. "Tomorrow's your birthday and I want you to help me pick out your surprise."

"Let's worry about that later. First let's get some lunch and then I'll tell you what my surprise should be."

There were a number of conventions in town and all the restaurants we tried were filled, so we wound up in a drugstore near the Supreme Court Building. I ordered a bowl of soup and had no sooner tasted a spoonful when I turned to Abe and said, "Something is happening to me." I felt dizzy and faint, and the next thing I knew I was looking up at a blurred circle of faces that mumbled, "What happened? . . . She fell off the stool . . . Give her air."

An ambulance took me to the emergency room of Washington's Casualty Hospital, where the intern said I should remain for observation. My husband asked that I be transferred to Emergency Hospital whose Chief of Staff was a close friend. Abe signed a release, and I was back in the ambulance again and on my way to the other hospital.

At Emergency the doctor concluded that I probably had an ulcer and placed me on the usual bland diet of milk and crackers. Despite the good treatment I was receiving, I felt weaker each day, so they began to give me blood transfusions. After each transfusion, my strength returned only to seep away again. Two weeks later the doctor decided to operate and found a duodenal ulcer. Everything seemed fine. But three days later I had a terrific pounding headache. Suddenly a curtain of black accompanied with what seemed like flashing pinwheels descended before my eyes, and that was the last thing I remembered for the next fifty days.

I was in a coma, paralyzed, and a neurosurgeon, Dr. Hugo V. Rizzoli, was called in. He took a spinal tap, which showed the spinal fluid was full of blood. He diagnosed it as an aneurism or distended blood vessel in my brain and explained that to confirm this diagnosis it would be necessary to fill the blood vessels of my brain with a special dye that would then show up on X-ray plates. This operation, a delicate procedure in itself, was complicated by the fact that my ulcer operation had been so recent. The surgeon advised that we wait for seven weeks and then go ahead with the X-rays.

This was a terrible period for Abe. He visited me faithfully twice each day but could only stare at me. I could not move a muscle, not even blink my eyes. I seem to recall his voice a few times, but I'm not sure of that, and he had no idea whether he was getting through to me.

Once, when my condition was almost at its lowest point, the nurse on duty received a long distance call from Palm Beach, Florida. It was the Senator asking about my condition and wanting to speak to me. The nurse told him that I was unconscious and couldn't accept the call. After she hung up, despite the fact that my condition was close to that of the living dead, she told me about his call. I don't remember this but the nurse later told me she believed I must have understood for shortly afterward my condition began to improve.

Finally, those horrible seven weeks were over, and the doctor went ahead with the X-rays of my brain. They were negative. The next day I was placed under the fluoroscope and the dye was pumped into my spine. The column of dye climbed slowly upward, past the lower vertebrae and then, at the eleventh dorsal, stopped completely. There was something blocking the passage of the fluid. The doctor marked the spot with a piece of adhesive tape and, as soon as the operating room was free, operated on my spine. He found a tumor—the cause of all the difficulty.

It was now April, and the first thing I recalled clearly since that Sunday afternoon in February was the doctor coming to see me shortly after I had been brought down from the recovery room saying, "I have just removed a tumor from your spine, and it was benign." I smiled weakly, but gratefully, and drifted off to sleep. The next day the black curtain was gone completely. I was conscious and could talk to my husband. I could move my toes slightly although I was too weak to do much more than that. But I was alive. It seemed I had been born again. During the time I was paralyzed, there was one thing that I could feel, and that was pain, constant and penetrating, but I couldn't tell anyone about it.

After a further examination the doctor told my husband that the operation was a success. "But I don't know how well she will be able to walk," he said. "She may be able to get around again in a year, but then there's a strong chance that she will never walk again."

Abe accepted this verdict but told me he would do everything possible to help me regain the use of my legs. He arranged for the aid of a physical therapist. After I arrived home, six mornings a week for the next nine weeks, the therapist arrived at nine o'clock, and I began to experience once again the struggle that I had won as an infant.

First I learned to sit, then to stand. At last there was the great day I took my first steps. I thought, "I'll show that doctor. I'm not going to be stuck in any wheelchair the rest of my life."

Soon I was pumping away madly at the exercise bicycle the physical therapist had brought. We walked up and down the hall. At first I had to lean heavily on the arm of the therapist. Later, I used crutches, then a cane, and finally I walked alone. I ventured up stairs, and then gradually moved from slippers into low heels. Eventually, I could walk anywhere on my own without any kind of support. Now my goal was to walk in high-heeled slippers, but I knew that was going to take some time.

Meanwhile I was keeping in close touch with the office by telephone. I learned that the Senator had returned to New York for another operation, and that he had left the hospital on February 25th, a few days after I became ill. He spent the period from February to May in Palm Beach slowly regaining his strength.

During the time of his greatest pain, before he left a year earlier, I was very sympathetic about his health. But I couldn't know how much he was suffering until my own illness. I remembered how angry he made me sometimes by his irritated manner. Now I knew and could feel the cause of that irritation and I felt deeply ashamed of myself for having thought about quitting the job.

"I'll make it up to him as soon as I get back to work," I told myself. I looked forward to the day when my strength would return completely and I could walk back into Room 362 and take up where I had left off in February.

About that time Abe received a call from the Senator. "Mr. Lincoln," he said, "I wonder if you would come over to my office; there's something important I want to discuss with you."

When my husband entered his office, he told me later, the Senator seemed lost for words. After asking about my health and some generalities about weather and politics, he said, "Mr.

Lincoln, although I'll still need these crutches for a while, the doctors tell me that chances are I won't have any more trouble with my back. That means that I'll be able to work a lot harder than I could before. And that means the pressure and the load on the staff is going to increase."

As he talked, Abe wondered what he was trying to get at. Then it came. "In short, Mr. Lincoln, whoever is my personal secretary is going to have to be in excellent health to keep up with the job. We know what your wife has gone through." Then he paused for almost a minute. "She's got a lot of courage and she's the best secretary I ever had." Another pause. "But it just wouldn't be fair to her to have her come back. I don't think she could take it, and I think it would hurt her health to try. So, that's what I asked you to come in for. I want you to tell her what the situation is."

"You mean you want me to tell her that she's through?"

"No, I didn't mean that. I'll always have a place for her in my office. But not as my personal secretary. That's what I want you to tell her."

"Senator, Evelyn's nurse told me that your call from Palm Beach helped her through a very bad period. And all those months that she's been learning to walk and regaining her strength . . . the thing that has carried her through was the thought of coming back here. I think my telling her this will break her heart. I don't think that I can do it. I think no one should do it but you."

Abe saw that the Senator was embarrassed and very troubled, and he decided that hearing it from the Senator might not be too good for me after all. So, a few nights later, after I started going through my plans to get back to the Senator's office, he told me what the Senator had said.

I felt a kind of numbness stealing over me as he went on. It was like a tornado that once passed close by when I was a little girl in Nebraska. Unexpected, and destroying everything. I didn't say anything to Abe, just walked into my bedroom and started to cry. He said through the door, "You didn't let me finish. He says he has another job open for you."

"Another job," I thought. "How can I go back there, just typing and filing? He's offered it out of pity. The way you find a job for the feebleminded or a cripple." I was too depressed and angry to cry; I just looked up at the ceiling, unable to sleep, my fists doubled up.

The depression lasted for several days. Every time I thought about everything I had worked for being thrown away just because I had been sick, a wave of anger swept through me and I couldn't think clearly.

Days later, still angry, I began to consider the future and what I would do. There was really no one else I wanted to work for, and even if there had been, jobs as personal secretary to a Congressman were hard to get. If I went to work somewhere else, I would be starting at the bottom of the ladder, and perhaps there would be no higher rungs on that ladder, or I might be working for a Congressman who had nothing to offer but routine and who had no great ambitions for his future.

Pride, I decided, was the only thing keeping me away from the Senator's office, and I began to wonder, can I afford pride? After all, I went to work for him not to help myself but to help him. I recalled how happy I was that day I was offered a job in his office. I didn't care what the job was then, why should I care now? I thought too of how he had kept me on full salary all during those months I was ill, and how ungrateful I would seem by refusing now to help where he thought I would be useful.

I recalled my childhood in Nebraska, how my grandfather and father had faced setbacks but worked on for what they believed. I remembered the dream I had so often while going to school from our home on the farm. It was of myself—Evelyn Norton—as a famous ballet dancer. When I was about ten years old I saw a motion picture of a ballet, and from then on I dreamed that someday I would be dressed in white, dancing for the whole world. Many times, Mildred Smith, the teacher who taught all eight grades in our one-room schoolhouse, would shout in her high-pitched voice, "Ev-A-lyn! Pay attention. You're dreaming again."

Evenings I would dance along the road on the way home from school, kicking up big clouds of dust. My mother would be very annoyed when she saw me. "Evelyn, I don't know how you get your stockings so dirty." Soon I would be helping her around the house, reluctantly laying aside my dream until bedtime.

Life on a farm can be dull, especially if you have only a brother who is several years older than you and who thinks you are too little to know what is going on. With no one to play with, I had plenty of time to dream and think and look at that flat, treeless horizon stretching on and on. The summers were especially long, with just the sounds of the locusts and the buzzing of the flies on the screen door at the back porch. The old piano that I learned to play sounded good breaking into all that silence, and sometimes on an endless summer afternoon I felt that the uncertain notes from that untuned piano proved there really was an Evelyn Norton.

Fortunately there was Grandfather. He lived across the road, and I loved to sit on his porch and listen to him tell about his experiences in the Civil War. Grandfather Charlie, or Calla, was what people called a "rugged individualist." You could always pick him out of a crowd for, unlike most Swedish people, his hair was coal black, and both my father and I inherited it. He possessed the kind of half-wild aristocratic bearing that would have appealed to the Indians, who were a problem in his early days on the farm. Grandfather was a pioneer, one of those men who really won the West.

When he was twelve years old his family and several others left their homes in the northern part of Sweden and together took the long, still dangerous, voyage to the United States. Just a few years before, John F. Kennedy's grandfather, Patrick Kennedy, had decided to leave New Ross, Ireland, and the potato famine that made the Irish feel the curse of God was on their land.

64

The mortality rate on board the crowded immigrant ships was terribly high in those days of primitive sanitation, and young Calla's mother was one of those who died on the way over. Although Swedish immigrants were among the first to come to America back in the 1840s, and for a while large numbers of them settled on the banks of the Delaware River in southern New Jersey where Swedesboro is still located, my grandfather, like most immigrant farmers during the 1850s, moved out to the Middle West.

First he stayed with a Swedish family in Illinois, and it was there in the land of Lincoln that he was caught up by anti-slavery idealism and volunteered to serve in the Union Army. Because he was so young, barely seventeen, they sent him to a quiet part of the battlefield and he served most of the war in an Army hospital in Texas.

After the war he came home, married, and moved on to Nebraska to stake out his claim.

I think my father, J. N. Norton, whose nickname was "Nate," must have inherited some of Grandfather Calla's rugged individualism along with his black hair, because he wanted to do a thing unheard of out there on the farm: continue going to school. Father and son had loud, violent arguments about it.

Father finally won; in winters he went to normal school and in the spring he came back to help with the corn planting. The thirst for knowledge stayed with my father, and he kept at his studies until he received his B.A. degree from the University of Nebraska.

He became deeply interested in good government and found politics a challenge. He began to read everything he could get his hands on about state government. He broke with his father, a Lincoln Republican, and joined the Populist Party of William Jennings Bryan. A few years later he was elected to the Nebraska state legislature, where he displayed such knowledge of the rules of the legislature that he became its parliamentarian.

One of his strongest views was that the system of having two houses of government was wasteful and just one more way to thwart the will of the people. So, during his first term in the legislature, he introduced a bill for a unicameral, or one-house, legislature.

My dreams of becoming a ballet dancer began to fade for lack of encouragement, and I was not happy in high school. In fact, I wanted to quit when I was a sophomore but my father persuaded me to go on, and I followed his advice and example. I not only finished high school but went on to get a B.A. degree, majoring in English and dramatics.

Father, in the meantime, was elected to the United States House of Representatives, and this meant moving to Washington. It was while attending George Washington University that I fell in love; suddenly it became more important for me to know how to fry an egg than to quote Shakespeare.

In Harold "Abe" Lincoln, also from Nebraska, I found my dream. A farsighted man who believed in open discussions and lived in the world of here and now, he had everything that my reserved home life lacked. As a girl I yearned for adventure, but my father was always busy reading and studying and mother was never well, so I was strongly attracted to this man who could give me all those things I had missed. Now life was fun. We went to school together, studied together, shared our dreams.

I was so proud when he graduated from law school, but then he left for the army. I thought the world had ended. But soon I found a way to be with him and took a job near his army post. It meant commuting fifty miles each day, six days a week, but that was a trifle compared to the chance to see Abe.

After the war was over and the khakis put away, we went to New Mexico, the "Land of Enchantment," to live. Getting married and moving away from my politically minded father didn't take me away from discussions about government and politics, however. Abe's job was at the University of New Mexico—teaching government. Between letters from Dad, previewing Abe's lectures, and entertaining the faculty and students of the government department, I found myself thinking about government almost all the time.

We were beginning to fall in love with the Southwest when Abe received an offer from New York University that he couldn't refuse. Soon we were fighting traffic and living in a Greenwich Village apartment. I thought I would hate New York after our good times in New Mexico, but I got accustomed to Greenwich Village life very quickly. We were fascinated with the way the Village came alive after dark and the variety of people that filled the streets.

It was then that Abe had an opportunity to get into the government work. He was offered a post on the staff of a committee of the House of Representatives. So we came to Washington, where my dream for John F. Kennedy was born.

I spent a week debating whether I would abandon that dream and go to work for someone else or return to my job in his office and be less than his personal secretary. I decided I would keep my dream and go back to work for him.

I telephoned his office that I would be back to work on September 1st, ready to do anything I could to help with the office routine.

CHAPTER 8

Past Is Prologue

Now I was determined to show Senator Kennedy—and myself—that I was physically fit, and the only way to do that was by producing. I remembered a letter he had written to one of his friends. He had remarked how impressed he was by the inscriptions that appear on the Archives Building: "What Is Past Is Prologue," and "Study the Past."

I decided to take my cue from these words. I would fill in the void that existed in my mind about what had happened during the months I was ill. I decided to read every note and go through every file, until I was completely up to date. When he came back, I'd be ready for him. "There won't be a thing he can ask that I won't know," I promised myself.

So I began. I made October 1954 my starting point—shortly after the first of his two operations. Reading the files of that trying time was like going back over the ruins after a disaster. But I could tell, as I read on, that somewhere along the line he had decided he couldn't just lie in bed and wait while time did its healing work. The files showed a growing desire to find something useful he could do. I wasn't surprised at his reaction; it was part of the pattern I knew: he hated to waste time.

During his recuperation Jackie did all she could to maintain his spirits and keep his mind occupied. She brought him magazines and newspapers by the armload, but his reading speed, once his friend, now became an enemy. He was able to get through the material so swiftly it was impossible to keep him supplied. Then he asked for books, and began to read such things as *The World's Great Orations*. Even this fare, useful though it would be when he started making speeches again, was not satisfying enough. He wanted to do something creative, and gradually the idea of writing a book was born.

I do not know what the original inspiration was. Perhaps one of the letters he received suggested a book; perhaps it was a suggestion by a friend or a member of his family. I remembered that ten years before, also in a hospital (the Chelsea Hospital near Boston) and also while recovering from a back operation (necessitated by an injury to his already weak back when his PT boat was sunk), he had received news that his brother Joe had been killed in action. This, too, was the making of a book into which he channeled his frustrations: *As We Remember Joe*, a collection of tributes written by those who best knew Joe, and his courage.

It was fascinating going over the trail of a book being born.

The files were full of letters he had written to Ted Sorensen asking for books from the Library of Congress and for Ted's reaction to drafts of chapters or material the Senator was considering.

In going through the files I discovered that after the second operation on his back, in February, he had developed a new zest and interest not only in the book, but also in the office. He kept asking for the mail and began using the dictaphone to draft his answers and instructions to his staff. I decided to go back over his dictation and transcribe every bit to make sure that I missed nothing.

The memos he wrote were like the line of a fever chart, clearly showing he was getting better and gaining strength and confidence.

Finally I came to his note telling the staff he would be back on May 23rd, after an absence of nine months. I was told there was quite a celebration when he returned. Television and newsreel cameras were on the Capitol steps to film his arrival, tourists stopped and cheered, reporters and photographers filled the office, and Senators and Congressmen kept dropping in to welcome him back. There was a basket of fruit with a card reading, "Welcome Home! Dick Nixon."

An office was ready for him near the Senate floor—this time seniority was overruled. Since the lease on their house had expired, he and Jackie had reserved rooms at the Congressional Hotel on Capitol Hill until they could find a home. Days later they announced they had found it: a beautiful old place called "Hickory Hill" across the river in McLean, Virginia, about ten miles from Washington. Formerly the home of the late Supreme Court Justice Robert Jackson, the white brick Georgian house once was used as headquarters by General George McClellan during the Civil War.

Soon the Senator began to travel again. On the 3rd of June he spoke at commencement exercises at Assumption College in Worcester, Massachusetts. The next day he went over to Hyannis to see his father and discuss his future plans.

In mid-June he went back to Massachusetts again, and he and his old roommate, Torby Macdonald, attended the fifteenth reunion of their Harvard class. In the file I found a large photograph of them in the reunion procession. It was a good picture of him—smiling, the wind blowing both his tie and his boyish mop of hair, while he and Torby strode along in the bright sun. He appeared to be enjoying the simple pleasure of feeling one foot following the other without paying the cost of pain that he had come to expect and almost to accept.

The Senate had adjourned on August 2nd. I could see that each time he came to Washington after September 1st, his new secretary was having difficulty keeping up with his demands— then I remembered how difficult it had been for me when I had first started.

I had now reached the point of telling myself that I would prove to him just how wrong he was about my ability to keep up with him. I didn't care if I worked eighteen hours a day and did nothing but dust and file, he was going to see that I was healthy as he. So I swallowed my pride and continued to do the routine chores.

Then he left for Europe. He had an audience with the Pope and he was going behind the Iron Curtain to visit Poland. The newspapers carried stories about his travels. This time he had gone to Europe to work and to learn, not rest and play. I felt an air of expectancy as I waited impatiently for the day he would be back in the office.

His return was preceded by his report on that trip to Warsaw. It contained his recommendations for American policy toward Poland, and he wanted the report released to the press on Monday, October 10, 1955. As I typed the press release, one paragraph stood out:

"If the Poles come to believe that we in the West have forgotten them, that we are willing to make an agreement with the Russians that does not provide for a free Poland, then their courageous struggle to maintain their freedom may cease. The show of friendliness at Geneva may indicate a change in Communist policy. The concessions they have made are extremely unimportant. They represent only the shadow of cooperation, not the substance; for the real face of Communism may be seen here in Poland. The barbarian may have taken the knife out of his teeth to smile—but the knife itself is still in his fist."

By the middle of October I had finished my excursion into the past and felt that I was up to date and ready to go. As far as I was concerned, the past had better be prologue, for I did not wish to repeat that period again.

He came to Washington for one day after his return from Europe. It was obvious that his stature as a Senator had grown, for he came back as an authority on the current situation in Poland. His secretary was visiting her parents at the time. I could tell that he was upset, but he did not say anything then. However, shortly after the first of November he again came to Washington and told Ted Sorensen while they were riding in from the airport that he was going to make a change as far as his secretary was concerned. I was glad that Ted tipped me off because when he called me into his office he acted as though there had never been a break in our relationship. I thought what a fool I would have been to let pride stand in my way. Once again, I was his personal secretary.

Then he left for his usual stay in Hyannis Port and Palm Beach over the Thanksgiving and Christmas holidays.

One day he called me from Palm Beach and asked me to order two rocking chairs from a company in North Carolina. "They say a rocking chair will be good for my back, so I want to give it a try." He had one sent to his office and the other one to his father down there in Palm Beach.

He returned to Washington on January 2nd for the opening of the new session of Congress on the third. Ted Sorensen rode out to the airport with Muggsie to meet him. The first big discussion was about the book, which Evan Thomas of Harper's had insisted should be entitled *Profiles in Courage*. Next he was concerned about getting an assignment on the Senate Foreign Relations Committee. He asked at the first of each session for this assignment, and after his report on Poland he hoped he would make it this time. However, he was still a first-term Senator, and again the seniority rule prevailed.

Soon cartons of his book began to arrive at the office. It was a study of notable examples of political courage in America, including such men as John Quincy Adams, Daniel Webster, Edmund Ross, George W. Norris, Sam Houston, Thomas Hart Benton, and Robert A. Taft.

He was proud of the book and wanted his fellow Senators to be aware that his time away from the Senate had not been a total loss. He asked me to give him a list of the Senators and put the books beside his desk. Then I would sit by his desk, hand him a book, and as soon as he had autographed it he would hand it back. After he had autographed about two dozen copies, he would get up and go in to talk to the men in the outer office. I would then see that these autographed books were delivered by hand to the Senators. Next he dictated a list of personal friends and prominent people to whom he wanted to send an autographed copy. He worked for hours at a time autographing books, checking lists, and adding more and more names.

There was great interest in the book, judging by the mail and the book reviews. I recall one review that said: [Also] notable is the fact that John Kennedy has set down so explicitly the standard of conduct that he thinks should guide a man in public office. Time will tell whether this was a rash thing to do. For, in making such a point of it, Mr. Kennedy may open himself to future harsh criticism. There will be those who will be ready to accuse him of hypocrisy and fakery if he deviates even slightly."

I thought, this man doesn't know the Senator or he never would have written this.

After *Profiles in Courage* won the Pulitzer Prize for biography in 1957, the Senator's prominence as a scholar and a statesman grew. As his book continued to be a bestseller, he climbed higher on public-opinion polls and moved into a leading position among Presidential possibilities for 1960.

At the time he was launching the book in 1956, Jackie was getting her house in McLean in order. There were constant rumors that she was making one of the rooms a nursery. That started speculation in the office about the Senator as a father. We all hoped they would have a boy.

We could tell by the mail that an election year was coming up. There were letters asking the Senator's views on the Democratic candidate for President. He always wrote back, "I have supported Governor Stevenson in the past and am supporting him for President in 1956." Then when they asked about his choice for Vice President, he was less specific. "I have made no decision," he would reply. "I think his selection will depend upon who will have been nominated for President and the part of the country from which such nominee may have been selected. There are several very capable persons to select from, any one of whom would make a good candidate for second place on the ticket."

Privately, he thought that Stevenson probably would pick a Southerner for a running mate but still he thought there might be a chance that he himself could get it. And there was much speculation in the papers about the possibility of Kennedy being named as the Vice Presidential nominee.

Adding to this speculation was the fact that the Senator was expanding his area for speeches. He went across the country to spend a weekend speaking at various meetings in Los Angeles. Ted Sorensen not only helped on those speeches, he went with the Senator on this trip to study his speaking techniques, help with last-minute revisions, and gauge the reactions. He came back with a valuable collection of names of Kennedy supporters in each audience.

Another boost for the Senator came on April 29th, when he spoke at the "America Salutes Israel" rally in Yankee Stadium in New York. This was the first time he had spoken to such a large visible audience and he came back pleased with the experience.

One morning he said, "I believe I will take a little time off

73

following the convention in Chicago. Will you arrange to charter a yacht to pick me up off the coast of France on the twenty-
first day of August. I would also like to have reservations from
Chicago to New York and from New York to Cannes." I went
to work on it immediately. It wasn't difficult to get the airline
reservations, but I could see that it was going to take a little
time to get the yacht.

He had earned a rest. This year he had worked hard on his
three interests—his Senatorial duties, his book, and politics. As
a result of the success of his book, he was made chairman of a
special Senate committee to select the five most outstanding
Senators in the nation's history. Named to serve with him were
such distinguished veterans as Senator Russell of Georgia, Senator Millikin of Colorado, and Senator Bridges of New Hampshire.

The five Senators they eventually chose, whose pictures were
placed in the Senate Hall of Fame, were Henry Clay, Daniel
Webster, John C. Calhoun, Robert M. LaFollette, and Robert
A. Taft.

CHAPTER 9

Water over the Dam

After Congress adjourned that summer, our office became
almost like a campaign headquarters. Everything was centered
on the coming Democratic National Convention and—we hoped
—on a Stevenson-Kennedy ticket. The question that was hashed
over and over again was how to get it across to the delegates
and to Presidential hopefuls that a Catholic would strengthen
the Democratic ticket.

"They only remember Al Smith," Senator Kennedy said, "and circumstances were different in 1928." With the Senator's blessing, Ted Sorensen began building up a detailed statistical report showing how important the Catholic vote was in pivotal states, and why Senator Kennedy would be the ideal running mate.

Meanwhile, the gears of the Kennedy organization began to move. Ted Reardon was making arrangements for hotel rooms in Chicago for members of the Senator's staff, and up in Boston Frank Morrissey was doing the same for the delegates from Massachusetts, whose backing would be crucial to the Senator. Working in the background was a team of strategists that included the Senator's brother, Bob, who at the age of twenty-seven had managed his campaign for the Senate; Lawrence F. O'Brien, experienced in Massachusetts politics; Kenneth P. O'Donnell, a former Harvard football star and a Boston political pro; Ted Sorensen; and Torby Macdonald.

Many times I heard the Senator say as they charted a course for him in Chicago, "We will go out there and we will try, but if I don't win I will still get out and work for the party." And once he said, "I think I have the best chance with Stevenson."

Because he wanted to stay in the background as much as possible, the Senator asked me to get him a suite at the Drake Hotel in Chicago and an adjoining room for myself so that I could handle his calls. I had never been to a national convention before and I was anxious to go. Abe, who was coming along, was just as enthusiastic.

Before leaving for Chicago, the Senator went up to Massachusetts to meet with the state's Stevenson-for-President organization and again to appeal to the Massachusetts Democratic delegation to cast their votes for Stevenson. In the office we were busy sending out invitations to the New England delegates for a breakfast at the Palmer House in Chicago on Monday, August 15th. Jackie was to be there with the Senator, and she would be staying at the Shrivers'.

He arrived in Chicago on the tenth and was immediately

besieged by reporters, who asked if he were a candidate for Vice President.

He replied, "I am not a candidate, and I am not campaigning for the office." But he added quickly, "I would accept the Vice Presidential nomination if Mr. Stevenson should happen to think me worthy of it."

As soon as I stepped into my room at the Drake Hotel the phone started ringing. I would no more than start talking to one person when the other telephone would ring. In between calls I managed to set up my office—Abe called it "a command post"—next to the telephone. I was in business, but worried about how I was going to learn from there about what went on at the convention.

Finally I said, "I just have to go down to the Kennedy head-quarters at the Palmer House and see about our tickets," and Abe, who had sprained a muscle in his back lifting a suitcase, volunteered to stay at the command post. I arrived at the Palmer House to find it just like election night at any campaign head-quarters: people milling around, hovering clouds of smoke, and here and there a large knot of politicians surrounding one of the party leaders. The Senator saw me as I was about to step into an elevator and asked, "Who's answering the telephone?" He seemed relieved when I told him that Abe was taking the calls and that I had just stepped out long enough to get the tickets we would need to go to the convention. "That's fine," he said. "I want you to stay over there. It's important."

I couldn't find Frank Morrissey, who was supposed to have our tickets, and I decided to go back to the hotel. By the time I got there the lobby was filled with a group of Harriman boosters complete with banners and buttons and accompanied by a regimental band. They were whooping it up for their candidate to a tune usually reserved for St. Patrick's Day—"Harrigan." What a funny thing, I thought, to use an Irish song for Harriman. They sang, "H-A-double R-I-M-A-N" with gusto, and occasionally in tune. They must have been working on this for months, I thought. If this is any sample, I wonder how much attention the Senator will attract with just a handful of people working for him, and no bands or theme songs?

When it was announced that President Truman had endorsed Harriman rather than Stevenson for President, there was a renewed burst of singing. I fled to the elevator before another burst of "H-A- . . ." began.

Frank Morrissey sent our tickets to us and that night we pushed through the mobs on the street into the International Amphitheater. Inside the crowds were worse than outside. My first reaction was shock. The hall was immense and covered with banners and bunting, and there were acres of people, all moving about in a continual swarming. Suddenly, I heard my name being called. "Hi there, Mrs. Lincoln." I turned and saw Ethel Kennedy. With her were Jackie and the Senator's sisters, Eunice and Jean. They looked as if they were having the time of their lives and immediately I began to feel better.

Seeing them and remembering that one of the calls I had received that afternoon for the Senator was from his father over in France, I said to Abe, "You know, the Senator might not have a big organization fighting for him, but with his family working for him, he doesn't need an organization."

Just then the lights dimmed and they announced the showing of the film, *Pursuit of Happiness*, the history of the Democratic Party, narrated by Senator John F. Kennedy. We groped our way to our seats, only to find they were occupied, so we had to take seats on the steps. There was so much walking up and down those steps we didn't get to see much of the film, but we were very disappointed at the few cheers we heard for the Senator. Favorite sons that we had never heard of before were getting more applause, it seemed to me, and if Adlai Stevenson was going to pick his running mate on the basis of applause, it seemed that Senator Kennedy had little chance.

All day Tuesday Stevenson supporters were busy lining up delegates. Several times they called and asked to talk to the Senator. Delegates pledged to other candidates were also trying to get in touch with him. I knew he was moving from one state caucus to another. I promised he would call each of them later.

And then on Wednesday they were calling me on the telephone.

"What do you know about Stevenson asking Kennedy to make his nomination speech?"

I hadn't heard anything about it.

"If he does that," Abe said, "the Senator will be out of the race for Vice President."

"Why?" I asked.

"It's the custom," he answered. "The nominating speech is a kind of consolation prize to the second choice."

"Well, John F. Kennedy isn't going to be stopped by any silly tradition, wait and see."

Stevenson did ask him, and if he was disheartened, he didn't show it. Far into the night the Senator and Ted Sorensen worked on that speech. While Abe held off most of the phone calls, I was taking dictation or typing until long after midnight. "It has to be good," the Senator said. When he had gone over the drafts several times, each time making corrections, he went to bed promising to look at it again in the morning. The first thing he asked for the next morning was a copy of his speech, and he read and reread it right up to the time of its delivery.

We went over to hear him speak. As his voice rang through that immense hall, I realized this speech was very important to him, not so much for the honor of being chosen to deliver it, but because he was deeply concerned about the future of the country. As he spoke, I knew he meant his words for the entire nation as well as the delegates in the hall.

"We here today are selecting a man who must be more than something of a good candidate, more than a good politician, or a good liberal, or a good conservative. We are selecting the head of the most powerful nation on earth—the man who literally will hold in his hands the power of survival or destruction, of freedom or slavery. . . ."

He showed how the critical nature of the world called for the

78

best we could give. "We have, therefore, an obligation to pick the man best qualified, not only to lead our party, but to lead our country. The nation is entitled to expect that of us." And then he reminded them that ". . . what we do here today affects more than a nomination, more than an election—it affects the life and the way of life of all of our fellow Americans. The time is ripe. The hour has struck. The man is here; and he is ready. Let the word go forth that we have fulfilled our responsibility to the nation."

The response was overwhelming. The cheering lasted for many minutes. Delegates marched up and down the aisle, bands blared. Most of it, I knew, was the expected reaction to having Stevenson's name placed in nomination; but some, I felt, surely must be for the Senator's masterful speech. When I got back to the hotel I discovered I was right. People called from all over leaving messages to tell the Senator they were for him one hundred per cent. They called me from the Kennedy headquarters and said that the wires of congratulations were pouring in from all parts of the country.

Now that Stevenson had been nominated on the first ballot, there was a fresh flood of rumors. Senator Estes Kefauver of Tennessee had campaigned throughout the country and won a number of primaries in his bid for the Presidential nomination. They were saying, "Stevenson will probably name Kefauver to heal the wounds in the party and add to Stevenson's strength." Some said, "It will be Humphrey. He's the kind of liberal Stevenson wants, and besides political leaders of the South would rather vote for him than for Kefauver."

More and more calls were coming, more and more messages of support were going down in my notebook. I talked to headquarters in the Palmer House and they said they were getting a fantastic number of messages.

"Did you know that Mayor Daley was so impressed by the Senator's speech that he has recommended him to Stevenson?"

"What did Stevenson say to that?" I asked.

"He can't make up his mind."

79

Later they said former Governor Battle of Virginia, Governor Ribicoff of Connecticut, and Governor Roberts of Rhode Island had also talked to Stevenson about Kennedy.

Stevenson walked up to the rostrum and made his acceptance speech. After he finished, he held up his hands for silence . . . and calmly dropped a bomb in the hands of the astounded delegates. "I have concluded to depart from the precedents of the past. I have decided that the selection of the Vice Presidential nominee should be made through the free processes of this convention."

It was now a free-for-all. Senator Kennedy got up from his seat and talked with some of the delegates. Then, as if realizing that he could never make a rational appeal in the middle of bedlam, even if he were able to reach a large portion of the delegates, he decided to return to his headquarters at the Palmer House. I called there and was told, "We're ready to go if he says the word."

"Where is the Senator?" I asked.

"He is closeted over here in one of the rooms with the leaders of his organization."

"Let me know if he leaves to come over here," I said.

He came over for a few minutes. He said he didn't have time to make any calls and promised to call me later. "Are you going to try for it?" I asked him.

"I just don't know."

Again I got a call from headquarters. The Senator had gone back there and had talked to New York's Mayor Robert Wagner. It seemed that Wagner was interested in the Vice Presidency himself. And then I was told, "Hold everything. Bob just walked in and said, 'It looks like we're in business.' So maybe you better come over and help."

The next twelve hours were a nightmare. "Where do we get a printer this time of night?" someone asked. They finally found one who would work all night printing banners, buttons, leaflets, placards, noisemakers—all the kinds of armament needed for the business of nominating a candidate. The Senator and

Bob were busy lining up friends and supporters to talk to the various delegates. All night long they went from one hotel room to the next telling about the statistical case for the Senator's candidacy, persuading and appealing. Never had I seen such a loyal, devoted little band of supporters.

The Senator stopped to get a little rest. Some of the others slept a few hours, but they were up bright and early using their salesmanship. The morning papers were giving an edge to Kefauver, but that did not dampen the ardor of the Kennedy group. I was back in my hotel room at the Drake answering the telephone. The girls at headquarters kept me up to date on developments.

"Did you hear that Louisiana will also support him? And Governor Ribicoff will make the nominating speech."

"Oh, that's wonderful," I said. "Who is going to make the seconding speech?"

I was told Senator Smathers would make one and there was the possibility that Congressman McCormack would make the other one, although he wasn't too keen about it.

The die was cast. As the Senator left the hotel to go to the Amphitheater, I told him that unless I would be helpful over there on the floor, I would stay by the telephones and watch the session on television.

"You will be better off watching it on television here in your hotel room," he said.

"Good luck, Senator," I added.

Governor Ribicoff gave a very impassioned nominating speech, which set off a wild demonstration by the Massachusetts delegation. The seconding speeches brought out the demonstrators again. What they lacked in numbers, they made up in noise.

I called out to the Stockyard Inn where the Senator had a room near the convention hall to see if I could find out how things looked to them there. I learned that the Senator was stretched out on a bed watching television himself.

They started the call of the states. "Ala-*bam*-a," boomed the clerk—and so on. It ended with Kefauver having 483½ votes, Kennedy 304. They were both quite a way from the required 686½. I called out to the Stockyard Inn again. "What's the good word?" I said.

"The Senator's calm. He's talking to Jackie now."

Then over the television they said, "Senator Kennedy does not have a statement, but the newspapermen are beginning to crowd around his door."

Again the clerk cried, "Ala-*bam*-a," and the second ballot began. Then the telephone rang. I said, "I'm not going to answer it."

Abe said, "It might be the Senator."

"What would he be calling me for at a time like this?"

It kept on ringing and ringing; I finally answered it to stop the noise. Someone screamed into the phone, "I have to talk to Ted Sorensen right away. I can't get through. You can. Give him the word to give me a call." He gave me a number. I didn't even get his name because I had one eye on the television screen and scarcely saw the pad before me. When I hung up I thought, maybe it is important. The least I can do is to call out there and give him the message. Then I can go on with my listening. So I gave them a call. A strange voice snapped, "Who do you want?"

"I'm Evelyn Lincoln," I said, and then he must have turned away from the phone because a moment later he said, "You can't talk to the Senator, he is taking a bath."

"A bath," I said, "how can he do that at a time like this?"

"Don't ask me, lady," he said, "and anyway no one wants to talk to you right now. Call back later."

I went back to the television and heard the report that Kefauver and Humphrey were crying, actually shedding tears, over the turn of events, and here was Kennedy taking a bath. Abe and I were far less calm.

His votes kept piling up, and he was picking up states that had not voted for him on the first ballot. When they got to the N's I wondered what would happen to New York's giant block.

When I heard, "New York casts its ninety-eight votes for John F. Kennedy," I jumped up and down and shouted, "Wagner came around! Wagner came around!" At the end of this ballot he was ahead—618 for Kennedy, 551½ for Kefauver. Only 68½ more votes and the nomination would be his.

They started the third ballot. I said to Abe, "I can't take this much longer." He said, "I've even forgotten the pain in my back." Kentucky gave him thirty votes; he was within thirty-eight votes. Congressman Sam Rayburn, the chairman, pounded the gavel. He recognized Tennessee Senator Albert Gore, who withdrew his name in favor of Kefauver. It was all over—they were now changing their votes to Kefauver. The announcer was saying, "Jack Kennedy just said 'That's it. Let's go.'"

I was mad. I said rude things about Gore, Rayburn, McCormack, and all the rest. "They couldn't do that to him," I said.

"But they did," Abe said.

And then out of the crowd Kennedy appeared, as humble as ever. He looked tired, he looked drawn, but in his gracious manner he stood before the rostrum. He was receiving a tremendous ovation. He started to speak but the words were drowned out. Finally he said, "Ladies and gentlemen of this convention. I want to take this opportunity to express my appreciation to Democrats from all parts of the country, North and South, East and West, who have been so kind to me this afternoon." He went on: "Recognizing that this convention has selected a man who has campaigned in all parts of this country, ...I hope this convention will now make Estes Kefauver's nomination unanimous." He started to leave and Rayburn called him back. He handed him the gavel. With the gavel in his hand the Senator said, "I move we suspend the rules and nominate Estes Kefauver by acclamation." Then he was gone.

The phones started to ring. Western Union boys pounded at my door. Then down the hall I heard two familiar voices laughing. I opened my door and there they were, the Senator and Torby Macdonald. "Senator, you were terrific," I said.

"I did pretty good, don't you think? Have there been any calls?"

"The phone hasn't stopped since you left the platform."

As he went into the suite the Senator said, "Let me know if I have any important calls. I'm going in to call Jackie." I was amazed at him. He looked as though nothing had happened and here I was furious. But I didn't have much time to be angry. They had now found out the Senator was in this hotel and the telephones were really screaming. Now the operator was saying, "Is the Senator there? Adlai Stevenson is on the line." I knocked on his door and he said, "Come in."

There he was in his shorts talking to someone on the telephone. When Torby, also in shorts, saw me, he scooted into the next room. The Senator moved the receiver away from his mouth and said, "Who's on the phone?" I told him it was Mr. Stevenson. Then he said to the person on the other end of the line, "I have to go. Stevenson is calling me." With this he hung up and followed me into our room. He settled down in a chair and very casually discussed what had taken place just a short while before. I heard him say that he would be glad to go all over the country and campaign for the ticket in the fall. He finished that call, then another one came in ... and another, and another.

Abe had gone in to talk to Torby about his campaign in the fall. On his way back into our room he passed through the Senator's room and noticed water all over the floor. He walked over to the bathroom and found the spigot on full blast and the bathtub overflowing. He turned it off and came in to tell me about the water all over the floor. All my pent-up emotion suddenly came out in hysterical laughter. Just then the Senator finished his phone call; as he started to leave I told him about the water. He said calmly, "Better get someone up here to clean it up."

He went in, took his bath, waded around in the water, talked on the telephone a dozen or more times, and then said to me, "Will you pack my bag and get this room cleaned up? What time do I leave in the morning?" I told him around eight o'clock; I promised to have the operator call him in plenty of time and to have a car waiting to take him out to the airport for his short vacation.

The Senator was going alone; it seemed best that Jackie remain close to her doctor, even though it would be some time before the baby was due.

As he walked down the hall I thought to myself, you would never know he had just finished a hard fight. He wasn't bitter. He didn't smash vases into little bits on the floor. I watched him until he turned the corner and disappeared out of my sight.

CHAPTER 10

Picking up the Pieces

We called the housekeeper about the water on the bedroom floor and soon the mop brigade was in action. To my surprise I learned that overflowing bathtubs were nothing new to them. It happened all the time: people were always leaving the faucet on and then taking a walk.

I sloshed around in the water gathering up various articles of his clothing—shorts, socks, shirts—that were festooned all over the furniture. When I got everything together and into his luggage I had some difficulty getting the bags closed, but one of the moppers lent me a hand.

His papers were also strewn about the room. There were a number of little scraps of paper with telephone numbers. I felt he might need these later, so I put them in an envelope and marked it "telephone numbers." I put it and his airline tickets atop his luggage where he'd be sure to find them. I also added a little note: "Dear Senator: I hope you have a pleasant trip

85

and I hope you enjoy your cruise around Capri and Elba. We will be looking forward to hearing from you upon your return." I signed it, "Evelyn L."

The room was getting dry. You couldn't tell that fifteen minutes before it had been covered with water. Nor could you tell that a man's hopes for the second highest office in the land had been born and had died in that room.

I started to pack my own luggage; Abe and I were going out to Nebraska for a few days before returning to Washington. Because our plane was due to leave the next morning, shortly after the Senator's, we were up when I heard the Senator's door open and shut. I peeked out the door and watched him until he turned the corner.

Before we left the hotel, I went into his bedroom to make sure he hadn't forgotten anything, as he so often did. There on his dresser was a note saying, "Mrs. Lincoln, make sure that everyone who helped us the last few days gets a letter of thanks, and especially the volunteers." I went back to our room and said to Abe, "Never have I seen such a good loser. He holds no grudges against anyone. All he can think of is how much he appreciates everything that's been done for him."

When we got to Nebraska I discovered how much of an impression Senator Kennedy had made by his sportsmanlike manner in conceding defeat. Almost everyone I talked to had words of praise for him.

"Abe," I said, "if they feel this way in Nebraska, where Catholic politicians aren't popular, how must they feel in other places?" I found the same feeling when we got back to Washington.

A few days later I heard the telephone ringing as I entered our apartment in the evening. It was a reporter from the Associated Press. "Where is the Senator, do you know?"

I asked him why he wanted to know, and he said something about Jackie being in the hospital. I was shocked to hear it, but didn't know how much I should tell him, so I was very noncommittal. After trying for a while longer to squeeze some information out of me, he gave up in despair. Then I got a call from Eunice Shriver.

"Yes, Jackie is in the hospital—she's lost her baby. How can we reach Jack?"

I told them, and soon I heard a radio report that he had been found and was coming home immediately. I was reassured to hear also that, after a very close call, Jackie was now out of danger.

Meanwhile letters of all kinds kept pouring in from those who had seen the Senator on television during the convention—political strategists who gave their views on why he wasn't chosen, personal friends who couldn't understand why he was bypassed, and people from all walks of life who felt that he should have received the nomination. Never had I seen such deep feeling shared by so many. They wrote of how they cried, how their children cried, and how they had prayed for him. And this was before the letters arrived sympathizing with them on the loss of the baby.

Shortly after his return from Europe he called me from Newport. I was anxious to hear about Jackie.

"She's coming along fine," he said.

I then told him about the letters and said that three-fourths of them came from children. He was deeply touched and said, "Send the letters up to me." I knew he wanted to share them with Jackie, so I sent a huge box full. The next day he called and said they had read every one of them.

Then he asked about the letters thanking those who had worked for him. They hadn't been sent out yet, and he dictated a letter saying: "This is a note of thanks to you for all your help in Chicago. It is on occasions like that you appreciate the helping hand of friends." He signed each one personally and in many cases added a postscript. To many of the personal letters he added, "I was, of course, disappointed at the time, but like everything in life you can't tell how it will be reflected in the future."

A friend of his wrote him a letter quoting what he had recently read in one of the newspapers. "The pertinent question is: Where does he go from here? Undoubtedly, his voice will carry more and more weight in party councils between now and the next national convention. And by the time that rolls around, a lot of people will undoubtedly be saying that Jack Kennedy in 1956 lost a battle but not a war. It could well be that in 1960 he will win the war."

Soon he was mapping a schedule that would take him all over the United States; I didn't see how he could do any more if he were a candidate himself.

Torby Macdonald had opposition in his bid for reelection to the House of Representatives, and since Torby represented a normally Republican district, he was working very hard. Abe, as his administrative assistant, was going up to Massachusetts for six weeks prior to the election to help in the campaign. He was going to live in the Senator's apartment in Boston while he was there.

I hated to be away from Abe, but I knew that there were so many arrangements to be made for the Senator's campaigning on behalf of the Stevenson-Kefauver ticket that I wouldn't have much time to be lonely. Besides, I was going to spend a couple of weekends in Boston before the election.

The Senator's first campaign stop was California. He spoke in Los Angeles, Santa Ana, San Diego, San Francisco, and Sacramento. From there he flew by private plane to Las Vegas to attend a reception for Senator Alan Bible. The next morning he was in New York, and the following three days were spent speaking in various New England states. He ended this tour by receiving an honorary doctor of science degree at the Lowell School of Technology, Lowell, Massachusetts.

After a brief respite, the Senator started on another campaign tour. This time he headed south—through Kentucky, North Carolina, Louisiana, and Florida. He spent a couple of days in Palm Beach, and then he and Jackie went to New York to see some plays.

When he came back to Washington he told me, "I don't think

we will be living in Hickory Hill this coming year. You know that Jackie spent so much time fixing up the nursery, and she doesn't want to go back there. She's terribly upset about the baby. It is also a little far out."

Soon he was on the campaign trail again. This time he went to Michigan, Rhode Island, Pennsylvania, West Virginia, Virginia, New York, and New Jersey, and back to Massachusetts again to a rally for Torby. Abe later told me that as Torby and the Senator appeared on the platform, the girls in the audience became very excited and started jumping up and down. "I've never seen anything like it," Abe said. "It was as if they were all cheerleaders and the home team had just made the winning touchdown."

Just as the Senator started to speak, he recognized Katie Griffin Murphy, one of the girls who had worked in his office in 1953. He interrupted himself and called out, "Katie, I wonder if you would come over here. I'd like to shake your hand." Then he introduced the flustered but proud girl to the crowd as one of his former secretaries. It was a gesture the audience appreciated greatly.

By now it was almost impossible to keep up with the speaking invitations pouring in from all over the country. I said to the Senator, "It's fantastic how popular you've become."

With the little smile that always preceded one of his witty remarks he said, "Yes, everybody loves a loser."

Most of the invitations were for the last and most crucial week of the campaign. To these he replied, "At the beginning of the campaign this fall I promised the national Democratic leaders I would make a nationwide campaign as well as tour my own state in an effort to bring about the election of Stevenson and Kefauver. In agreeing to make such a campaign I reserved the last week of the campaign, which to my way of thinking is the most important part of the campaign, for my own state. During the final week, then, I shall exert my very best efforts toward the election of the Democratic ticket in Massachusetts as well as toward winning the state for Stevenson and Kefauver."

During this time I spent a couple of weekends with my husband in Boston. It was fun staying in the Senator's apartment. It was like stepping backward in time and seeing him during his college days. There were pictures of him at school, and of his brother Joe and beloved sister "Kick" (Kathleen, who had died in a plane crash in England). It was sad to look at those bright young faces so full of the love of life, and then to think that only a few years after the pictures were taken both Joe and "Kick" were dead.

When I opened his closet to hang up my things I found to my surprise that it still held a number of his textbooks and other school articles, as well as his Navy uniform and sword. Although he had used that apartment many times since his Navy days, he had never bothered to clean out the closet.

"Look," I said to Abe, "all his things from before he entered politics. He's just never had time to clean them out."

"You think that's the reason?" Abe asked.

I thought for a moment and said, "No, I guess you're right, he would have cleaned it out, but it just never occurred to him. He's like that poem, the one by Holmes, about the chambered nautilus—he just seals off the past, and moves on from there."

The Bowdoin Street apartment was by no means a sumptuous one, but it fascinated me just the same. Certainly those walls had heard more politics than almost any other place in the country, and, like notches on a gun, the furniture and rugs wore the dark smudges and burns of a hundred political smokes.

It was a comfortable place for a man. Though the Senator had a kind of elegance that made him at home with the antiques Jackie collected, I thought he would feel much more relaxed with this old furniture, the kind that invited a man to throw a leg over a sofa arm and not worry about where the ashes were falling.

I promised Abe I would come back to spend election night with him, and so back to Boston I went on Saturday, November

3rd. This time the Senator was using his apartment, and we stayed in the Bellevue Hotel. As soon as the Senator heard I was there he called and said, "Why don't you come over to the apartment? I have some dictation."

When I arrived the room was filled with clouds of smoke. All sorts of politicians with cigars were moving around and looking wise. But there were no "deals" going on there. All the political deals were over; now the voters all over the country were making the deal as they marked their cards "victory" or "defeat."

Nightfall, and the first returns began to come in. The Senator watched television in his apartment while I watched with Abe at the Macdonald headquarters in Malden. It was soon obvious that Stevenson and Kefauver had been defeated, but we were not sure until 3 A.M. that Torby had bucked the Republican tide.

The Senator had done his best for the campaign, but it was now apparent that his career would have been badly hurt, perhaps finished, if he instead of Kefauver had won the Vice Presidential nomination. Everyone would have said, "Stevenson might have made it if it hadn't been for a Catholic running mate." Now they couldn't say it, and from his reaction to the encouragement Senator Kennedy was receiving in the mail, it seemed unlikely he would try for anything but the top place.

I think he was beginning to believe the story he often told of Finley Peter Dunn's "Dooley on the Vice President." It went something like this:

"It's strange about the Vice Presidency," said Mr. Dooley. "The Presidency is the highest office in the gift of the people. The Vice Presidency is both the highest and the lowest. It isn't a crime exactly—you can't be sent to jail for it—but it's a kind of disgrace. It's like writing anonymous letters. At a convention nearly all the delegates leave as soon as they have nominated the President for fear one of them will be nominated for Vice President."

PART II

CHAPTER 11

Young Man on the Move

IT was apparent to Senator Kennedy that his fight for the Vice Presidency at the 1956 Democratic convention had been shared with considerable sympathy by the American people. The enormous number of letters and telegrams he received following the convention, especially from the younger people, made him more determined than ever to reach the goal he had been thinking about for several years.

The more speaking invitations he received, the more he accepted.

Someone had once told me that his speaking style was ineffective. Not only did he talk too fast, his voice was also flat and unmodulated. Furthermore, he nervously chopped the air with his right hand like a pendulum on a clock—a very distracting motion. So one day I decided to watch the crowd as he spoke. I understood what my friend meant, but he had missed the point entirely. It was the man, all of him, that made the voice, and whenever he spoke people listened.

Although he could think and speak easily on his feet, Senator Kennedy wrote most of his speeches and read from prepared texts, digressing from time to time. He had a great reservoir of ideas from which to draw when he began working on a speech, and he was constantly tearing things out of the paper and saying to me, "Save this, I'll use it sometime." He would forget about one of these; months later he might say, "Do you remember that item I gave you on Indochina?" Sometimes when he got an idea, he would dictate it to me and ask me to put it in the file for future use.

I remember one time the Senator was leaving for New York. As he flew out the door, he asked me to find out about a Richard Rush. I thought, what an appropriate name—everything is rush, rush, rush these days. But I did find out that Richard Rush was the United States Attorney General from 1814 to 1817; Minister to Great Britain from 1817 to 1825; Secretary of the Treasury from 1825 to 1829; and unsuccessful candidate for Vice President with John Quincy Adams in 1828. I wired the information to him immediately so that he had it when he arrived in New York. I learned later that he wanted it in planning a speech he was to give at the senior class banquet at Princeton University the next night.

He usually dictated a rough draft of his speeches and then went over the draft with Ted Sorensen. He had great respect for Ted's mind. Ted's Midwestern thinking began to have an impact on the Senator. Ted was a student of history and brought to the Senator's attention the progressive thoughts of some of the Midwest's great men—like Robert LaFollette and George Norris—and gradually the Senator took on a national rather than just an Eastern point of view.

Ted, who was a graduate of the University of Nebraska and on the staff of a subcommittee of the Senate Banking and Currency Committee before Senator Paul Douglas recommended him to Senator Kennedy, was intensely loyal and would work around the clock if the occasion demanded it. He and the Senator would bat ideas back and forth several times before deciding how they should be used. Sometimes other members of the staff would be called upon for an opinion, particularly Mike Feldman, a friend of Ted's who later came to work for the Senator.

The Senator liked to have close to him people on whom he could test his ideas and get frank and honest replies. He also liked to have around people with different views so that he could have the benefit of more than one approach to a subject. He would listen to all the divergent ideas and then come to his own conclusion. He had a way of prodding his staff to see just how firm they were in the thoughts they presented to him. He would say again and again, "Are you sure?" He used the same technique with me sometimes. A poor speller, he would call through the open door from his office, "Mrs. Lincoln, how do you spell collapse?" I would tell him and he would say "Are you sure?" I always ended up checking the dictionary before he was satisfied.

His inquiring mind and search for all the facts reflected, it seemed, the training he received around the family table when he was growing up. His father would assign a subject—Algeria, for example—to one child and instruct him to find all he could on the subject. Then he would tell the other children to do the same so they could question the first one when he made his report and see how much he really knew. Both father and mother tried to develop alert minds in their children by giving them mental exercise, just as they encouraged physical exercise. And the same competitive spirit prevailed at the table discussions that was apparent in the touch football games on the lawn.

Following the election, now that Jackie had recuperated from the loss of her baby, the Senator took her on a vacation to France and England. I could tell she was storming the antique markets when I received letters telling me I could soon expect some shipments.

Upon their return they went to the Round Hill Hotel, Montego Bay, Jamaica, and stayed until Christmas, but flew back to Palm Beach to be with his family for the holidays. Jackie remained in Palm Beach for a while and the Senator returned to Washington after January 1st. We could tell she did the Christmas shopping for him that year because she had asked me for the dress size of every girl in the office. The gifts were lovely quilted dressing gowns.

When Jackie returned to Washington it was not to Hickory

Hill, their former home in McLean, but to a furnished house at 2808 P Street in Georgetown, leased from Mr. Joseph Bryan.

One day I received a call from Jackie.

"Mrs. Lincoln, I don't believe Jack is eating the right food. I think it would be better to send his lunch to him from the house. Perhaps you could serve it to him in the office. Muggsie could come out to pick it up and perhaps you could get a hot-plate to keep it warm until it is time for him to eat."

I said I thought it was a wonderful idea and would be happy to do it. But after I put the receiver down and got away from the charm of her voice, I began to have doubts.

Once we got the system going, however, it didn't seem to take any time at all. We arranged it so he would eat at 1:15 unless he had to be on the Senate floor for a roll call. He liked the idea of my serving him at his desk. Then he decided to share his food, and we began having guests for lunch. I got a card table and set it at one side of his desk. Jackie arranged for tablecloth and napkins to come with the food basket, and he and his guests dined in style.

The Senator liked simple food. Sometimes there would be baked chicken, mashed potatoes, and a green vegetable. Or there might be a broiled lamb chop, or a slice of roast beef, or perhaps a broiled steak, with some kind of fish on Friday. He drank milk with his meals, and although there was generally a slice of cake, a dish of fruit, or some other kind of a dessert, many times he did not eat it.

One morning in early January 1957, when Senator Kennedy was going over his invitations to speak he was surprised not only at the large number he was receiving but also by the fact that they were coming from all parts of the country. He said, "Mrs. Lincoln, why don't you keep a tally on these invitations? If we continue to get them in such large quantities, I am sure the reporters would be interested."

I went to work on it, and the results amazed him. The total was in the hundreds. He released the figures to the press, and he was right—they were interested, and they kept checking back at intervals to get the latest count. Soon the columnists began to analyze the significance of these figures. They all drew the same inescapable conclusion: he had made a deep impression everywhere. He no longer was merely the junior Senator from Massachusetts, he was becoming a national figure—and it meant working seven days a week.

Therefore, when I received a call from him one bright Sunday morning asking me if I could come out to his house at eleven o'clock, I was not surprised. He said, "I want to give you some dictation on the Hoover Report (the Reorganization of Government report prepared by a group headed by former President Herbert Hoover). And," he added, "bring a dictaphone."

Abe and I put the papers aside, gulped down a quick breakfast, and like firemen, we were soon on our way. The first stop was the Senate Office Building to pick up the dictaphone and then out to Georgetown, where the Senator was then living.

We arrived five minutes early, and I went inside while Abe waited in the car. The Senator was in the backyard where two photographers were taking pictures of him.

He came in from the yard a few minutes later and said, "Glad to see you. Did Abe bring you?" I said yes, and he said, "Why don't you ask him to come into the house." He waited until I brought Abe in. After greeting him he said, "I'll be back in a few minutes. They want to make some more pictures. Provie will give you some coffee." While he was outside smiling at the cameras, I set up the dictaphone machine and Provie, Providencia Paredes, Mrs. Kennedy's maid, served us coffee.

The next time he came in, his dog, Tippie, was with him. Tippie went around the room licking everybody's hands, but when the Senator sat down at the dictaphone, he curled up at his feet. Senator Kennedy loved dogs—in fact, he loved all animals—but he was allergic to them. If they were around him too much, his nose would fill up and he would have difficulty breathing. When it got too bad, he would keep the dog outside or send him out to Jackie's mother in McLean.

99

The Senator started to dictate into the machine. He had a few notes scratched out on a piece of paper and from them dictated for a solid twenty minutes. The ideas and phrases just tumbled out. When he finished, he said, "I should be in the office by 9:45 tomorrow. Will you have this typed up at that time so I can go over it."

I said yes, and he then went back to the waiting photographers. Tippie was close at his heels.

It took me most of the afternoon to type the dictation. I didn't want to wait until the morning because there were always so many interruptions and I wanted to have it finished for him. The very first thing he said to me when he came into the office was, "Do you have that material I dictated yesterday?" I handed it to him and he started reading it as he walked into his office.

A few days later while he was sitting in his office going over his schedule, he looked at me with a sly expression and said, "Aren't you from somewhere in the Middle West?"

He knew as well as I did that I was from Nebraska, so I answered, "How did you guess?"

"I am seriously thinking of taking a trip out that way. How would you like to go with me to Omaha for my speech at that Democratic dinner on May 17th?"

I drew a deep breath and answered, "I'd love it."

I could hardly wait to get home and tell Abe. He was as delighted as I was. We called my brother, who was planning to attend the dinner, and we also called Abe's folks in Lexington. "Maybe I can get out to see you," I told them.

The day finally arrived. When I walked out of the office beside Senator Kennedy and Ted Sorensen wearing my new dark blue suit and matching hat, I felt really important. Jackie was waiting in the convertible to ride with us to the airport. When she was in Washington it had become a practice with her to ride to the airport with the Senator. The Senator was at the wheel and this time we didn't dash madly through the streets

—probably because Jackie was at his side, and as she was again expecting a baby, everyone was taking extra care to protect her from any possible upset or harm.

At the airport the Senator got his usual stack of magazines and packs of chewing gum, which he asked me to carry for him. After saying goodbye to Jackie, the three of us got on the plane. Ted sat with the Senator and I was directly in front of them. As we changed planes in Chicago, there was, as usual, a reporter waiting at the airport for an interview with the Senator, and some photographers were trying to take his picture as he descended from the plane. Ever since the convention it seemed he couldn't step outside the Senate Office Building without attracting newspapermen.

Soon we were aloft again, and the closer we came to Omaha the more excited I became. There were only a handful of people to greet the Senator, and the first one to shake his hand as we stepped from the plane was Bernard Boyle, the Democratic National Committeeman. Mr. Boyle introduced the Senator to several of the local politicians who were there to welcome him. In a few minutes we were being whisked away in a big limousine. The Senator was sandwiched in the front seat between the driver and Mr. Boyle while Ted and I shared the back seat. All the way from the airport to downtown Omaha, Bernie was telling the Senator about various sites of interest and briefing him on the difficulties the Democratic party was facing in Nebraska.

How well I understood him! My father, many years before, had had the same problems—perhaps worse ones—for many people in the state had been wooed to the Republican party by Abraham Lincoln with his "Homestead Act," and Democrats almost always found themselves in the minority.

As soon as we entered the Fontenelle Hotel, we were directed to the Senator's suite and told there would be a press conference in a few minutes. There seemed to be a little more interest in him here, for a small crowd had formed in the lobby to await his arrival. Ted Sorensen's family, and my brother and his wife were there. I guess both Ted and I had that hometown-boy-makes-good feeling.

Since I was going home with Bill and Catherine after the dinner, I didn't have a room assigned to me at the hotel. I had to use the Senator's bedroom to change my dress. And since Ted and the Senator were going on to Lincoln after the dinner, Ted did not have a room either, so he also had to use the Senator's room to change his shirt and suit. The three of us kept coming and going out of his bedroom. It was almost like a game of musical chairs.

After the Senator dressed he called Catherine, Bill, and me into his room and talked to us for about five minutes. Then he said, "Mrs. Lincoln, will you see that my bag is packed and ready to go? I enjoyed meeting your brother and sister-in-law, and I'll see you all down at the dinner."

As an indication of the growing national interest in the Senator, the dinner was a sellout and people were even standing in the balcony.

As my brother looked around the banquet hall, he said, "It is amazing how many people are here. You can't imagine how difficult it was in previous years to sell tickets." I thought, these are my people. I came from this state and now I'm back. Then all of a sudden I heard, "And down on the floor is the Senator's personal secretary. A daughter of former Congressman John N. Norton from the old Fourth District, a sister of Bill Norton, and a staunch Democrat. I now introduce to you Evelyn Norton!" As I was standing I saw the Senator tug at Toastmaster Jim Green's sleeve and whisper something, and then Jim said, "Excuse me ladies and gentlemen, the Senator just reminded me that her name is now Evelyn *Lincoln*." I stood in a glow of pride—proud to be honored because I worked for John F. Kennedy.

After I returned to the office and got into the mail I found an invitation for the Senator to speak at the annual Gridiron press dinner the following March. This dinner is an institution peculiar to the United States. The prominent men who appear are unmercifully ribbed and held up to scorn and derision, and then they are expected to deliver a brilliantly witty speech in honor of the occasion.

The Senator, who could take as well as give ribbing, knew it was an honor he should accept. Never will I forget the preparations for this dinner. "I want this to be a real good speech," he said, and for weeks he worked on it. He went over it and then over it again, for draft after draft. A typical session would begin, "Let me see, Mrs. Lincoln, do you have that quotation by Dooley?" Then he would add, "Take this down, Mrs. Lincoln." And he would pace the floor, walk into the bathroom, take a look at himself in the mirror, push his hair to one side, dictating all the time. He said, "No, strike that, take this down" so many times my notebook looked like a racing card.

On the day of the dinner he said, "I believe this dinner is white tie, and if it is will you have somebody check to see if I have everything I need?"

As soon as I could get in touch with Muggsie, I said, "Muggsie, you have work to do. Will you check and see if the Senator has everything he needs for the dinner tonight? After you have checked his room, please call me." Then I started to transcribe some last-minute dictation.

The Senator was at my desk a few minutes later. "How about my suit? Have you checked on that yet?"

"I should have a report on that any minute."

Finally, Muggsie called. He couldn't find a white tie and there didn't seem to be any studs. And here every Christmas I had gone through torture trying to think of a gift for the man who seemed to have everything.

"The stores are still open, Muggsie," I said. "I will call down and order these things and tell them you are going to pick them up."

I went back to my dictation. We finally got everything together, and Muggsie called me from the Statler Hotel to say they had arrived and all was well. "And the boss really looked sharp," he added.

There was still another sign of his growing popularity. He was continually being asked to make radio or television tapes for other Senators to use in their home states. And one of the networks asked him to read the Declaration of Independence for a tape to be used on a Fourth of July program. Since these tapes were always done far in advance, the network crew arrived one morning in the latter part of May to set up the equipment. When the Senator came in a little while later, he said, "What's this for?" I told him and he nodded approval. He stepped over the cords and groped his way through the equipment until he reached the chair behind his desk. He didn't pay any attention to them, just kept on reading an article he had brought with him from home. Finally they were ready. Just as the lights were turned on, he called out to me, "Mrs. Lincoln, do you have a comb?" I ran in with a comb, he raked it through his hair, put the comb in his pocket, and signaled that he was ready. As I closed the door I heard his deep, clear voice say, "We hold these truths to be self-evident, that all men are created equal. . . ."

Each day the pace was picking up momentum and it seemed as though he was leading a triple life. There was a carefully laid plan for making quick speaking tours in one or two states each time he left Washington. He would then come back to Washington to do some intensive work on legislation. In between he would go to Massachusetts to work on his campaign for reelection to the Senate in 1958.

I have never seen anyone with so much energy. Yet despite the many things he was doing, he never seemed harried. He still took an interest in the mail, and, as always, each delivery brought its share of interesting letters. His replies were diplomatic and sometimes filled with dry wit. For example, in answer to an inquiry as to whether he would serve as a patron for a debutante ball, he answered, "I feel that it would be more appropriate for someone with a debutante daughter to serve on this committee. And I have a few years to go...."

Sometimes the girls on the staff read aloud the letters they thought unusual or particularly interesting, or ones that contained impossible requests. One morning I read one from a junior woman's club asking the Senator what he would be most interested in reading if marooned on a desert island for an indefinite period. I showed the letter to the Senator and he said, "You write and tell them the four books I would choose are: the Bible, *Pilgrim's Way* by John Buchan, the *Oxford Book of American Verse*, and the *Oxford Anthology of American Literature.*"

Occasionally the mail contained hidden pitfalls for an over-zealous secretary. One morning I found my annual letter from one of the Senator's Boston constituents asking if he could obtain a pass for the Florida race tracks for the months of January and February for his mother. One thing I learned quickly in working on the Hill is that you always try to help a constituent with his request. So I went to work on it immediately. I was assured that I could get a pass for her, and I wrote a letter saying I would forward it in the very near future. I then dismissed the matter from my mind.

A few days later as the Senator was going through the news clippings he came across an item in one of the Florida papers stating that he had requested and received a free pass to the Florida race tracks from the State Racing Commission. Angry, he rushed into Ted Reardon's office.

"Did you see this, Ted?" he shouted. "Where did they get that?"

"Maybe somebody in the Boston office asked for it," Ted calmly suggested.

I overheard the words "Hialeah" and my mind went into focus. I thought they must be referring to the lady's request for a season pass. When he got back into his office, I went in and said, "I am the one who wrote for the pass for a constituent of yours in Boston."

"Take this wire: 'You stated that I had personally requested for myself and received a free pass to the Florida race tracks from the State Racing Commission. Inasmuch as this statement is wholly inaccurate, I would greatly appreciate your setting the record straight to your readers at the earliest opportunity.' "

The article charged that with all his wealth he was asking for a free pass to the race tracks.

Often a letter would send his spirits soaring, like the one he received after returning from a trip South. He had been to Georgia for a tremendous reception in Atlanta and on his way back stopped in South Carolina to deliver the commencement address at the state university. A few days later he received a letter from one of the professors at the University, who told him an applicant for entrance into the law school had answered the question: "Why do you want to study law?" by saying, "I heard Senator Kennedy make his address at the commencement, and I want to prepare myself seriously to be of service in our government." The Senator showed the letter to Ted Sorensen and said, "It is letters like this that seem to make all this speaking worthwhile."

The Senator had learned early that it was almost impossible to buck the rules that prevailed in Congress. Many said that it was this confusion that had spurred him on to make the race for the Presidency. During his first term as Senator he had pressed hard—for the second time—against the invisible anchor that holds down ambitious young men in the Senate, namely, the seniority system. He knew that the assignment on the Foreign Relations Committee that he wanted so much was barred to him by the seniority rules, but at the beginning of every session he requested it anyway. He finally won out, however, and when I heard it I ran into his office exclaiming, "You made it! You made it!"

"Made what, Mrs. Lincoln?" he asked.

"Made the Foreign Relations Committee."

"Yes, I know," he said very matter-of-factly—and went on reading. But he was obviously pleased. And he was delighted over the many letters he received congratulating him on the appointment, especially the one that ended, "To use an old Gaelic saying, 'May your shadow never grow less.'"

He received another honor that made him very happy. He had mentioned that his name was among the nominees for the Board of Overseers at Harvard, but he was not optimistic he would be chosen. Once before, the Alumni Association Committee had voted unanimously to nominate him but he had not received sufficient votes for election and was extremely disappointed. Then one day in June I opened the mail and saw the good news.

When he came in the door I had the letter in my hand and I followed him into his office. Thinking that he already had the news, as he did concerning the Foreign Relations Committee, I just handed him the letter when he sat down at his desk. This time he didn't know. A smile spread across his face. He read the announcement that he had been elected to the Harvard Board of Overseers and said, "I not only received the most votes, but I am the youngest ever to have been elected as an Overseer. Very good. I wonder if I am the first Catholic?" He asked Ted Sorensen if he was the first Catholic.

"No, you are the second," said Ted, who always seemed to know everything.

Then with a twinkle in his eye, the Senator said to me, "This means that I will have to wear a top hat at the commencement exercises next June. Be sure to order one for me."

When I brought the hat into the office the Senator was away, but each of the men in the office tried it on and everyone thought it looked right. When the Senator came in he put it on and rushed to a mirror. In a moment he came back beaming. Like a little boy wearing his first "grown-up" clothes, the Senator sat at his desk the rest of the afternoon and never once took off that top hat.

After a few months at 2808 P Street, Jackie was househunting again. They wanted to own a house in Georgetown and Jackie was looking them over. She would call the office and say, "Could you send Jack out? I think I've found something he would really like." So, off he would go, and when he came back I'd say, "Did you find one?" Sometimes he would say, "It was too small"; another time he would say, "It was too large." It reminded me of Goldilocks and the three bears. It wasn't too long before they found what they wanted—a three-story Federal style at 3307 N Street in Georgetown.

Jackie was spending a lot of time in New York now because her father, Jack Bouvier, had not been well. Thinking that he was much better, on the weekend of her birthday, July 28th, she went over to Newport to be with her mother, and the Senator flew up to meet her.

The following week while he was in the office he received a call that Jackie's father had died. He turned to me and said, "Mr. Bouvier just died. I'm terribly sorry about this." We all shared Jackie's loss, for her father used to drop in the office often and he was a very attractive and gentle man whom we all liked very much.

When Jackie returned to Washington, she began fixing up their new house with a nursery they hoped would not be empty very long. The Senator was pleased at her interest in the house and commented, "All Jackie has to do is to walk into an empty room and she can visualize immediately how it should be furnished."

She was so busy transforming her visions into chairs, tables, rugs, and other items to fill the big empty house she didn't have time to answer her mail. The Senator brought huge envelopes of it every morning for me to handle. She had read it through and often I'd get a note or call telling me her thoughts on how it should be answered.

As the Senator crisscrossed the country in his travels that fall, I could tell he was worried about Jackie, who was awaiting the birth of their much-wanted baby. He would caution me each time he left to "keep in close touch with Jackie in case you need me in a hurry." As it happened, her doctor told him he thought it would be best to take the baby by Caesarean section, and he set the date. So on November 27, 1957, the Senator called me from New York and said, "Jackie just gave birth to a little girl and they are both doing fine."

At last he was a father. "What do you suppose they will name her?" we pondered. The next time he called, I asked.

"Caroline Bouvier Kennedy," he said, and a note of pride slipped into his voice as he told me the color of her eyes and how much she weighed. "And," he added, like every other proud father, "not just because she's mine, but she is the prettiest baby I have ever seen."

Just as Abe and I were getting ready for bed on Saturday night, December 7th, the phone rang. It was the Senator, and he sounded upset. "I'm down at the office. Where are the notes I gave you to keep? You know, the ones on the chapters I wrote for *Profiles in Courage*."

I told him they were in the bottom drawer of the file cabinet in the southwest corner of his office. He said he couldn't find them. I remember that he had given me the yellow pads and notebooks covered with his scrawlings and other material he had put together in compiling his book some time in 1955, and I had filed them away for safekeeping. I could not imagine why he wanted them, particularly at that time of the night. After all, the book was published, was already a bestseller, and had won a Pulitzer Prize.

Then he said, "Could you come down here and show me where they are?" Abe drove me down, and we found Muggsie there, too, trying to help him find the notes. I walked into the Senator's office, he was talking on the phone. I don't know who he was talking to but he was saying that someone had claimed his book was written by a ghost writer. Now it was beginning to make sense. I found what he wanted, and he went over all the notebooks and manuscripts carefully. He asked me to keep them in a secure place and then thanked me for coming. He seemed relieved.

There was constant turmoil in the office the following week. We learned that Drew Pearson, in a broadcast over the American Broadcasting Company television network, had charged that *Profiles In Courage* was written not by Senator Kennedy but by some other person.

The following Saturday night, Mr. Oliver Treyz, Vice President of the American Broadcasting Company, made a statement on the same program that the company had inquired into the charge made by Pearson. The charge was unfounded—the book had indeed been written by Senator Kennedy. He extended the network's apologies to Senator Kennedy and his publishers.

On December 13th, Caroline was christened in St. Patrick's Cathedral in New York City with the Senator's brother Bob and Jackie's sister, Lee, as godparents.

Soon little Caroline was at home in the third-floor nursery with Maud Shaw, a competent, red-haired Englishwoman to take care of her.

Life magazine had heard about Caroline's pretty little room and wanted to make some pictures of her there. It caused a great deal of commotion in the office because we were eager to see her pictures. It also caused some commotion in the Senator's home, but for a different reason.

Jackie always had a strong sense of individuality and valued her privacy very highly. Jackie was not at all interested in exposing her private life to the press for political reasons. The Senator understood what a sacrifice it was for her, and he asked her to make it as seldom as he could.

Jackie wanted to shield Caroline as much as possible from public intrusion and any influence that could make her childhood difficult. Here she was, only three months old, and already a national magazine wanted to invade her nursery. But the Senator wanted it, and Jackie agreed.

CHAPTER 12

He Makes It Official

At the beginning of 1958 it was apparent that Senator Kennedy had two major goals. He wanted to win reelection to the Senate from Massachusetts by the biggest majority in the history of the state, and he was determined to get a labor reform bill enacted by Congress.

All the while he was keeping an eye on the national scene and the big target for 1960—the Presidency. Every action was geared in that direction. He was traveling all over the country making speeches and meeting with special groups. His staff was expanding to keep up with the influx of mail that increased the more he traveled.

In Washington he held open house in his office for all the Democratic party bigwigs who came to town. He made special appointments with many of them to sound out their support of him and his chances in their home state. Some whose support seemed essential were invited to breakfast or dinner at his home.

As the year wore on, his hectic schedule made it more difficult for him to see the groups of school children from all over the country who continually asked to see him. I would ask, "Do you want to see this group from Gardner, Massachusetts?" And in spite of the many demands on his time, his answer nearly always was, "Sure, if you can work them in."

One day he was scheduled to have two guests for lunch, after which there were appointments every fifteen minutes until 6:30 that evening. When he looked at his appointment schedule, he said, "What are you trying to do to me, Mrs. Lincoln? I'll never be able to see all these people."

"Well, these are people you wanted to see. They are all here for a Democratic meeting."

Then he looked at the list again for a moment, hit his right fist against his open palm with a slight grin, and said, "I guess you are right." As he walked into his office he added, "Let me know when my luncheon guests arrive."

Not only did he see everyone on the schedule, he seemed to enjoy it thoroughly. After they had all gone he sat down with Ted Sorensen and began analyzing what he had learned from the afternoon of political talks. I think he would have talked until midnight if Jackie hadn't called and said, "Mrs. Lincoln, will you please tell Jack that his dinner guests are here." I told him. He got up, put on his coat, but kept right on talking. Ted Sorensen walked to the door with him and they both strolled down the hall, still talking politics.

In consultation with his brother Bob, who was Chief Counsel of the Senate Labor Rackets Subcommittee, the Senator started to draft a bill to curb corruption in labor unions. He consulted experts on the subject, including professors at Yale, Harvard, and Massachusetts Institute of Technology. He called in labor leaders and they would argue and bounce these ideas around. After their departure, he would call his brother Bob or he might call his father. The next day would be more of the same. He leaned heavily on Professor Archibald Cox, who would come down from Harvard for a couple days at a time. When he had the bill in acceptable form, he discussed it with Senator Irving Ives, a Republican from New York, and shortly thereafter it was introduced by them jointly.

The Senator was chairman of the subcommittee of the Senate Labor Committee to which the bill was referred. When the hearings began on this bill, morning after morning labor leaders and labor technicians filed into our office to hold conferences with him before he went over to the committee meeting. Arthur Goldberg, it seemed to me, spent as much time in our office as he did in the AFL-CIO office, for which he was counsel. As soon as the Senator came back from the committee meeting he would again go into a huddle with these men.

Whenever he worked past his lunch time, he would grab a bite to eat between conferences.

Occasionally he clashed with union officials testifying on the bill. He would come back to the office from the committee meeting still worked up over the opposition he was getting. He was impatient. It was a fight to the finish for him. He would ask for another conference in his office and once again there would be an effort to reach an agreement. While they were working he would walk from one office to another like a panther in a cage. When he passed the conference table, he would stop and listen to the discussion and perhaps add a word or two.

Finally, a union control bill moderately stronger than the labor leaders wanted was reported out of the subcommittee, and a few days later it cleared the full committee.

Next came the battle to win full Senate approval of the measure. Little by little he had been reasoning with the Senators individually on the advantages to be gained by the passage of this bill. He would talk to them in the elevators, in the corridors, in the Democratic cloakroom, as well as formal visits in their offices. He never let an opportunity pass. The day it was scheduled for consideration on the Senate floor he went into action. He entered the Senate chamber well in advance, armed with papers and material. He sat down at his seat at the back of the chamber and started to write—no doubt putting down some last-minute thoughts. You could tell he was impatient with the slow pace in the Senate; he moved restlessly in his chair, swinging his crossed right leg back and forth, sometimes twisting his foot. He watched every movement, every action, every amendment. As debate on the bill wore on, at the end of every day he would go into a huddle with the labor technicians and labor representatives to gather ammunition for the next day's debate. And many a night, just before leaving the office, he would call his brother Bob, who generally worked until nine or ten o'clock, and talk it over with him.

Each day he was gaining. If a point was raised on which he needed clarification, he would call from the floor or send

Ralph Dungan, a member of our staff who was working closely with him on this fight. Then the information would be given to him after the labor technicians had been contacted. During the days the Senate was not in session he would have Senators for lunch and discuss the labor bill all during the meal.

After three days and four nights of debate the Senator felt confident that it would pass. He returned from the Senate floor deep in thought, and I made no mention of the lunch that had been sitting on the hotplate for hours. He walked into his office and closed the door. Then a call came. It was Speaker Sam Rayburn. After he hung up the receiver I went into his office; he was slumped in his chair as though he had won a great battle.

"You did it?"

"Yes," he said, "how about a little lunch?"

The bill passed the Senate by a vote of eighty-eight to one; he had received assurances from Speaker Rayburn that it would be passed by the House.

Wires and letters poured in congratulating him for winning the almost unanimous approval of the Senate. His fellow Senators gave him the sincerest form of flattery by asking him to make tape recordings explaining the bill for use in their states.

Senator Kennedy greatly appreciated the time and effort that Professor Cox had given during this time. He asked me one day to "order a watch like the one I purchased a few days ago and have it sent to him. I think he is going to teach at the summer session at Stanford University, so perhaps you can send it to him out there."

He never forgot the efforts of Arthur Goldberg, either, and the warm relationship they formed during this cooperative project lasted through the years.

The bill was rejected by the House. The Senator vowed he would bring it up again in the next session of Congress and "this time I will work on the House members myself." He also voiced his protest in a speech on the Senate floor.

He did reintroduce substantially the same bill. Again he had consultations with Professor Cox and Arthur Goldberg in pilot-

114

ing it through the legislative processes. This time it passed the Senate by a vote of ninety to one.

Senator Kennedy began exerting his influence to win support for the measure in the House. He invited members of the House Labor Committee to his office for lunch to discuss the bill. He went over to the House chamber and talked to various members in the Democratic cloakroom. He went to Congressmen's offices to talk to them personally. He worked tirelessly. However, as often happens, the House members had their own ideas of what should be law, and they substituted their own bill.

The fight wasn't over. He was selected to preside at a House-Senate conference to bring the two bills into a form that would be acceptable to both legislative bodies. For twelve days he worked. Many times it looked as though he faced a stone wall, but he kept on trying. He talked to the conferees personally, he talked to them collectively, and then he consulted the experts. And all the while he was in close communication with his brother Bob. They finally reported out a bill that was passed by both the Senate and the House. The Senator was not satisfied. "But," he said, "taking it as a whole, it is the best bill we can pass."

The main thing was that he had won his battle and had proved to the doubting Senators and Congressmen that he was a good legislator.

Now Senator Kennedy turned his attention to his campaign for reelection. Shortly before the primary in September he set up headquarters at 150 Tremont Street in Boston. Ted Reardon was sent to get the organization rolling. Many people asked why the Senator was working so hard when "he's certain to win." He simply never took anything for granted. Nonetheless, his opposition did not seem very threatening. At the Republican State Convention Charles Gibbons, who was first selected to be his opponent, withdrew from the race, and the new Republican candidate was Vincent J. Celeste.

The Senator selected his brother, Ted, then a senior at the

University of Virginia Law School, as his campaign manager. Stephen Smith, his brother-in-law, left the family's business in New York to help in the campaign, and Lynn Johnston, an attorney with the Kennedy Foundation in New York also went to Boston to help. Others who joined the campaign staff later were Ted Sorensen, Mike Feldman, and Bob Thompson, a Washington newspaperman who later covered the White House for the New York *Daily News* and Los Angeles *Times*. He handled the press for the campaign.

The Senator had tried to keep intact the organization that had elected him to the Senate originally. Once each year he had met with the organizing secretaries in each county to get their reports on his strength in their areas and to advise him about any fences that needed mending.

People were beginning to volunteer their services for the campaign. In Washington a campaign film of the Senator's life was being made, and almost daily he dictated instructions on how the campaign should be run. One day he said, "Write them up there and tell them that in working out my schedule they should be sure to see that it covers each section in a definite pattern, and that we don't lose any time by crisscrossing from one part of Massachusetts to another."

Everything was going fine until the bills began rolling in. Then the Senator started worrying about the cost, more from a sense of good politics than concern for his pocketbook. He sent memo after memo to Boston emphasizing that "the lower we can keep this spending the better off we will be."

The Republicans also criticized the amount of money he was spending, and he shot off a memo to Boston pointing out that they (the Republicans) had started out with $1,000,000 and had already spent $500,000 before the campaign had hardly started.

Meanwhile Jackie had gone to France and was anxiously waiting for the Senator; he had promised he would vacation with her there before plunging into the Senate race. I received a cable from her one day: "Is Jack arriving tomorrow Saturday.

Please wire immediately." The Senator wired back: "Arriving Sunday afternoon at 3 P.M. via Air France Airlines." I had made the arrangements for his flight and also for his return on September 9th in time to vote in the Massachusetts primary.

His journey to Paris indicated how confident he was of victory—few Senators would think of taking a European vacation in an election year.

Before he settled down to a concentrated campaign in Massachusetts, he scheduled a trip that would take him to Louisiana, Nebraska, California, Nevada, Colorado, Wyoming, Kansas, Missouri (for a visit with former President Truman), Oklahoma, Michigan, Indiana, back to Washington for one day, and then out to Ohio. I had my work cut out for me: airline reservations and hotel accommodations for each stop.

Jackie accompanied him on part of the tour, and they spent their fifth wedding anniversay in Omaha.

During his one day in Washington he mapped final plans for his campaign swing through Massachusetts. He was always looking for ways to save time.

"I want to take a dictaphone with me and I would like to have it fixed so that I could run it in the car. That way when I am going from town to town, I can dictate the names and addresses of the people I have just met. Then at the end of the day the girls at headquarters can write personal letters from me to these people."

Then he added, after a pause, "I would also like to have the secretary in each town make up a list of people who attend the various meetings and send them to headquarters, making sure that they designate whether or not they should be called by their first names."

New ideas developed as he talked. "Would you see also that they set up a system of poll watchers for the voting places that do not have machines so that they can explain where my name is on the ballot."

A few days later, when he left for Massachusetts, I asked him if he wanted me to come up and work in the headquarters.

"No, with everyone else up there it is important that you stay here in this office. I've told everyone throughout the country that if they wanted to get in touch with me they should call you and that you would be able to tell them where I am. I will call you every day to find out if there are any messages."

I appreciated his confidence in me but I also wished I could get into the thick of the campaign. I didn't want to miss the excitement.

Toward the end of October I could stand it no longer. While I was talking to the Senator on the telephone one day I said, "I would like very much to come up there."

"Why don't you come up tomorrow?"

That was all I needed. The next morning Muggsie met me at the airport in Boston and drove me to headquarters. It was good to be there working with everyone else. There were volunteers all over the place—speeches were being written, press releases were being prepared, posters and brochures were everywhere.

On the day before election the Senator made a speech in downtown Boston and I went to hear him. He was scheduled to make a television appearance immediately thereafter and I followed him to the television station. As soon as he saw me, he asked, "Do you have a comb?" I fished around in my purse and finally found one. He combed his hair and asked, "How does that look?"

I thought of the letters he kept getting from people who commented on his hair. They were always asking why he didn't get a haircut or buy a brush or use some pomade. One letter he really enjoyed asked, "Why don't you have a hair style of your own instead of copying Mamie Eisenhower?"

Election day was perfect voting weather—cold but clear and crisp. We spent a quiet day and that evening gathered at headquarters to await the returns. As each new tally was announced, it was marked up on the board and a cheer went up in the crowd. By midnight the winner was obvious, and someone came through the crowd announcing, "Jackie and the Senator are on their way over here." Their arrival was marked by the popping of flash bulbs and the happy throng pushing to get close enough to touch them. He made a short speech thanking everyone for their help.

It was not until later we learned how well he had done. The official election returns showed he received 73.6 percent of the votes cast, a plurality of 874,608 votes. He had broken all records for the state and had a larger plurality that year than any other Senator in the country. Towns that had voted Republican as long as anyone could remember, such as Melrose, went for Kennedy. It was the kind of victory the leaders of the Democratic party couldn't ignore—which was exactly what he wanted.

Now that the Senator had been reelected, there were rumors he would be entitled to more office space. Happy news—our office was beginning to look like a storage closet. The Senator looked at space in the new Senate Office Building but decided it was too far from the Senate floor. Finally he was told he could have part of the office suite next door; it had previously been occupied by Senator Ives, who had not run for reelection.

In the reshuffling of space, I got an office of my own right next to the Senator's and directly behind the reception room. I was now working in style. I had an unlisted telephone on my desk in addition to a private line and three extensions from the Senate switchboard. I looked like Hollywood's idea of the girl executive, especially when all the phones buzzed at the same time.

Each Senator is supplied with a refrigerator, and since there was no space for it in the Senator's office, I inherited that, too. There I was, with a refrigerator in one corner of the room to keep his food cold, and a hot plate in the other corner to keep his food hot.

The girls who handled case mail, who formerly worked in an office in the basement of the building, came up to occupy part of the new space. They were happy to feel part of the family again. They included Dorothy McCann, Helen Lempart, Eleanor Elhajj, Edwina Brown, and Pierrette Spiegler. Pamela

Turnure, a pretty girl who many visitors said looked like Jackie, was our receptionist. Another addition to the staff by this time was Fred Holborn, a scholarly-looking Harvard graduate who handled anything that had to do with Harvard for the Senator and also replied to students who wrote asking for his views on subjects for term papers. Fred shared an office with Ted Sorensen's secretary, Gloria Sitrin, and with Mary Durkin, Sue Mortensen, and Joan Delaney. The staff at this time also included Ralph Dungan, who had joined to help the Senator on the labor bill.

One Friday afternoon Ted Reardon sent a memorandum around the office announcing a staff meeting for 9:30 A.M. Monday. This put all the girls in a dither; such conferences were rare. One of them speculated, "Maybe they are going to increase our hours, but it seems to me we work around the clock as it is."

The Senator was not there on Monday morning, and Ted presided. He started out by giving a pep talk, emphasizing that we were all in this fight together and it would mean hard work, long hours, and close cooperation. He was preparing us for the long campaign that was beginning for the Presidency. The meeting had been inspired by a letter the Senator had received from a former employee who claimed, "Too many of the employees keep what they are doing to themselves. And therefore, there is not a close working relationship between employees."

A few weeks after his reelection, the Senator suddenly became interested once again in wedding attire. I soon discovered why. He was going to be in his brother Teddy's wedding to the lovely Joan Bennett. He spent a weekend in New York, flew to Hyannis Port for Thanksgiving, and was to be back in New York on Saturday for the wedding.

On Monday, Lem Billings, one of his friends from prep school days, asked me to find out where the Senator's wedding attire was located. He said it might be at the house in Georgetown. First I called Hyannis and asked the maid if the clothes were there.

"Not here, sorry."

Then Jackie called. "I understand you are trying to find Jack's clothes. You can find them on the third floor of the N Street house in the closet."

Out to the house I went. I searched the third floor, but they were not there. I looked in his bedroom. They were not there. I wondered if they could be at his apartment in Boston and had the closet there checked. Still no wedding attire.

I spent the next couple of days calling and checking, but everyone I talked with referred me to the third floor in Georgetown. The wedding was only two days away and I was getting desperate. The only thing I could think of was to rent an outfit and air-mail it to New York. It arrived safely and was placed in the family's New York apartment.

I heaved a sigh of relief.

Early Saturday morning my telephone rang. It was the Senator.

"Where did you get this suit?" I told him I couldn't find his wedding attire, so I had rented one.

"But these don't fit," he said. "They hang like a sack and it's too late to go out and buy something that does, so I suppose there isn't anything else for me to do but wear these."

With that he hung up.

I was feeling rather frustrated about the whole business. When the Sunday papers arrived, however, there on the front page was a picture of the Senator and Teddy. The suit didn't look too bad. The following Monday the suit was returned to me, and soon it was back on the rack at the store. I wonder who wore it the next time.

December came and so did the annual Christmas card project. By this time his "list" ran into the thousands, for he was sending them to the key political people in every state. Ted Reardon hired some part-time typists to address the envelopes. The card was a picture of Caroline, looking like a little doll; the wording inside read, "May the Blessings of Christmas be upon you and yours. Senator and Mrs. John F. Kennedy." Printed below, in his handwriting, were the words, "Warmest regards, Jack."

With the beginning of 1959, the political tempo was speeding up. Some of our office staff moved to the Esso Building, at the foot of Capitol Hill, to work on the Senator's unannounced campaign for the Presidency. We didn't discuss outside the office that we were setting up an office in the Esso Building, but I am sure nearly everyone of any consequence in Washington knew about it.

Stephen Smith, the Senator's brother-in-law, was to be in charge, and Jean Lewis, who had been working on gathering lists of people all over the United States, was going to help him. Helping to fill in information about the people on these lists was Larry O'Brien, who was to have a special campaign assignment. He was going to travel all over the United States, talking with leading citizens and laying the groundwork for the campaign. He would make reports on what he found in each town and keep a file so complete that anyone going into that town would know not only who was friendly toward the Senator as a Presidential candidate, but also what they did, where they went to school, and what their special interests were. It was essential to build an organization of supporters who would be willing to work when the time came.

On January 10th, President Truman came to town, and the Senator wanted to see him. I made the appointment at the Mayflower Hotel at 11:15 A.M. When the Senator returned he said that Truman had told him, "The present administration has put this country in a terrible condition and it is vitally important that we have a change in power." The Senator added, "I was unable to find out which candidate he is going to back in 1960, but he did say that he would never do anything to hurt me." He seemed pleased at that assurance.

We received a letter that brought up an issue the Senator found he was going to have to face frequently in the next two years. The letter asked whether or not he had attended a parochial school. He replied: "There was no edict in our parish which made it mandatory for us to attend parochial schools and, therefore, neither my brother Joe nor I attended a parochial school. My brothers Bob and Ted did, however, and so did my four sisters. I am not sure of the importance of all this information, although I am glad to provide it. What is important in this particular regard is whether you hold to the tenets of your faith. I do and so do the other members of my family. In any case I appreciate your interest."

One day the Senator burst into the office and said, "Take this memo. 'I noticed in the paper this morning that Mr. Drew, who was Governor Stevenson's barber, and who was a delegate in 1952 and 1956, again stated that he wanted once more to be a delegate to the next convention. This raises the question of how the delegates are selected. Therefore, perhaps it would be better for us to seek our own delegates rather than waiting until candidates have expressed an interest.'" Then he added, "Save this memo for me. I will use it later."

Occasionally the girls in the Esso Building office would call us on the direct line to tell us about the magnificent view from their window or about the coffee wagon that came around daily.

For several months Professor James M. Burns was a familiar figure around the office; he was writing a book about the Senator. It was to be a "campaign biography," and the Senator was concerned that it should be a good book as well as a useful one. He told us, "Help Jim as much as you can to get the material he needs, including both political and personal material."

Soon we discovered we were living by the public opinion polls. We were not unlike the people who check their horoscope each day before venturing out. The polls indicated that Kennedy was narrowing the leads held by Adlai Stevenson and Senator Symington of Missouri. One day we would read that Nixon and Stevenson were seen as the strongest potential Presidential candidates for 1960. The next day they would say that Rockefeller and Kennedy were favored.

We received a letter from someone in New York suggesting that the Senator include Richard Nixon in his next edition of *Profiles in Courage* because he had the courage to risk the displeasure of labor unions by his vote on the labor bill. The Senator answered that he appreciated the letter but "inasmuch as my book only included those who had passed away and Mr. Nixon is strong and well, the matter will have to wait for some years."

An article appeared in one of the newspapers saying that although the Vice President and Senator Kennedy were neighbors in the Senate Office Building and on a "Hi, Dick"-"How are you, Jack" basis, they no longer stopped to chat when they met in the hall. Accompanying the article was a cartoon showing the Vice President peeking out of his office on one side of the hall, and the Senator peeking out of his door on the other side. I wrote to Bill Pause, who drew the cartoon, and asked if the Senator could have the original, and he very graciously sent it. When the cartoon arrived the Senator asked me to get Dick Nixon to autograph it. He wrote: "To Jack Kennedy, my good friend, who I wish the best in almost everything. Dick Nixon." I had it framed and hung it in my office, it never failed to get a chuckle from visitors.

The Senator was not only using his lunches for political sessions, he also had dinner meetings with politicians, and dictated while driving and flying. Yet he was still looking for ways to get more working time out of each day. It was obvious to him that time was being wasted while he toured around the country. Like everyone else, he had to wait when planes were late or connections were missed. It was decided that a private plane was the best solution. "It is just too difficult to make speaking engagements without one," he said. His brothers and sisters were eager to help him in every way possible, and so they decided to form a corporation to buy a plane jointly. The

Senator was given the privilege—or responsibility—of selecting the plane and Jackie would determine the interior decor.

For several weeks letters went back and forth between our office and the Kennedy family's New York office concerning the most suitable kind of plane. The Senator spent hours looking through advertising brochures put out by airplane manufacturers, and finally made his selection. On July 17th we put out a news release: "Kenaire Corporation, a company jointly owned by the Kennedy brothers and sisters, announced today that it had purchased a Convair airplane from Frederick B. Ayer & Associates of New York." It was to be decorated in light green and beige, and was named *The Caroline*. The family also hired the pilot, Howard Baird.

During July, 1959, Jackie went to England to visit her sister, Lee, but the Senator stayed behind. She was in Switzerland on her birthday. As soon as the Senator arrived at the office that morning he said, "See if you can get Jackie on the phone." I placed the call, but it was several hours before it was completed. He was eager to wish her a happy birthday and kept checking to see if I could do something to rush the call through.

His father also went to Europe, but before he left he called me about a secret project. He asked me to go to the Senator's house and see if a certain chair was there. He described it to me and I found it easily. Then he explained: "Jack liked that chair so much he asked me if he could have it, and I told him he could. But, to tell you the truth, I found it pretty comfortable, too, so I want to have one made just like it, but I don't want him to know this, or he will think he's causing me trouble and will send it back. So, I'd appreciate it if you would get another one made exactly like it and send it to Hyannis by the time I return from France."

I had a time finding someone to go to the house to photograph and measure that chair so that it could be duplicated. The Merchandise Mart finally took over the business of having it made, and I left it up to them to get it to Hyannis on time. As far as I knew, the Senator never learned what was going on.

Jackie returned from Europe, and they went to the Cape together for the weekend. Later they went to Southampton on Long Island for another weekend, and then he flew to San Francisco. Before leaving he had me wire an old friend from his Navy days, Paul (Red) Fay: "Arriving San Francisco to speak at Building Trades meeting Thursday morning. Could you play golf with me Thursday afternoon. Leaving at 10 P.M. that night." Then as an afterthought he said, "You know that's Grand Old Lovable." It was his favorite nickname for Fay.

He was back in time to spend his wedding anniversary with Jackie in Hyannis, then he was gone again on a speaking tour.

He called me from Indianapolis, not to talk about politics, but to ask me to get some samples of light-weight gray flannel for a suit and to have them by the time he got back. That same morning's mail brought a letter from Jackie, asking me for two copies of the Senator's complete schedule for fall, and mentioning also the gray flannel for the Senator.

When the samples arrived, he went through them, laying them on his sleeve, one by one, until he had chosen two. They looked exactly like suits he already had, but he wanted two more.

While he was in Washington, he telephoned Bob and discussed the campaign. I heard him say: "Pennsylvania remains frozen and I have no suggestions at the present time. Ohio should be left alone for the time being, as should Michigan. Other than that everything looks good."

He was working hard on California, however. He went there again on October 18th and again in November. In between he visited in Nebraska, where the response was not always good. In Scottsbluff he walked from his hotel to a dinner at the Pan Handle Club alone and unnoticed—something unusual for a man used to cheering crowds and a welcoming escort everywhere he went.

He was not critical, however. When I asked him how it was out there, he replied, "I haven't met enough of them to be certain yet. But they seem to be friendly in a skeptical way."

He went back to Hyannis Port the latter part of October to map out the strategy for the rest of the campaign.

Early November; people were beginning to think about Christmas. Jackie came to the office one day and spotted in the hall a black leather padded chair that had been set aside by one of the Senators. She asked me to check to see if it could be purchased.

"It doesn't seem to be in use, so you should be able to get it for practically nothing."

I found it a little more complicated than merely offering a price. First, the chair had to be declared surplus, then I had to go to the Government Procurement Office, where a price would be set. And it would be no bargain. I was told, "You know, these chairs are very valuable. We don't buy that kind any more so they have become a rare item." Finally I was notified the chair had been declared surplus and could be purchased. When I relayed the news to Jackie she said, "Buy some wide red ribbon and tie a big bow on the chair and put a card on it saying, 'Merry Christmas, Mark.' Then send it to Mark Shaw in New York City." I remembered that Shaw had taken pictures of them at the beach the summer before. The pictures apparently had pleased Jackie very much.

After spending the Christmas holidays in Montego Bay, the Senator and Jackie arrived back in Washington on Friday evening, January 1, 1960. It was no secret that he was about to announce his candidacy for the Democratic Presidential nomination. The newspapers had been speculating about it for weeks. When the announcement was made that he would hold a press conference the next day at 12:30 P.M. in the Senate caucus room, everyone knew what to expect.

To the staff, it marked a long-awaited milestone. We could sense his exuberance when he arrived at the office a little after ten that morning. His barber, David P. Highley, was waiting to cut his hair. When he sat down he said to me, "Mrs. Lincoln, I'd like to dictate to you."

"I am announcing my candidacy for the Presidential nomination in 1960," he dictated, and suddenly the impact of what he was doing hit me. I realized that it was a turning point in my life as well as his.

He calmly went on dictating while the barber snipped his hair. "I am convinced after touring every state in the last forty months, most of them several times, that I can win both the nomination and the election—and I do not intend to relax my efforts until both have been accomplished." Then the telephone rang. It was Arthur Goldberg, and he talked to him before finishing his announcement speech.

After he had his haircut, he went to the recording studio in the Capitol to make some one-minute radio and television tapes for New Hampshire. All morning people had been walking up and down the hall hoping to catch a glimpse of the Senator. When he stepped out into the hall, they rushed up to shake his hand. There were so many of them he was late getting to the recording studio.

He was back in time, however, for his appointment with Lawrence Spivak, who wanted to discuss the Senator's appearance on the "Meet the Press" radio and television programs the following night. After Mr. Spivak left, the Senator was fidgety. He walked from room to room, picking up papers, reading a little. Then he would sit down at his desk, move the papers around, lean back in his chair, stare up into the ceiling, then thump his fingers on the arm of his chair and look at the clock. He was like a thoroughbred racing horse waiting for the starting gate.

At 12:15 Mike Feldman, Ted Sorensen, Ted Reardon, and I went into his office. Ted Reardon said, "I just took a poll in the office and I have good news. They are all for you." This brought a smile to the Senator's face. Then he suggested that we four walk down the hall and he would follow.

When we reached the caucus room it was packed. I thought every reporter in Washington was there. I finally found Abe and went to stand with him. In the distance, down the corridor, we could hear a ripple of applause growing louder and louder as the Senator approached. Jackie was waiting for him at the door, and they entered the caucus room together. She was beautifully dressed in a red suit. As they started toward the front of the room there was a great burst of applause. He moved toward the podium with Jackie at his side, and they stood for a moment while the photographers took pictures. Then, with an occasional flashbulb lighting up his face, he started to read what I had typed for him earlier.

"I am announcing today my candidacy for the Presidency of the United States." He ended with the statement: "For eighteen years I have been in the service of the United States, first as a naval officer in the Pacific during World War II, and for the past fourteen years as a member of the Congress. In the last twenty years I have traveled in nearly every continent and country, from Leningrad to Saigon, from Bucharest to Lima. From all of this, I have developed an image of America as fulfilling a noble and historic role as the defender of freedom in a time of maximum peril—and of the American people as confident, courageous, and persevering. It is with this image that I begin this campaign."

When he finished speaking, he asked the reporters if there were any questions. The crowd was silent for a second and then there was a thunder of applause. Then everyone was crowding around, trying to get near enough to say a word or shake his hand. I was so thrilled that Abe gave me a little push to bring me back to reality. Suddenly I realized I had work to do; the Senator was flying to Boston that afternoon. I raced back to the office and the ringing telephones. People were calling from all over offering their support.

The Senator, Jackie, and her mother and stepfather came back to the office for a little while after the press conference. While I was setting up the table in his office for lunch, the Senator went into another room to tape a short interview for

CBS about his announcement. I began putting things in the black briefcase I knew he would want to take to Boston. He was going to tape a recording with Mrs. Eleanor Roosevelt at Brandeis University.

On Sunday morning he was going to meet with his advisory group, the informal "brain trust" with whom he and Ted Sorensen had been working. I could see this group was playing an increasingly important role in his campaign. Among other things, it served as a kind of sieve through which ideas from the university thinkers filtered and were transformed from impractical hopes to practical politics. I once heard him say, "Just as the road to hell is paved with good intentions, the pages of history are studded with countries that disappeared because they couldn't turn their good ideas into action."

He believed that the low opinion many people had of politics and politicians was not only incorrect but positively dangerous. He once dictated his thoughts on this:

". . . the fact remains that politics has become one of our most abused and neglected professions. It is this profession, it is these politicians who make the great decision of war and peace, prosperity and recession, the decision as to whether we look to the future or the past. In a large sense everything new depends on what the government decides. Therefore, if you are interested, if you want to participate, if you feel strongly about any public question, whether it is labor, what happens in India, the future of American agriculture, whatever it may be, it seems to me that governmental service is the way to translate this interest into action, that the natural place for the concerned citizen is to contribute part of his life to the national interest."

The Senator came back from Massachusetts Sunday afternoon in time for his appearance on "Meet the Press" at six o'clock that evening. Several members of the office staff went to the studio. A few minutes after we arrived, the Senator came through the door with Jackie and Caroline.

The program started easily enough, then the tough question; "Would you, Mr. Kennedy, accept the Vice Presidency if you failed to get the Democratic nomination for President?"

He answered in all sincerity: "I am not going to accept the Vice Presidential nomination. I shall support the Democratic ticket, I will work hard for it, but looking at the history of the last sixty years, I don't recall a single case where a Vice Presidential candidate contributed an electoral vote. . . . The Vice Presidential candidate does not contribute. That is what is going to happen in 1960. They presume that the Presidential candidate is going to have a normal life expectancy. They don't say 'We don't like the Presidential candidate, but we will vote for the Vice Presidential candidate.' "

There had been a number of telephone calls between our office and Columbus, Ohio; and the day after he made his announcement, I heard the Senator say, "I believe Mike DiSalle is going to endorse me for the Presidency." It seemed that the seats on the bandwagon might be beginning to fill up. Governor DiSalle did indeed endorse him, and the next morning the Senator dictated a wire expressing his gratitude.

The Senator's announcement seemed to overshadow the opening of Congress four days later. The first day was the usual handshaking session. The following day brought both President Eisenhower's State of the Union message and the Democratic conference, the annual strategy planning meeting of the Democratic members of the Senate. The Senator attended to make sure that the minimum wage and education bills were given high priority on the legislative agenda.

A few days later he asked me to get him a list of the primary dates in the various states. I knew he had decided to enter the New Hampshire race. Later that day at lunch I heard him telling Torby Macdonald, "I may go into Wisconsin, but I must say that I find it difficult to do when it means I will have to go into Humphrey territory while he confines himself to those states in which he is known, and Symington will not go into any primaries. I guess I'll have to wait and see how things progress."

As an announced Presidential contender, the Senator was very much in the spotlight when Democratic National Committeemen and Democratic governors arrived in Washington for the annual party get-together and the Jefferson-Jackson Day dinner on Saturday, January 23rd.

Arrangements had been made several weeks earlier for California's Governor and Mrs. Pat Brown to have lunch with the Senator and Jackie at their home on the 23rd. After lunch the Senator brought them down to the office and had a further talk with them there. After the Browns left he came out to my desk and said, "Take this down. I might want to refer to it later. 'I talked to Governor Brown today and he said that he is for me as of today. He said that he would not be a candidate for Vice President, unless at the end of the balloting for President, if I asked him to be, he would consider it. He said that he would make no effort after he had received the first ballot vote to influence the votes of the delegation, if he [Brown] were for Symington [at that time]. In other words, he would release the delegation to vote as they wanted and would take no action to impose his judgment on them. He would hold them under the unit rule for me. He agreed to send me the poll he is taking on Brown versus Kennedy. I agreed to send him mine.'" Then he added, "Remind me to send that poll to him."

The Jefferson-Jackson Day dinner was to have a program of four speakers in addition to the principal speaker, former President Harry Truman. The four speakers were Senator Hubert H. Humphrey, New Jersey's Governor Robert B. Meyner, Senator Lyndon B. Johnson, and Senator Kennedy. So many people wanted to attend the dinner that it had to be held in two banquet halls and each speech given twice. The order of speaking was determined by a spin of the wheel. On the first go-round the Senator was the fourth speaker, and on the second he was to be first. His first speech drew noticeably greater applause than the others, and as soon as he moved to the second banquet hall, many people got up to follow him.

Stories about Caroline were becoming more numerous in the newspapers, probably because her father liked to talk about her. Some said she was Kennedy's "secret campaign weapon." People loved to hear that she called him "silly Daddy" and ran to him when he came home at night. I smiled at the memory of the times we had wondered if he would make a good father.

She adored her "silly Daddy" and he adored her. His Irish laughter was never more unrestrained than when they were together, and I know he missed her when his schedule kept him away from Washington.

He was flying all over the country in his campaign for support. After one trip he rushed in and said to me, "Take these down, Mrs. Lincoln: 'One, check with Steve Smith about possibility of going to Nevada's State Democratic Convention on April 30. Two, tell Steve no new dates in Oregon until after Wisconsin primary. Three, call Congressman McCormack. Four, talk with the West Virginia Senator and Congressmen concerning the West Virginia primary. Five, call Jim Patton about National Farmers' Union.'" Then he began to read the mail. Suddenly he looked up and added, "Oh, yes, you'd better order five white broadcloth shirts with French cuffs." Later that day he walked by my desk and said, "Tell my tailor that I will pick up the coat he is altering for me on Saturday."

He seemed caught up in a whirlwind. One day he came back from a Labor Committee meeting and said, "Come into my office." I could tell something was bothering him. "I just passed Senator Dodd's wife in the hall and I didn't speak to her. Let me give you this letter for her."

Pacing the floor, he dictated: "'I am extremely sorry that I was in such a hurry today that I didn't recognize you. I am afraid that the same thing will happen to me with my wife one of these days. I have always had a warm feeling for you and I was delighted to see you looking so well.'"

He stopped pacing. "Get that out right away. Have it hand delivered."

133

The Senator spent so much time in the air and in various cities it was surprising that he did not sometimes forget where he was. Fortunately he liked to fly. The pilot of *The Caroline* told me once that Kennedy was the perfect passenger. "He never worries about flying or tries to second guess me about the weather. He just climbs aboard and relaxes."

CHAPTER 13

The Bandwagon Rolls

New Hampshire's primary is always the first one, and this year it was to be held on March 8th. All the newspaper reports conceded that, as a native New Englander, the Senator would have no difficulty winning the votes of his neighbors. But he was taking no chances, particularly when these same papers, following their own strange logic, also agreed that if he didn't win decisively, he really would not have won at all.

He spent the three days just before the primary walking— hatless—through the chill, snow-covered streets of New Hampshire cities and villages. The Sunday papers showed him waving to one of the many groups of children who came out to greet him wherever he went.

On the morning of the primary, he left New Hampshire and flew back to Washington, arriving at 1 P.M. He had made a luncheon date with Torby Macdonald, and Torby was waiting for him when he came into the office. The Senator was in an exceptionally good humor, confident he would win by a big vote.

He was going to rest only that one day in Washington before hitting the campaign trail again, and he left the office a little early to go home and listen to the results. Abe and I also stayed up to listen that night, and each report was more gratifying than the one before. It was soon obvious he had sailed over the first hurdle. But more difficult ones were coming up.

When I congratulated him the next morning, he seemed almost surprised, as if New Hampshire were already ancient history. His mind was now in the Middle West—Wisconsin, April 5th.

He went out to Wisconsin for three days. The first letter he dictated to me when he returned was to Bernie Boutin, who had been in charge of his campaign in New Hampshire. "Dear Bernie: You have no idea how much the New Hampshire results helped around the country. You did a wonderful job and I want you to know how much I appreciate it."

He knew that in Wisconsin he would not find the same immediate sympathy he had found in New Hampshire, but he was there to win, and his sense of organization was helping to make up for the lack of enthusiasm he expected to find among Wisconsin voters. For months Kennedy supporters had been working feverishly for him throughout the state, and now several members of the staff were also going there. To avoid any possibility of misunderstanding, the Senator insisted that all of his staff workers be removed from the Senate payroll before they went to Wisconsin.

By now the Kennedys—his mother, brothers, sisters, and in-laws—were popping up all over the state of Wisconsin. They were at teas, they were at receptions, ladies' clubs, supermarkets, and on television. And everywhere they were both charming and effective. The newspapers were filled with cartoons showing them taking over the state. The Senator enjoyed these cartoons, and I wrote many letters to political cartoonists asking if the Senator could have the originals for his parents, for Eunice, or for himself. I covered the walls of his office with these cartoons, and he took a great deal of pride in showing them to visitors.

When April 5th arrived, I was jittery all day. I turned on the television in the Senator's office and ran in every few minutes to see if there were any reports. There was an hour difference in time, and the returns came in slowly. I talked to the Senator on the telephone. "How does it look?"

"Can't tell yet," he said very noncommitally. "We will know more later."

I resigned myself to waiting at home. After what seemed hours the Milwaukee results began arriving. As soon as they were announced I gave my husband a hug. "Abe! He's leading!" The next morning we knew he had won. But not by enough to make it a clear-cut victory. He had 56 percent, giving him six districts to Senator Humphrey's four. Now, as expected, the papers said that the real victory belonged to Humphrey since he had kept Kennedy down to only 56 percent, ignoring the fact that the primary was held in Humphrey's back yard.

When he returned to Washington, again his mind was already on the next primary; he had to prove all over again his ability to win. He had already filed in the West Virginia primary, and also in Indiana and Maryland. Jackie accompanied him to each state for the filing.

On March 16th he had opened West Virginia headquarters in Charleston. Since that time there had been plenty of activity by campaign workers in the state, and, after the Wisconsin primary, the main organization moved down to West Virginia. He was concerned with the importance of the religious issue. When he read the newspaper comments on the Wisconsin primary, he said, "Okay, if that didn't prove anything, West Virginia will—it has the lowest percentage of Catholics in the United States."

The Senator was visiting West Virginia whenever he could, and he was bearing down hard on economic conditions in that state. He told audiences that if he was elected he would work toward helping people in the depressed areas get back on their feet. I heard stories about boys back in the West Virginia mountains going barefooted until they were in their teens.

We had once received a letter from a mother whose four-year-old son had seen Caroline on television, in her bare feet.

He had looked up and asked, "Mommy, are her parents too poor to buy her a pair of shoes?" He wanted to share his shoes with Caroline. When the Senator saw the way the people of West Virginia lived, he felt the same way. He was really determined to help them, win or lose, and I think they knew it.

He stopped off in Washington one afternoon long enough to refill his briefcase with campaign material and dictate a few letters. The letters showed that though he was pleased about Wisconsin, his mind was grappling with the problems of winning elsewhere. In answer to one he said, "As for Wisconsin, I am reminded of the story of the old Frenchman who was asked what he had done during the French Revolution. He replied, 'I survived.' That's the way I feel about Wisconsin." To another he wrote: "Thanks you for the cognac. I would like to say that I am planning to keep it to sip during the warm spring nights. Unfortunately, last night I began to think about West Virginia and drank the whole bottle."

The political cartoons were getting funnier. One showed "Humphrey Dumpty" sitting on a wall holding his head. The wall was split by the Kennedy vote, and the cartoon was entitled "Wisconsin Wall." And then there was one entitled "Strange Clubfellows," showing a group in front of a sign reading "Stop Kennedy Club." The club members were Hu, Sam, Morse, Lyndon, H.S.T., Stu, Den Mother (Mrs. Roosevelt), KKK, Dixiecrats, and Hoffa.

The Senator took a few days off and went to Jamaica. He had once said, "In arranging my schedule, you should provide one full day off per week in a pleasant surrounding, preferably a beach. Every three weeks I should have four days off. Every six weeks I should have five to seven days." This was his plan— or should I say dream?—but things never worked out that way; once he started he rarely took any time off.

When he returned he spent three days in West Virginia and came back with his briefcase filled with bits of material he had clipped out of the papers. One clipping read: "There has been no real test of the so-called Catholic issue in an election since

Al Smith lost West Virginia in 1928. Some Democrats believe there is anti-Catholic sentiment, but are awaiting the May 10th primary to learn how much, if any."

Another article discussed why James H. Rowe, Jr., a Washington lawyer who was a close friend and political advisor to Lyndon Johnson, was working for Hubert Humphrey. The article said, "When Humphrey was asked what implications should be drawn from Rowe's backing, he replied with a grin: 'Well, I don't know what kind of implications you want to draw, but you know he is a close friend of Lyndon's and Lyndon has said all along he would not be a candidate.'"

I once heard the Senator say, "Lyndon is helping Humphrey. Senator Robert C. Byrd of West Virginia is urging the delegates to be for Lyndon Johnson, and President Truman is backing Symington. It all adds up to one thing—they would like to stop me."

May 10th was another day of waiting and worry. I sat at the typewriter, but I was listening to the reports on the television in the Senator's office. I kept telephoning headquarters in West Virginia. They couldn't tell me anything except there seemed to be a large turnout of voters. We rushed home, ate dinner, and started the long vigil of waiting for the returns.

While the ballots in the West Virginia primary were being counted, Senator Kennedy was in his home on N Street awaiting the returns. He had returned to Washington to have dinner with Jackie, who was expecting another baby in the fall. By ten o'clock it was fairly certain that he had won, but Humphrey, at the Ruffner Hotel in Charleston, did not concede until around 1 A.M.

He sent a wire to the Kennedy Headquarters in Charleston. The Senator's brother Bob received it, and went over to the Ruffner Hotel to make a courtesy call on Senator Humphrey. About the same time Humphrey started for the Kennedy headquarters. When they met, they shook hands and then headed for the Kennedy Headquarters to await Senator Kennedy. He had telephoned he would arrive from Washington around 3 A.M.

138

He and Humphrey met at the Kanawha Hotel. The next morning Humphrey issued a statement saying he was no longer a candidate for the Democratic Presidential nomination; he had decided to concentrate his efforts on reelection to the Senate.

The next primary was Maryland. The Senator asked Torby Macdonald to head the organization in that state. Instead of choosing an old Maryland hand to run the Baltimore headquarters, Torby surprised everyone by selecting Joe Curnane, an Irishman from Everett, Massachusetts. Joe's winning ways and shrewd political sense soon made him very popular among Maryland Democrats, and he showed that he was an effective campaign leader.

My husband was also working with Joe, acting as a liaison between the Maryland headquarters and the state's Democratic Congressmen. When the Senator was scheduled to make a tour of Maryland, Abe helped with the advance arrangements and Torby traveled with the Senator.

Before the Maryland campaign was over, the Senator was campaigning in Oregon. Both these states, and Indiana and Nebraska as well, repeated the victories he had won in New Hampshire, Wisconsin, and West Virginia. In each state he took his cause to the people and they rallied behind him.

Now that he had demonstrated in seven primaries his ability to get the votes of the people, he began working on the party leaders and on the delegates. He never let up.

Convention time was drawing nearer. We established a direct line to Los Angeles, where the convention was to be held. Robert Troutman, an attorney from Atlanta and a good friend of the Senator's late brother Joe, was out there getting things started. With him was Jean Lewis, a very efficient Alabama girl, who had worked in the Senator's Esso Building office.

Soon she sent us a report that the headquarters in the Biltmore was functioning smoothly. They had a switchboard installed and were interviewing operators. She was working in the Kennedy office in southern California, lining up drivers for cars. They had obtained the Music Room on the first floor of the

Biltmore as the hospitality room, and they had reserved the Main Ballroom for a one-to-four P.M. reception on Sunday, July 10th.

While the Senator kept traveling all over the country attending state Democratic conventions to line up delegates, I began making plans to go to Los Angeles. He had told me he wanted me to work in his suite at the Biltmore. One day I asked Jean Lewis where I would be staying and reminded her that Abe was coming with me. She said all I had to do was check with her when I arrived and she would give me the key to our room, and also send a driver to bring me in from the airport.

Suddenly I discovered I had nothing to wear. At the last moment I dashed out for a special dress to wear to Senator Kennedy's reception.

The Senator was back in Washington at the end of June. When he left the office on June 30th, he asked, "What do I have tonight?"

"There is a fund-raising reception for Senator Hubert Humphrey at the Broadcasters Club on DeSales Street tonight. You know, to raise funds for his Senate campaign."

"Oh, that's right. I can't miss that one."

And off he went to help raise funds for the man who fought him so hard a few months before.

CHAPTER 14

California, Here We Come

There was much to be done before the Senator left for California and the convention. He was still concerned about the Maryland delegates; his primary victory did not bind their votes. He went to Annapolis to see the Governor, Millard

Tawes. When he returned, he said, "It was a pleasant visit, but he doesn't want to commit himself."

While he was gone, Stewart Alsop called to ask if the Senator would give him permission to use in the "Keeping Posted" section of the *Saturday Evening Post* an interview he had had with the Senator.

"ALSOP: I think that the most likely alternative would be a Stevenson-Kennedy ticket if you don't make it and Johnson and Symington don't make it. My God, the pressure you must be under from Stevenson.

"KENNEDY (with some heat): Look, I'll make you an offer—if I take the Vice Presidency under anybody, I'll send you a check the next day for $25,000.

"ALSOP: A useful sum. I wonder if I would have to pay income tax on it?"

When I showed this to the Senator he immediately crossed out the words "send you a check the next day for $25,000" and wrote instead "give you my next year's Senate salary." Then he said, "Call Alsop and tell him to make the change."

The Senator and Jackie decided it would be better for her to remain in Hyannis Port with Caroline during the hectic days of balloting. There she could follow the convention on television in a more restful atmosphere. He was to join them for the July Fourth weekend. What began as a peaceful few days ended with a great display of fireworks between former President Truman and the Senator.

In a scorching television statement at noon on Saturday, July 2nd, Truman asserted that he did not want to be a party to a convention that had been rigged by Kennedy and therefore would not attend. He also said that Kennedy was not Presidential timber; in fact, he ". . . wasn't even dry behind the ears."

Senator Kennedy went into action at once, and fought back with the facts. He was hopping mad when he called the office. "Imagine making a statement like that on the eve of the convention." He got in touch with the television networks and demanded equal time under the provisions of Section 315 of the Communications Act. They advised him the Section did not apply because Truman was not a political candidate.

Then he announced he would hold a press conference in New York City at 4:30 P.M. Monday, July 4th, where he would present a statement and be available for questions. The National Broadcasting Company wired that they were willing to broadcast his statement. Ted Sorensen flew to the Cape, and they went to work on the statement. I was kept busy Sunday and Monday trying to answer questions from the curious public and newspapermen about what he was going to say.

On Saturday Herbert Klein, Vice President Nixon's press secretary, had invited us to hear Truman's statement in their office because our set was not working. I had a repairman fix our television Monday morning so that we could hear the Senator at 4:30. He was calm and confident, and answered Truman directly. He said it was "time for a new generation of leadership to cope with new problems and new opportunities." Then he demolished Truman's main argument by pointing out that, far from being controlled, his votes came largely from his primary victories. He noted that he entered and won all that were open while neither Symington nor Johnson had entered a single primary, although they did support Kennedy's opponents. He ended by saying, "I do not intend to step aside at anyone's request." Now he was ready for the convention.

Arrangements had been made for the rest of the Kennedy family to stay either at Marion Davies' house or at the Beverly Hilton and the Biltmore. Jackie's sister, Lee, and her husband were going to stay at the Beverly Hilton. Airline reservations were staggered from Tuesday, July 5th to Sunday, July 10th. I decided I would go out on July 8th, and Abe would follow me on the 10th.

The morning of July 8th came quickly. When I kissed Abe goodbye he said, "Be careful, don't get your fingers in any car doors, and I'll see you Sunday." I stopped by my parents' apartment to say goodbye. "Be sure to watch for me on TV."

I rode over to Friendship Airport, near Baltimore, with Agnes

Mathiesen, secretary to Congressman Eugene Keogh of New York, who was also en route to the convention. In Chicago we changed planes and I rushed out to buy a paper. On the front page of the Los Angeles *Examiner* was a picture captioned "Kennedys Come to Town." It said nine members of the Kennedy clan, including four nephews and a niece, arrived in Los Angeles Thursday to give moral support to Presidential candidate John F. Kennedy. Also in the picture was Louella Hennessey, the Kennedy family nurse.

When we arrived at the International Airport in Los Angeles, I saw girls with Kennedy hats all over the place. As we waited for our luggage, I asked a boy with a big Kennedy button, "Where do I find the cars?"

"Is someone going to take you to headquarters?" he asked.

"Yes, they told me someone would drive me in."

"What is your name, Ma'am? I'll check it for you."

When I told him, he said, "Oh, for Pete's sake, I am supposed to drive you in." He carried our luggage to the car and soon we were speeding down the freeway.

A bellboy came out for our luggage and asked if we were planning to stay at the hotel.

"Well, it may sound funny, but I don't know. I'll have to check with Jean Lewis."

"Ma'am," he said with a grin, "in Los Angeles and during a convention, nothing, but nothing, sounds funny."

He took my luggage and put it in a room behind the desk until Agnes and I could find where we were staying.

We looked around the immense lobby already filled with people, then walked up a flight of steps to the main floor and into the Music Room. A bright young boy hopped up and said, "You are now in Senator Kennedy's Hospitality Room. Is there anything I can do for you?"

"Yes, can you tell me where Jean Lewis is?"

He directed us to Jean, who told me my hotel room was a couple of miles away, out on Wilshire Boulevard. But I was not ready to go there yet. I first wanted to find out where I was going to be set up for the "strenuous work" I was going to do for the Senator. I opened one door and heard people directing cars: "Send one to the airport to pick up Steve Smith's briefcase. It is coming in on the flight from New York, arriving around 6 P.M." Then I saw Leo Racine, who worked in the Kennedy Foundation office in New York, and I knew things were under control.

"Where is the Senator's suite?" I asked one of the girls.

"Oh, we never go up there, but it is 9335." I walked down to the elevator and rang the buzzer. When the doors opened out popped Scotty Peake, Senator George Smathers' administrative assistant. He asked where I was going and I told him to the Senator's suite. He wanted to know when Senator Kennedy was coming in, and I said, "Tomorrow at 12:30."

I finally found 9333, 9334, and 9335. The door to 9335 was locked, but I got in at 9333. It was a very pretty bedroom done in a warm orange color. I opened the door to Room 9334 and stood entranced. It was a decorator's dream, a blend of lavender and green with touches of pink here and there. A fireplace was at one end and a beautiful television set nearby. Directly opposite a wall covered entirely with draw draperies was an alcove with mahogany table and chairs.

The Senator's bedroom was decorated in the same style and colors as the sitting room. Draw draperies at the windows matched the bedspreads. There was a huge bathroom, and I knew he would like that.

All the time I was taking in the beauty of this suite I was wondering where I was going to work. I decided on Room 9333. I ordered telephones and asked to have the bed taken out.

While they were removing the bed I remembered that the Senator had told me to send a telegram to a dinner party that evening for Red Fay in Woodside, California; it was his fortieth birthday. The message he asked me to send was, "Life begins at 40, so they say, so go, Grand Old Lovable, this is your day. Jack."

I called for a desk and supplies. The telephone men arrived

and I asked them to put two phones in my room, one in the sitting room and one in the Senator's bedroom, all with connecting lines. They said things would be in order the next morning. Soon I was on the way to my hotel.

The key was waiting and the desk clerk showed me to my room. I had a sitting room as well as a bedroom. It didn't look like the Senator's but it was very nice. I looked around for a moment and suddenly realized how tired I was. I hurried into bed, and before I closed my eyes, I offered a little prayer that we all would have the strength to carry us through the next few days.

I awakened with a start the next morning. For several seconds I couldn't remember where I was. I looked over in the other bed. Under those blankets someone was sleeping, and it certainly wasn't Abe. Then I remembered Agnes was staying with me until Sunday, when Abe would arrive from Washington.

I dressed, had breakfast, and by eight o'clock I was at the Biltmore Hotel. When I entered Room 9333, the maid said, "You must have the wrong room. This suite belongs to Mr. Kennedy." I told her I was Mr. Kennedy's secretary and her face lit up. "Oh, it must be wonderful working for him."

Somehow the operators learned I was in the room, and the calls began to come one after the other. Everyone wanted to know when the Senator was coming. I told them he was due to arrive at 12:30 P.M. at International Airport via American Airlines, Flight 1 from New York City. Flying with him would be Torby Macdonald and the Ben Bradlees. Ben and Toni Bradlee were Georgetown neighbors of the Kennedys and they had become close friends. Ben was associated with *Newsweek* magazine and Toni was a niece of the late United States Senator Gifford Pinchot of Pennsylvania.

One of the liaison men called me from the airport when the plane arrived; the Senator was coming down the ramp. The noise of the demonstration for Kennedy was so deafening we had to hang up. After he left the airport, I was called again. "We've never seen people so enthusiastic. People were fighting to get near enough to touch him. It was like those old news-reels of Mahatma Ghandi, except that most of these were girls ... they kept jumping up and down and squealing and scream-ing. He went out of his way to go through the crowds shaking as many hands as he could. The motorcade is now on its way and should be there before too long."

The operator called to say, "The motorcade is nearing the hotel." I ran into his bedroom and looked down from one of the windows. His car was moving at a snail's pace through the crowd. A tremendous cheer rang out every time he waved his hand. Finally, his aides managed to get him out of the car and into the hotel.

"He's now in the Music Room," the girl on the telephone reported. "He was mobbed out in the lobby and now it is just as bad in here. Wherever he goes, there's a crowd."

I could tell by the scramble outside my door that he was approaching. He came through the door looking perfectly calm and at ease, looked over at me as though he knew I would be there, said, "Hello, Mrs. Lincoln," and went into the next room. The people following him were shoving and pushing and show-ing all kinds of credentials to the policemen, who kept shaking their heads.

In a few minutes I stepped into the sitting room to give the Senator a message about one of the incoming calls. He was sitting in one of the easy chairs with his leg thrown over the arm, looking exceedingly comfortable for a man who had nearly caused a riot. He was talking to Larry O'Brien.

The talks continued and the messages piled up. Now there was concern about the door that led into Room 9334. Someone suggested putting a strong man on the door to keep people out. Elected for the job was Jim McShane, who had been with the police department in New York City and later served with the Senate Rackets Committee. Jim, who seems carved out of solid oak, was in charge of protecting the Senator. He was very pleasant, but he could also be very stern; we were sure the two doors would be properly guarded.

146

Senator Kennedy held a strategy session with his top staff to discuss the state delegate liaison assignments. Key men, including Steve Smith, Ted Kennedy, Bill Walton, Larry O'Brien, Kenny O'Donnell, Byron White, John Bailey, Joe Tydings, Bob Troutman, Bill Battle, Dick Donahue, and Hy Raskin were each assigned several states and told to be available for anything a delegate from those states might want. They were expected to interest the delegates in the Senator's candidacy.

They went over the caucus lists and tentatively decided which ones the Senator should attend. They asked me to work out the schedule of each day's activities the day before and type up the schedule so that it could be given to the press the night before.

It wasn't long before I had a mimeographed copy of the state delegate liaison assignments, where they were staying, and their room numbers. I also sent a memorandum to all delegate liaison men saying, "To make it easier for you in reporting delegate changes, a girl at HEADQUARTERS has been assigned to YOUR state." When they called, all they had to do was to ask for the girl assigned to their state. There was also a memo stating that all liaison men were to meet each morning in one of the conference rooms where the day's activities and progress would be discussed. Bob Kennedy was to preside at these meetings. I said to myself, "If the Senator doesn't get the nomination, it is not going to be for lack of organization."

In the midst of all the confusion in my room, the NBC television crew was badgering me about getting into the living room to set up their equipment for the Chet Hagan interview with the Senator scheduled for 6:30 P.M.

Mike Prendergast of New York came out of the living room, and George Meany, who had been waiting for a few minutes, went in to talk to the Senator. As I took Mr. Meany in I said to the Senator, "NBC would like to set up their equipment for your interview in a little while. Is that going to be okay?"

147

"Whenever they want to set up, tell them to come in. We can talk in the bedroom."

After the Chet Hagan interview, the Senator came out and told me he was going to his sister Pat's house and asked when his first appointment was the following day. I told him at 9:30 with Governor George Docking of Kansas. On his way out he spoke to several people, and I returned to work on the caucus list. The states were divided into three groups: "No," "Perhaps," and "Yes." The liaison men for the "Yes" column were trying to find out when these states were going to hold their caucuses.

Finally I returned to my hotel, telephoned Abe in Washington, and slipped into bed and to sleep. I tried not to awaken Agnes the next morning but she was awake anyway. She said she was going to work in the news release section and that she was moving in with one of the other girls since Abe was arriving in the afternoon. As I left her that morning I said, "I'll see you at the Senator's reception this afternoon."

I fully intended to go to the reception, but the day turned out to be too busy for that. First, Bob Kennedy called to ask if the Senator had arrived. When I told him he had, he said he would be right up. By the time he got there the office was so full of staff people he had to squeeze through.

It looked like Governors' Day for the Senator. After his first appointment with Governor Docking, he saw Terry Sanford, the Democratic nominee for governor of North Carolina, who came with his close friend, and an early Kennedy supporter, H. L. Riddle. They were followed by Governor Herschel Loveless from Iowa. After seeing him the Senator went to a breakfast that Bart Lytton, the financier and industrialist, gave for the California delegation, and then came back for a television interview with Edward R. Murrow.

The reception was supposed to start at one o'clock. I kept thinking I could skip down to see how it looked, but every time I tried to leave, the phone rang or someone came in with a memo about caucus changes. With a reluctant look at my new dress, I gave up.

Following the reception, the Senator made a television appearance on "Meet the Press," and was interviewed for television by Edward P. Morgan.

He then went to the Shrine Auditorium where he talked briefly at a meeting of the National Association for the Advancement of Colored People, and returned to the suite for appointments with columnists Joe Alsop and William White, and Ohio Governor Mike DiSalle. He also had a conference with Ted Sorensen before going to the Democratic Committee dinner at the Beverly Hilton.

That evening Abe took me to dinner at a little restaurant near our hotel and told me about his flight from Washington.

"Senator Eugene McCarthy was on that plane and he is certainly against Kennedy."

"That's funny. I thought he would be for Kennedy because he is a Catholic."

"He is strongly opposed to him. There must be a reason. Perhaps it is that question of oil depletion allowance. I believe he votes with the oil-and-gas Senators."

Before I went to bed the Senator called to ask what time his first appointment was the next day. I told him he was due at the Alexandria Hotel at 8:30 A.M. to attend the Nevada caucus.

He had nine caucuses to attend that day. From my office I checked first to make sure that a car was ready to take the Senator to the Alexandria Hotel. One of the liaison men went along with him to carry the schedule so he would know which caucus he was about to attend. Men were stationed at each caucus; they called me when the Senator left, and I notified the man at the next caucus that the Senator was on his way and would arrive in x number of minutes. Sometimes he was a few minutes late, but everything ran almost like clockwork.

The previous day I had received a copy of a wire sent that morning to the chairmen of the Alabama, Florida, Georgia, Kentucky, Louisiana, Mississippi, North Carolina, South Carolina, Tennessee, Texas, and Virginia delegations. It read: "I am most grateful for the support and friendship of my Southern friends in 1956. As a candidate for President I would appreciate very much the privilege of meeting your 1960 delegation in your caucus to explain my views and to answer their questions. If this privilege can be extended to me, please telephone my personal secretary, Mrs. Evelyn Lincoln, Phone MAdison 6-3592, Ext. 27. Sincerely, John F. Kennedy."

The response was good, but one reply was quite unexpected. Lyndon Johnson wired: "I am very happy to know that you are grateful for the support and friendship that your Southern friends gave you in 1956. It is interesting to know you need them now. Personally, I believe that the problems before us are far too important to be determined on the basis solely of regional and sectional issues. As a firm believer in the democratic process especially as it relates to national party conventions, may I suggest that in response to your request we appear together before a joint session of the Texas and Massachusetts delegations in caucus and debate the major issues on which these bodies solemnly will act later this week. It would be in the interest of our party that this session be open to a free coverage by press, television, and radio. I propose that we meet at 3 o'clock on Tuesday, July 12, at a place to be determined and of which I will advise you promptly. Best regards. Sincerely, Lyndon B. Johnson."

The Senator talked to Bob and several other liaison men about the message, and then Congressman John W. McCormack, chairman of the Massachusetts delegation, sent a wire to Senator Johnson rejecting his invitation. Among other things, Congressman McCormack said this proposal was inconsistent with the seriousness of this convention and "it tends to create unnecessary emotionalism."

However, Senator Johnson did not give up. He set the time and the place—3 P.M. in the Grand Ballroom—and said he would be there. The Senator arrived promptly. The debate had caused so much interest that long before it was to take place, delegates from other states had started to fill the room. According to Abe, who called me from downstairs to tell me that he was going to be there, there were a lot of Texans on hand to hear the debate.

As soon as the debate was over Abe came up and gave me a report. "The Senator was simply terrific. He really answered Lyndon Johnson. Johnson spoke first and expounded at great length about his qualifications and experience as Senate Majority Leader. And then when Kennedy got up, about all he said was since Lyndon Johnson is such a good Senate Majority Leader I think we should keep him there. That brought down the house and finished the debate."

The Senator had sandwiched this into his schedule of attending caucuses of state delegations and seeing the stream of governors and Senators who came to his suite. Every time I went into the sitting room, the Senator would be telling the one he was talking to about his qualifications and his ability to win the election. This was no time for modesty.

Someone came out and told me the Senator wanted me to come into his bedroom to take some dictation. As I entered the bedroom I heard the Senator and California's Governor Pat Brown talking. The Senator was trying to persuade the Governor to come out for him, but the Governor hesitated. Then the Senator turned to me and said, "Take this down. 'One. I am not asking this delegation to indicate their individual preferences today. I have called you together to hear my views on the situation. I can assure the members that I will call another meeting of the delegation within the next day or so, sometime before the nominating begins, in which the members of the delegation can make known their individual views. I think by then we will all have a clearer view of our situation. Two. I can also assure you that I will make my final decision known to you sometime before the nominating session on the matter of my name going before the convention and my judgment will be motivated on what I feel will be for the best interests not only for my own state of California, but also for the nation.' "

Then he turned to Governor Brown and asked, "Is this what

you would like to say?" The Governor nodded. Then the Senator turned to me and said, "Would you type that up right away so that we can look it over." I rushed out of the bedroom and typed it quickly, ignoring the ringing phones. I took the statement in to the Senator, and he handed a copy to the Governor. After they read it over the Senator said, "I will see you at 1:30." With that Governor Brown left.

Late that afternoon Senator Kennedy and Ted Sorensen met at the Beverly Hilton and began work on the Senator's acceptance speech. It was only Tuesday afternoon, but they were sure he was going to need one.

CHAPTER 15

A Special Night

The day for the 1960 Democratic National Convention to select the party's Presidential candidate had arrived. During the morning Senator Kennedy was attending as many state caucuses as he could, and he was running a little late. When he showed up at the office in the Biltmore Hotel I gave him a message from his sister, Pat Lawford, saying that all the family was having dinner with Ambassador Kennedy at Marion Davies' home that night. "If you plan to be there we should let them know," I told him.

"Call Pat and tell her that I will have dinner at Dad's tonight. And as soon as I leave here I am going out there to swim until suppertime."

He had a string of appointments that afternoon. Soon he had seen all except one, a Hawaiian delegation. There were twenty-three in the group. I went into the living room to speak to the Senator, but he wasn't there. I found him in the bedroom, standing before the window staring into space. He didn't notice that

I had entered the room. I stood motionless for a couple of minutes and then said, "Mr. President."

He turned and looked quickly at me and then, with a slight smile, said, "Thank you, Mrs. Lincoln."

"Whenever you are ready I'll call downstairs and tell the Hawaiian delegation to come up."

"You can do that now."

The Hawaiian delegation came in through my office and went into the living room. When they passed in front of the fireplace where he was standing, each delegate shook his hand. He made a little speech that seemed to impress them, for they all wore smiles when they left.

Shortly thereafter the Senator came out and said he was leaving and could be reached at Marion Davies' house if he was needed.

Abe and I had decided to watch the balloting on the television set in the Senator's sitting room, and I ordered steaks sent up for our dinner.

I knew the Senator was going to watch the balloting at the hideaway where he and Torby Macdonald had been staying, the apartment of actor Jack Haley out on North Rossmore. He was going to have dinner at his father's and then slip back to Haley's apartment to watch the balloting.

Around five o'clock I got a call from Charles Roche, who was handling the press from the hideaway. He said that the Senator would like to have me come out there with my typewriter because he might want me to take some dictation. Chuck who worked at the Democratic National Committee, said, "I am sending a boy up to get your typewriter, and he will also bring you out since it is a little tricky getting out here."

"I'll be there."

Now I had to find Abe and tell him the change in plans. I called down to the Music Room and, fortunately, he was there. He came right up to my office and I told him what I had to do.

"Would you like me to stay here to answer your phones and to cover this end of it?" he asked.

153

"That would be wonderful. I have already ordered dinner and the television is on."

Charley Bartlett called and asked me how things were going. When I told him that I was asked to be with the Senator during the balloting, he said, "Write down the exact words the Senator says when the balloting is over. Remember now, Evelyn, it is important that you do that. And save those words, Evelyn; someday they will be historic."

There were a hundred and one things to do before I left. I had calls to make. At least I had to comb my hair and wash my face. I looked down to see what I had worn that day. Oh yes, my red-and-white-striped dress. I also had on the white sweater Abe had bought as a surprise for me after he arrived in Los Angeles.

The boy came for my typewriter. I turned to Abe. "Keep your fingers crossed. This is it. I'll come back here after it is all over."

We went down the back elevator and got into the car. I sat in the front seat with the driver, and the boy who had been helping me as a volunteer sat in the back. There was a lot of traffic on the streets through which we raced. The boys talked about what they were studying in college and how exciting it was for them to be able to help Kennedy at this convention.

I had not seen much of Los Angeles since I arrived, and I enjoyed this little ride through the streets with block after block of pastel-colored houses. I had no idea where we were going; it seemed we were weaving in and out of the same streets. Finally I saw a crowd of about two hundred people gathered in front of a three-story apartment house in the midde of one block.

"What is that crowd doing there?" I asked. "Must have been an accident."

"No, that is where we are going."

"How can that be? No one is supposed to know where this place is."

154

The boy laughed. "I guess you can't keep anything secret. They have been milling around this place since noon."

The police were trying to keep the people from getting too close to the house, and when we drove up they were not sure we could go in. But after the boys showed their cards, they told us to drive up in the driveway. I was carrying a little bag in which I kept my shorthand book, some white letter-size paper, carbon paper, copy paper, a couple of pencils, and a pen. I had also put in some notes I thought the Senator might want to see.

In front of the building was a patio crowded with people. I recognized some of the reporters, but when they started to come toward me I ran like a scared deer. I didn't want to talk to them. A doorman opened the door, and we walked in and out of a couple of rooms until we came to an elevator. I learned it was the only way to get up to Jack Haley's top-floor apartment.

I stepped out of the elevator into another decorator's dream. There was a massive baby grand piano in the room and a bar one step up from the living room. In the bar room was the television they planned to use to watch the balloting. I saw Chuck Roche and asked, "Are you alone here?"

"No, I think Torby is back in his bedroom."

"I am going to look around a bit before the rest of them come," I said.

I went into the dining room, which was also very beautiful. When I went into the kitchen, for the first time I realized how hungry I was. In the refrigerator were some eggs and a little cheese, some milk and butter. I then went out into the hall and into the Senator's bedroom. From the look of the rumpled bed-spread, the Senator had been doing some reading and telephoning on that bed. He had little slips of paper on the night table by the telephone and newspapers were strewn on the floor, on top of the bed, and in the chairs. I didn't look into Torby's bedroom before I went back into the living room.

Chuck was just closing the draw draperies because he didn't

want anyone to see us. He told me that the press had finally won out and they were holding forth in one of the rooms on the ground floor. They were calling Chuck every five minutes, asking where the Senator was and if he would watch the television here. He had a hard time stalling them. We kept peeking out around the draperies; every time we looked, the crowd seemed to get bigger. I helped Chuck answer the phone until I got so hungry that I went out to the kitchen and made myself a cheese sandwich and some coffee.

Before the boys left to go back to headquarters at the Biltmore they made sure my typewriter was all set ready to go. While I sat there and waited, I suddenly felt the fatigue of the last few grueling days. My body felt drained of energy. Then I thought, "If I am tired, what about the Senator? He must be at a stage beyond tiredness."

Just then the telephone rang. Chuck answered and said "Fine, we are waiting for them." He turned to me and said, "The Senator is on his way."

The telephone in the Senator's bedroom was ringing. I ran to answer it, but was too late—the party had hung up. As I came into the hall, Torby asked me. "Where's Jack?"

"He's on his way."

"Good, it will soon be time for the balloting to start."

Just before ten o'clock the Senator arrived. He was relaxed and in very good humor. That swim in the afternoon must have been good for him. He went into his bedroom, took off his coat, came out to the living room, and said, "How are you doing, Mrs. Lincoln? Have you had anything to eat?"

I told him I had a sandwich a while ago.

"Good."

He walked up to the bar and checked the television set. He was humming a little tune as he went back into the bedroom. I soon heard laughter and talking. He and Torby were kidding each other again. A few minutes later Jim McShane showed up, then Buz Sawyer, a volunteer who had been driving the Senator.

156

Just then Chuck hollered, "They are getting ready to start balloting." The Senator and Torby came out of the bedroom. The Senator had a tally sheet in his hand. The Senator, Torby, Chuck, and Jim sat down in wicker chairs in the bar, and Buz and I sat near the step leading up to the bar.

We all became silent and very intent when at 10:07 the clerk began to call the roll: "Ala-*bam*-a!" Then, all of a sudden, the lights went out and the television went dead. "Damn it," the Senator said, "who blew a fuse?" Someone struck a match, and I could see a figure groping its way out to the kitchen. He put a penny in the fuse box and the lights came back on.

Once again we sat down. We were still in time for the tail end of the count from Alabama. Again the lights went out. "Good God," the Senator shouted. "What in hell's name is going on here? This is impossible. Mrs. Lincoln, maybe it is your typewriter that is doing this."

Chuck's voice came through the dark. "It couldn't be her typewriter 'cause it isn't even on." Once again they got the lights fixed.

It happened again. The Senator was furious. "The convention will be over and we won't know what happened."

Someone said, "I know what is wrong. That air conditioner we brought in here today is taking too much electricity."

"Turn it off," the Senator ordered.

With the air conditioner off, the lights and the television stayed on, and Senator Kennedy was again making marks on the tally sheet. There was still a lot of balloting to be done. I was getting more nervous by the minute as the votes for Kennedy kept piling up. Buz said, "I have butterflies in my stomach."

Now the count was coming down to Washington, then Wisconsin—I couldn't stand it any longer. I jumped up and shouted, "You need only eleven more votes!" It was 10:51 and the Wyoming delegation appeared on the screen.

The Senator said, "And there is Teddy with them. This should be it."

And it was. Wyoming put him over the top. We all jumped up in unison and shouted, "Hooray!" The Senator's first words were, "That's fine. Let's go. First, Mrs. Lincoln, call Jackie on my phone in the bedroom." I went into his bedroom and placed the call.

It took a few minutes, and while I was waiting for her to answer, the Senator dialed his father on the living room phone. I held the line open, talking to Jackie until he came into the bedroom. "Isn't it wonderful," she said in her soft, warm voice. "I'm delighted." As soon as I handed the phone to him, I went out to the living room.

The men there were making plans to go out to Convention Hall, where the convention was being held. I was in a daze. I couldn't realize we had come to the end of the first part of the journey. I was still clutching a packet of papers in my hand. I thought, if he decides to dictate now, I will never be able to take it. A minute or two later he emerged from the bedroom. He had changed his shirt and suit, and he looked like what he was: the Presidential candidate.

Right away he said to Torby, "Are you ready?" Then he said to me, "Mrs. Lincoln, you are going to ride in my car." Meanwhile the newspapermen, photographers, and other people outside the house were going wild. "We want Kennedy. We want Kennedy," they chanted. Buz Sawyer had gone down to get the car ready, and Jim McShane, Torby, the Senator, and I got on the elevator. The Senator turned to Jim and said, "Keep in the background. I don't want them to think I have a muscle man with me."

We stepped out of the front door to a thunder of cheers and the lighting of dozens of flash bulbs. We pushed through to the car, where Buz was waiting. The Senator said, "I will sit up in front. The light is better up there and I might want to do a little writing." I got in the back with Torby, and we backed out of the driveway and started up the street.

Motorcycle police cleared the way, and soon we were out on the freeway, moving fast, with the screaming sirens of our police escort loudly announcing that Senator John F. Kennedy was now someone special. This was my first motorcade ride, and I was excited. But the Senator paid no attention whatever to the sirens—he took a slip of paper from his inside pocket, wrote a few words on it, looked ahead, wrote some more, hit his knee, folded the paper in his hand, opened the paper again, read some more, tapped his fingers on the dashboard, and finally put the paper away. The rest of the trip we rode in silence.

When we neared Convention Hall, I could see the traffic being pushed back on the streets leading to the freeway. There was a great honking of horns, and people craned their necks around their windshields to catch a view of the car that was speeding by.

We neared the trailer where Bob and the liaison men had been working so hard. The Senator wanted to shake their hands, and he stopped there before going into the room behind the platform where convention officials were awaiting him.

When I got that far I was caught in the crowd beside David McDonald, President of the United Steelworkers Union. He took my arm and said to the policemen who were trying to keep people back, "This is Senator Kennedy's secretary; for God's sake let her through." We got through and up the stairs and managed to stand with our backs against the railing where the Senator would pass on his way to the platform.

He soon appeared and waved to us as he went by. We tried to follow him, but again the guards gave us a hard time. Once again Mr. McDonald, a very forceful man, was able to get through to the back of the platform.

Soon the Senator was standing calmly before the huge crowd and the words were rolling out of his mouth as though he had written them weeks before, instead of only a few minutes ago in the front seat of the car. His speech was not long, but the crowd was pleased; they cheered him again and again.

When I thought it was just about over, I edged down from the platform. Again I stood along the rail as he passed to go

159

into the reception room. This time he had his mother and his sisters Eunice and Pat with him, and he waved to me once more. As soon as they had passed, I thought I should go back to the car. A path was roped off and I walked back through the crowd with no trouble. I saw Charley Bartlett against the rope and waved to him. At the car I told Buz, "This time I am going to ride in the front seat and the Senator and Torby can ride in the back." We didn't have to wait long for the Senator to come out, and once again the motorcycle police cleared the way.

When we got out on the street the Senator said, "Look, there's Ann Gargan. Let's pick her up." We stopped and the Senator hollered to her, "Ann, why don't you come along with us." Ann, a first cousin of the Senator's, got into the front seat with me. She was carrying a Kennedy hat, which she said she had worn in the demonstration parade.

"Isn't it exciting?" she said.

"I still can't believe it," I answered.

By 2 A.M. we were back at Jack Haley's apartment. I said to the Senator, "I will see you in the morning."

"Oh, no, why don't you come up for a while. This is a special night."

There was much kidding and laughing in the apartment. The Senator said, "I'm hungry." Ann and I went out to the kitchen to fix him some scrambled eggs, toast, and milk. While he was eating, I went out into the living room. Buz was sitting there waiting to take me back to the hotel.

It was hard to leave and break the happy mood we all shared, a mood that combined the sweet taste of the victory with the pleasure of being able, at last, to give way to the fatigue we'd pushed aside for so long. I found myself walking over to the baby grand piano. I couldn't think of anything to play for a second, and then my fingers began almost on their own to hit notes that said, "When Irish Eyes Are Smiling." It somehow seemed just right.

When I got back to the Kennedy suite at the Biltmore, I

found that Abe had had little time to watch the convention because the telephones gave him no peace. "And to top it all," he said, "I had to take dictation from the Senator. He called about twenty minutes ago and asked for you. When I told him that you hadn't arrived yet, he dictated a message he wanted me to deliver to Lyndon Johnson."

"I guess I left them too soon," I said, "but there didn't seem like there was going to be any more activity." When I left the apartment, the Senator was in his bedroom making one telephone call after another; I guess he automatically called the hotel, thinking I would get back there in less than five minutes.

Abe showed me the Senator's message he had scribbled on an envelope and also the telegram, which he delivered personally to Senator Johnson's room, telling Johnson that Senator Kennedy wanted to see him the next morning.

Abe said that before he delivered the message he had called down to see if Senator Johnson was in his suite. The operator said he didn't want to be disturbed—he had retired. So Abe had given it to someone at the door.

We went out the door of the suite and saw chairs and television equipment strewn all around the hall, the dregs of the earlier excitement. When we walked out on the street, the night air washed over us like a cool shower. This had been the climax of our work, and things could not have turned out better. We stopped on our way to our hotel room for a hamburger and a cup of coffee. We talked and talked, too tired and too excited to sleep.

Finally I said, "I think I'd better go to bed; tomorrow is going to be another busy day."

Before we turned in, Abe said, "You know something? I'll bet the Senator will name Lyndon Johnson as his running mate."

When I asked why, he said, "I am sure that the liberals and the labor leaders would be against Johnson. Then why would he pick someone so distasteful to his liberal supporters? The answer is simple, and spells the difference between a professional politician and a dreamy-eyed amateur. He wants to win.

He will feel that selecting someone like Governor Orville Freeman or Senator Henry Jackson would give the ticket a kind of
'whiz kid' flavor, because of their age. Adlai Stevenson would
pull in liberal votes, but Senator Kennedy knows he has the
liberal votes anyway, and with Stevenson as a running mate
he would lose people who might be favorable to him, but anti-
Stevenson." And so he went, down the list of possibilities. He
weighed each name carefully, and kept coming back to Lyndon
Johnson. "He knows he must have the South to win, and that
the strong civil rights plank in the Democratic platform, a plank
Kennedy has supported, is not going to help bring in the Southern votes. Also, Johnson has done much to help President Eisenhower get his legislation through the Senate, and his presence
could be counted on to draw the votes of middle-of-the-road
conservatives who do not care for Nixon. And of course, Johnson is older than Senator Kennedy."

At this point I was getting sleepy and didn't much care who
was going to run as Vice President. The main thing to me was
that Kennedy had proved to the people that he was the man
for the number-one spot.

CHAPTER 16

Picking a Running Mate

When I arrived at the office around 8:30 the next morning,
the volunteers were bringing in the telegrams, hundreds of
them. Thumbing through them, I found one from Lyndon Johnson. It was a night letter and addressed to the Senator at Democratic Convention Hall. Since it wasn't delivered until 6:48 this
morning I knew the Senator had not seen it.

Among the papers on my desk I found a memo someone had

left for the Senator to read. It was entitled, "Here are eight good reasons why Humphrey's nomination for Vice President is good for Kennedy." I looked them over. One of the points read, "The breakdown of the summit conference will weigh heavily on the coming campaign. Nixon is to be expected to capitalize on his record of having stood up to Khrushchev. Humphrey's presence on the ticket, by virtue of his famous interview with Khrushchev, will negate to some extent the benefit Nixon can get out of this issue."

One of the newsmen stopped by and said, "I hear that it is going to be Senator Jackson of Washington for Vice President."

"Don't ask me," I said. "I don't know anything about it."

I was still trying to dig out from under all the telephone messages and wires when the Senator came through the door. I suppose he was too keyed up to rest, or that he was eager to get about the business of picking a running mate.

When he arrived in Los Angeles on Sunday, the newspaper headlines were predicting that Senator Stuart Symington of Missouri was leading the list of possible nominees for Vice President acceptable to Senator Kennedy. The Senator had said many times that he would not leave the nomination wide open as it had been in 1956, and, without mentioning any names, he had frequently indicated a preference for a running mate from the Middle West or the West who would balance the ticket and who was familiar with farm issues, since he had no background in that field.

As he rushed in that morning he had that special "I-have-work-to-do" look on his face. Following him through the door were his brother Bob and some of the liaison men. They went right into a huddle in the sitting room. The Senator was seated in a comfortable chair and the others were standing or seated around him. Also in the group were his brother Ted, Ted Sorensen, Kenny O'Donnell, Larry O'Brien, Stephen Smith, and Sargent Shriver.

Every time I went into the room with an urgent message I heard snatches of heated discussion about who should be the

163

Vice Presidential nominee. Several names were mentioned: Governor Orville Freeman of Minnesota, Senator Henry M. (Scoop) Jackson of Washington, and Senator Symington. But the name that seemed to come up most often was Lyndon Johnson, which shocked and surprised me. I remembered how hard Johnson had fought to deny the nomination to Senator Kennedy. Then I recalled Abe's comments of the previous evening and thought, "Well, I suppose that's the way politics works."

I went into the living room with another message, and the Senator and Bob were no longer there. I asked where they were and was told, "in the bedroom." In the bedroom I found the Senator pacing up and down while Bob sat on one of the beds. They were both completely unaware of my presence; neither of them said a word. The Senator walked into the bathroom, took a drink of water, and came out again. Still silence. I could tell they were deeply involved in making some decision, so I went back to my desk.

Then another urgent message had to be delivered; back to the bedroom I went. Each time I walked through the living room the liaison men were still sitting around sipping coffee and arguing about the Vice Presidency. When I entered the bedroom this time, Bob was picking up the phone.

"See if Lyndon is in," the Senator said. "And tell him I will be down to see him."

As I gave my message to the Senator and turned to leave I heard Bob say, "He'll be available in a few minutes."

"Okay," the Senator said. "I'll go down in a little while."

About eleven o'clock the Senator went through my office and took the back stairs down to Johnson's suite on a lower floor. He was back via the same route in about twenty minutes. When he came through my office I told him that someone—and I cannot now recall who it was—was on the line for him. "That can wait," he said, brushing past my desk into the living room, where Bob and the other men waited for him.

I also had a message for him to call his father; I trailed him

into the living room to hear him say only one word: "accepted."
There was an electrifying silence among the small group of men
who had recently been so vocal. I could sense this was no time
to interrupt the Senator, not even with a message to call his
father—for which he always permitted interruptions.

I turned to one of the men seated in the closest chairs and
asked, "What did Johnson say?"

"He said yes."

I walked out and telephoned the news to Abe. Despite his
prediction of the previous evening, his reaction was: "I can't
believe it. I can't believe he would accept." He put into words
what I had read in the silence of the men in the adjacent room.

The choice of Lyndon Johnson for Vice President struck
like a bombshell among many, and there were all sorts of reactions, ranging from "cynical deal" to "stroke of genius."

Senator Kennedy announced the selection at a four o'clock
news conference in the basement hall of the Biltmore with
these words: "We need men of strength if we are to be strong
and if we are to prevail and lead the world on the road to freedom. Lyndon Johnson has demonstrated on many occasions his
brilliant qualifications for the leadership we require today."

The Senator had dictated the statement to me and then read
it by telephone to Johnson for his approval earlier in the afternoon. Before releasing it he also talked to most of the other Vice
Presidential possibilities—Symington, Freeman, and Jackson—
and explained to them the reason for his choice. He made it
clear that there was a place for them in his administration and
that he wanted their help and their talents.

Not everyone among the small group of Kennedy strategists
was happy with the choice of Johnson. Some feared it would
bring labor opposition and result in a floor fight that could have
serious consequences in the election. In the afternoon Bob Kennedy went to the Johnson suite, offering to let the Texas Senator
withdraw his acceptance and become chairman of the Democratic National Committee instead. However, the word was

brought back that Johnson had declined, saying, "If Jack wants me, I'm willing to make a fight for it."

It was a strange day, with many big decisions and much running around. Through it all I still had to take care of the delegations who wanted to have their picture taken with the Senator, and newspapermen and photographers who tried every possible gimmick to get in for an interview or picture.

The day wore on into night, and the nominating speeches for Vice President began. By a predetermined strategy designed to avoid any opposition, a motion was made to approve Senator Johnson's nomination by acclamation. The ticket for 1960 was set.

Senator Kennedy invited all the leading Democrats—President Truman, Adlai Stevenson, Governor Harriman, Governor Williams, Terry Sanford, and other Democratic Governors, Senators and Congressmen—to sit on the platform during his acceptance speech. Wires went out to all of these men, each one like a bandage to cover the scars and scratches they had given one another during the struggle for the nomination.

Friday was to be clean-up day. There were still a few delegations that had not been photographed with the Senator. Senator Smathers invited him to a luncheon for the Florida delegation in his suite, and Congressman William Dawson from Illinois arranged for a Negro group to stop by and see the Senator.

He took a break in the afternoon and came back in time to be in a motorcade that would take him from his hotel to Convention Hall. Abe and I had tickets to hear the Senator speak, but we decided it would be just as good to watch him on television from our hotel room.

His eagerness to meet the challenges of tomorrow shone forth in his speech. ". . . the problems are not all solved and the battles are not all won. . . . We stand today on the edge of a New Frontier—the frontier of the 1960s—a frontier of unknown opportunities and perils—a frontier of unfulfilled hopes and threats. . . . The New Frontier of which I speak is not a set of promises—it is a set of challenges."

In closing, he said, "As we face the coming challenge, we, too, shall wait upon the Lord, and ask that He renew our strength. Then shall we be equal to the test. Then we shall not be weary. And then we shall prevail."

He had sounded the starting gun. As the Senator moved back from the podium, Abe turned from our television screen and said, "Evelyn, that speech will go down in history."

When the Senator arrived at the office the next morning, I could see he was restive. He wanted to get going. But there were still some final formalities. He attended the Democratic National Committee breakfast and then held a press conference at which he announced that Senator Henry M. Jackson of Washington would be chairman of the Democratic National Committee until after the election. Then the convention was over and he was ready for the future.

CHAPTER 17

A Trying Interlude

After the convention we flew to Nebraska for a brief visit with relatives. At Lexington, a Republican stronghold, I was honored at a tea attended by two hundred women, including Mrs. Frank Morrison, wife of the Democratic candidate for Governor. I was very proud to take a bow when they introduced me as the personal secretary to "our Democratic Presidential Candidate, John F. Kennedy."

We didn't stay long, however, and on Monday, July 25th, I was back in my office in Washington. One look inside was enough to make me want to turn around and walk out again. Mail, packages, magazines, papers, and telegrams were piled so high I couldn't see out the window behind my desk. And soon the Senator would be calling to find out how things were coming.

First I made little stacks out of the big ones. There was a pile of hundreds of wires of congratulations; there was a pile of magazines, a pile of newspaper clippings, and a pile of letters marked "personal." These I opened first. I stacked the boxes on the floor near my desk. Then I began making still smaller divisions. I sorted through the wires and put the ones from friends, relatives, Democratic leaders, and prominent people on top. Then I went through the newspaper clippings. Some showed that the Stevenson people were now pushing Adlai for Secretary of State. They never stop working for their man, I thought.

One of the letters was from Senator Estes Kefauver of Tennessee, and my mind went back four years to the previous convention when he won the nomination for Vice President over Kennedy. This year he didn't attend the convention; because he was busy campaigning for reelection, and the primaries in Tennessee were on August 4th. He had been invited to sit on the platform with the other senators on the night of the acceptance speech, but he couldn't make it—he was out in a "Campaign Caravan."

Following the convention Senator Kennedy had flown to Massachusetts; Jackie welcomed him with a painting of his victorious return she had done during the convention. After a brief rest with Jackie and Caroline, he began binding the party wounds and planning the campaign ahead. He was eager to turn the special session of Congress coming up in August into an advantage to the Democrats in the campaign. But this took some doing.

First he started on his task of unifying the party. Sometimes in ones, sometimes in twos, the party leaders went to see him in Massachusetts. He met them all in the big white summer house he and Jackie had bought some four years earlier, which Jackie had decorated attractively in early American style. The first leader to arrive was Adlai Stevenson, followed by Lyndon Johnson, Michigan's Governor G. Mennen Williams, Senator Henry M. Jackson, and New York's Mayor Bob Wagner.

Perhaps the most important telephone call was with former President Harry S. Truman, who pledged his active support in the campaign.

There were meetings of the strategy group headed by his brother Bob. They decided to launch a massive voter-registration drive. Larry O'Brien was placed in charge of organization, and Kenny O'Donnell was in charge of scheduling trips.

As plans developed they were announced to the press. One day the headline read, "Kennedy Sets Organization for Big Push"; the next day it would be, "Kennedy to Take to Whistle Stops."

One afternoon he took the newsmen and photographers covering his vacation headquarters out on the Kennedy yacht, *The Marlin*. They took pictures of Jackie, the Senator, and Caroline, and of neighbors making a call on him.

One day I received a memo from Bob Kennedy addressed to all persons representing or speaking of Senator Kennedy in public. It asked them to refer to him as "Senator Kennedy" rather than by his first name. So many of them called him Jack.

When the Senator returned to Washington, we had another problem: where was his office to be for the remaining session of Congress? Was he going to be in the Senate Office Building, or would he have an office in the Capitol near the Senate floor? Ted Reardon got in touch with Joe Duke, the Senate Sergeant-at-Arms, who solved the problem. He said the Senator could use his conference room, located across from the Majority Leader's office and just a few steps from the Senate floor. Soon I had a desk and telephone in there, too.

The day before the Senator returned to Washington he called me from New York and asked me to call Lyndon Johnson, "Scoop" Jackson, and Matt McCloskey, treasurer of the Democratic National Committee, and ask them to meet with him in his office at 9:30 the following morning.

At that meeting they discussed the strategy to be used during the session of Congress, and the tentative campaign schedule after adjournment. At the end of the meeting the Senator and Lyndon Johnson issued a joint statement:

"We have discussed the legislative program for the forthcoming session. The agenda is long. The unfinished business covers a wide range of fields—all of them of key importance to the American people. There are such key issues already on the calendar as medical care for the aged, housing, aid to education, mutual security appropriations, and minimum wage legislation. We intend to devote our full energies to the enactment of this program and we will leave our principal campaigning until the end of the session. We hope to have the cooperation of the Republicans and their candidate in the enactment of this program. The short three-week period will not allow for partisanship. The American people will be quick to spot obstructionist tactics aimed at keeping us from enacting much of this legislation."

I had the tentative schedule covering the period from September 1 through November 8, 1960, and it was staggering. I was glad that the Senator looked so well—he had a rugged time ahead.

Things were moving in on us, pressure groups were beginning to act. They wanted appointments. They had to see the Senator, they said. Democratic Congressmen wanted pictures taken with him. And groups from all parts of the country wanted to present their views. I always tried to be sure they got a chance to be heard.

I thought of the time Franklin D. Roosevelt was campaigning for President and my father wanted to tell him about crop insurance for farmers. This was new then, and he thought perhaps Roosevelt didn't know about it. So my father got the National Democratic Committeeman from Nebraska, a close friend of the then Governor Roosevelt, to see that he got five minutes with him aboard a train at Kansas City.

I remember my father reporting, "Mr. Roosevelt was very

attentive and let me explain my mission. He made some notes and thanked me for coming." And the next day he said, "I see where Roosevelt mentioned crop insurance in his speech last night. So my interview was successful." Crop insurance was important to my father, and through his efforts the Federal Crop Insurance Corporation in the Department of Agriculture was established.

While I listened to the people who wanted appointments, I was mindful of my father's experience. I heard their views, and then made summary notes so that the Senator could decide whether or not he wanted to make an appointment with them.

One day I noticed a hoarseness in his voice, but he kept right on with his appointments—talk, talk, talk, all day long. On Saturday morning his voice was a little better, but he decided he would see a doctor in New York on Sunday. He was going up to Hyde Park to speak at ceremonies at the grave of Franklin D. Roosevelt.

He asked me to telephone Jackie, then at her mother's home in Newport, and tell her he would join them for dinner that night. Then I was to call Bill Walton and tell him to meet the Senator at Hyde Park Sunday and ride in with him to New York.

The Senator seemed anxious to get up to Newport. I think he felt a little rest might help his voice. I filled his black brief-case with memos, polls, and notes concerning the meeting at Hyde Park. One of the notes read, "When you meet with Mrs. Roosevelt on Sunday, sit on her left side—that is her good ear." Another said, "Someone very close to Mrs. Roosevelt called and said she is going to press you for a private commitment to appoint Governor Stevenson as Secretary of State."

When he returned to the office on Monday, he carried a little pink pad around with him and wrote notes to the people who came in instead of talking. His throat was no better, and the doctor in New York had told him not to use his voice.

When Senators Hubert Humphrey, Philip Hart, "Scoop" Jackson, and Joe Clark came in, he just listened, wrote notes, and nodded his head. He did the same when Douglas Dillon, the Undersecretary of State, came to see him. After the Senator left that evening I went through the waste-paper basket and picked out some notes he had written to visitors that day: "Have had an infection." "Is there a big industry there?" "What part of Michigan?" "I spoke there last fall." "I have lost my voice." "Did it shake you?" "I'm glad to see you. How are you doing."

He didn't come to the office until almost noon the next day. When he arrived, he wrote me a note saying, "Keep my schedule to the minimum." As the day wore on I could see that he was becoming very irritated about his voice. By the middle of the afternoon I saw something I had never seen before, not even in 1954 when his back was the most painful: he was completely unnerved. He paced the floor, brushed his hair back a hundred times, and kept hitting his fist on the table.

Finally someone suggested calling a throat specialist in New York. He agreed to come down to Washington at 5:45 that evening. Meanwhile the Senator had taken my appointment book and written "nothing" on the pages for the next four days.

When the doctor arrived, he examined the Senator's throat and assured him that things were going to be all right. They went to the Senator's house. The doctor wanted to run some tests to see if the problem was an infection. After they left I said a little prayer that his throat would soon be better.

There was also a suggestion that he get a speech therapist so that he might use his weak voice more efficiently. The next morning a therapist arrived from Massachusetts.

The next three days were rugged ones. He managed to keep most of his appointments. He now seemed to be in control of himself and was making an effort to speak.

But when a reporter telephoned and asked, "Do you plan on taking your rocking chair with you to the White House if you are elected President?" he wrote his reply for me to give: "Whither I goest—it goes."

A few days later the Senator, pawing through some papers on my desk, came to a little card I had written but had never shown to him. It said, "Governor Ribicoff wanted me to tell you. In your picture on Sunday, Truman took your arm by his left hand. This is a gesture by Truman when he wants to be friends with you." The Senator didn't say anything but he flashed a grin and gave me a little nod.

There were conferences galore on September 1st, the last day of the Congressional session. The Senator held a press conference, was interviewed by various newspapermen, met with Paul Nitze, one of his consultants on national security, and then with Adlai Stevenson. Obviously his voice had come back.

I watched the Senator and Governor Stevenson with their heads close together in a corner of the office. Then the Senator came over to me and said, "Adlai would like to dictate a statement to you." I wondered if he would dictate as fluently as he spoke. But he took his time, speaking carefully, and then asked me to read it back to him, making sure that was what he wanted to say. The statement read:

"Governor Stevenson will be advising me on foreign policy and on campaign strategy generally. I want to take advantage of his Presidential campaign experience. I expect to see him periodically and will talk to him by telephone from time to time. Because of his recent experience in Latin America and his extensive travels in Africa I have sought his views on the current crises in those areas. I have also asked him for a review of the principal problems that will confront a new President."

After Governor Stevenson left I typed the statement and handed it to the Senator. He nodded and told me to read it to Pierre Salinger, his press secretary.

The Senator was glad to see the Senate adjourn. Now he could get on with what was uppermost in his mind—the campaign. I had been hoping that he would ask me to go along on the campaign caravan, but he never had, and now he was about to leave.

"Senator, what am I going to do now that you are going out to campaign?"

"Mrs. Lincoln, don't you realize how important it is for you to be in the office here in Washington? You are the only one who can get me on a minute's notice. And I can get you on a minute's notice. And, believe me, there will be plenty of important calls coming through."

Ted Sorensen, who was waiting to leave with the Senator for a meeting of the speechwriters, turned to me and said, "What a recommendation, Evelyn. You should have a tape recording of that."

CHAPTER 18

The Campaign

The Senator was right when he said he would be calling me often. And I was continually relaying calls and messages to him while he campaigned from town to town. I had the numbers of the mobile phones in the cars they used, and could telephone him at almost any time. By calling the station master I was also able to speak to the Senator when he was on the whistle-stop trip through central California for two days early in September.

I received a copy of a speech he delivered from the rear platform at Marysville, California, on that whistle-stop tour. In conclusion he said, "And I can assure you that if we are successful we are going to move again in this country. We are going to assume the leadership again of the free world. We are going to move in this valley, and we are going to move again around the globe." He was certainly moving himself.

Although it was impossible for him to have an entirely new speech each time he spoke, he often said new and eloquent things that I found very moving. I could imagine what an impact he must have made on people who saw and heard him for the first time. For example, in Oakland, California, he said, "I am in this campaign of 1960 remembering the words of a great American a hundred years ago in the election of 1860. In that election Abraham Lincoln wrote to a friend: 'I know that there is a God, and that he hates injustice. I see the storm coming and I know His hand is in it. If He has a place and a part for me, I believe that I am ready.'"

The Senator opened his campaign on September 3rd in San Francisco with a speech that placed the blame on the Republicans for Congressional inactivity on civil rights, medical care for the aged, a higher minimum wage, housing, and school aid. He asked voters to remove the threat of continued Republican Presidential vetoes that had blocked previously this legislation.

He flew to Alaska, keeping his promise to campaign both there and in Hawaii, the two new states. Then he flew back to Detroit for a Labor Day address. A week before going to Detroit he telephoned me from Boston and dictated a letter to Senator Frank J. Lausche of Ohio asking him for material he needed for the Labor Day speech. He was giving all Democratic Senators an opportunity to help him in the campaign.

After the whistle-stop tour in California, the campaign began picking up speed like a prairie tornado. But my mind was really elsewhere. My father's health had been declining for some time, and now it seemed obvious he would have to go to the hospital. Abe and I drove him to the George Washington University Hospital. I was glad I was not out campaigning with the Senator, for I could visit my father in the hospital every evening and tell him about the day's activities. I also telephoned him several times a day. In my eyes Dad was a hero, and I idolized him for the things he had done not only for me but for his state and his country. I was encouraged to know that even though he was ill he was interested in how the campaign was going. I read him the Senator's speeches and he would say, "That's great, Evelyn. He's a fighter." He was especially interested when I told him that the Republican candidate, Richard Nixon, was not drawing nearly so many people in California as Kennedy had when he was there. And he smiled when I told him how the hatters were still after Senator Kennedy because he wasn't wearing a hat.

Even in the midst of campaigning the Senator remembered little details that were politically important. On September 14th he said, "Don't forget to send a wire to Congressman and Mrs. Mike Kirwan on their fortieth wedding anniversary." Mr. Kirwan was the very influential Representative from Ohio.

From California the Senator went to Texas, where he was to discover that the West Virginia primary had not settled the religion issue. He explained his religious views before the Greater Houston Ministerial Association, and then answered the Protestant ministers who questioned his freedom from Catholic domination. He told me about it the following Monday, when he returned from campaign trips to New York City, Baltimore, and Greenville, North Carolina.

The Senator felt that the meeting with the Houston ministers was the most important of the campaign. He hoped he had finally erased the doubts many Protestants had about voting for a Catholic for President. When he went into the meeting, many of the ministers were hostile to his candidacy; when he left, they were friendly and agreeable.

In his speech, he assured them that he would resign as President if he could not make a decision in the national interest without regard to outside religious pressures or dictates. "I do not speak for my church on public matters and the church does not speak for me." That speech and the question period following were filmed and shown repeatedly all over the country throughout the rest of the campaign, and the Senator seemed to regard it as an early turning point in the campaign. Thereafter, he seemed much surer of the course the campaign would take.

On his one-day visits to Washington, Jackie and Caroline would meet the Senator at the airport and ride home with him and then ride back to the airport with him when he departed.

While he was away Jackie made her contribution to the campaign at home. She held weekly teas for women reporters and women leaders from various sections of the country to exchange campaign techniques and discuss the issues.

On September 26th, 1960, the Senator turned his attention to his first debate with Nixon the coming Monday night. He asked me to fill his black briefcase with various articles and books to study during the week. We were anxiously awaiting this debate. I told my father when it was scheduled, but as each day passed he seemed less and less interested, and more concerned about his illness. Often I went to the hospital and spent my lunch hour with him, trying to cheer him up, but he didn't seem to be getting any better.

On the day of the debate I asked him if he wanted a television so that he could watch it, but he didn't think he had the strength, and I left his room feeling very discouraged.

When Abe and I sat before the television that evening, we were amazed at the appearance of these two men. The Senator looked fresh and relaxed, while Nixon looked gaunt and actually frightened. I was so shocked at Nixon's appearance I could hardly listen to what he was saying. There was the same contrast in their delivery. The Senator was prompt and clear in his answers, but Nixon hesitated and stammered.

The response from the debate was enormous. The next day the newspapers were full of it. Despite the different conclusions about the outcome, the columnists agreed that the American people for the first time had had a chance to compare the two candidates directly.

Although I was elated about how well the Senator had done in the debate, when I went to work on October 5th, my heart was troubled about my father. He seemed to be slipping away from us. I had not been at the office long when the doctor called to tell me Dad had just passed away. I called Abe, told him, and said I was going to be with Mother. I closed my desk and walked out. Although I knew it was coming, it was the kind of shock that no one can—or probably should—prepare for.

We made arrangements to take my father back to Nebraska to the small cemetery near the Swede Plain Methodist Church, which his father had helped build. It seemed right to bring him back to that little church that had meant much to him as a boy and had given so much to his parents and the other pioneers who tamed that lonely land.

We buried Dad there on Sunday, October 9th, and Abe took me back to Washington on the 10th. My mother decided to stay in Nebraska with my brother Bill until after the election.

When I came back to the office, I learned that the Senator had been trying to get in touch with me. When I called him he said, "Mrs. Lincoln, I want you to join us in the campaign on the 16th. I've decided we can't do without you." I was thrilled. I think he felt the constant excitement of the campaign would get my mind away from brooding over my father's death, and I was very grateful for his thoughtfulness.

Though I hated to leave Abe, I welcomed this chance to lose myself completely in the campaign.

I was told to be at National Airport at 10:15 P.M. on October 16th, where I would board *The Caroline*. Everyone else on the plane was so used to traveling that this was old hat to them, but to me it was different. I didn't know what clothes to bring. We were going from Ohio to Florida to New York City to Michigan to California and so on—and on. Surely I couldn't wear the same clothes everywhere. But where could I ever put as many as I would need?

When I got aboard, I saw a seat by a desk, and on the desk a typewriter. Janet Des Rosier, our stewardess, told me that no one was sitting there, so I said I would. Soon the speechwriters arrived, Ted Sorensen, Dick Goodwin, and Willard Cochrane. They greeted me and went to seats I was sure they had been occupying during the entire campaign. Right away they started reading the evening papers to see what ammunition they could get for firing at Mr. Nixon.

While Janet bustled around getting sandwiches for the speechwriters, Howard Baird, the pilot, sat down next to me and told me he was glad I'd be going along. Howard, a thin, wiry man who looked every inch a pilot, told me about his children and how proud they were that he was piloting *"The Caroline."*

A few moments later I looked out the window and saw a series of car lights coming into the airport. "Well, here he is," Ted said. I heard car doors banging and people talking, and then the Senator came aboard. While he walked down the aisle, hitting his right leg with a rolled-up newspaper, he spoke to each of the staff as he passed by. When he came to me he said, "Glad you're here, Mrs. Lincoln." I was glad that he didn't mention my father; I would have burst into tears if he had. He went right into his compartment with Ted Sorensen following him. Pilot Baird started the engines, and in a few minutes we were in the air and I was entering my first Presidential campaign.

The Caroline was to be my home for the next few weeks. At first I felt like a fifth wheel—useless and in the way. Even the Senator had somehow got used to not having me there, and that was something I'd soon have to change. I began to make myself useful. It wasn't long before the speechwriters started to dictate to me while we were flying between stops. I typed the drafts and they would be shown to the Senator. He went over the drafts and called me in for dictation. Then the drafts and his comments would be pieced together into a final version and given to me for typing on a special, large-type speech typewriter. It was really quite a job keeping far enough ahead that we weren't always pulling the last page out of the typewriter while he walked up to the speaker's platform.

It was hectic, and it was hard work—but it was interesting.

While we went from town to town, the Senator always tried to get a little rest before the plane landed at the next stop. He could leave the speaking platform, where he was the picture of drive and excitement, and a few moments later be sound asleep. I don't think he could have gone for more than a few

179

days if he had not had that remarkable ability to take his rest where he found it.

As soon as the plane landed, he would come out of his compartment, brush his hair to one side, and look out the window to see how many people were there. There was always a tremendous ovation when he appeared at the door. People would try to force their way through the ropes that had been put up to keep them at a safe distance. Hands would be outstretched in the hope that he would reach out and shake them.

And then there were the girls. They screamed and hollered the whole time he was in their presence. We had the "squealers," "the jumpers," "the leapers," and the girls that did nothing but just stand and beam—although I think they were just out of breath from their earlier exertions.

It was both frightening and quite wonderful. He was very pleased about the reaction of the young people. Their cheers and admiration were a kind of fuel that kept him going as much as did his catnaps on the plane. He waved to them, smiled at them, shook their hands, and returned their affection.

Soon he was in a car. Generally it was an open convertible, and he usually waved as he passed the immense crowds that lined the streets. Sometimes he would stand up and greet people standing at the windows of buildings. At each stop local Democratic leaders followed him in the motorcade so that the people would see them riding along with him.

When we reached a town where we planned to stay overnight, we generally rode to the hotel in the motorcade. By this time we were so well organized we knew the number of our hotel room before we left the plane. Often we scooted in through the rear door of the hotel; we had learned that it was murder to be caught in the lobby while the Senator was going through.

Then I went right to my room. If there was work to do, I would have my typewriter sent up. Occasionally I went to the dinner or rally where he was speaking, but generally there was such a mob that it was much easier to watch it all on television.

180

I'll never forget the night we landed in Waterbury, Connecticut. We were three hours late and it was almost two A.M., but the people had waited. The motorcade could hardly get through the crowd at the airport, and the streets were lined all the way to the hotel. When we reached the hotel, it was virtually impossible to get through the crowd to get into the lobby. When we did get into the lobby, we couldn't get near the elevator. We finally reached the floor where our rooms were located, and corridors were just as crowded as the lobby. And by now it was almost three A.M.! I was hungry when I got to my room, but I knew the room service had closed, and I decided I'd rather be hungry than to buck that crowd down in the lobby again. Anyway, I thought, we will be leaving early in the morning.

The airport stops began to assume a pattern. The huge crowds were always there. Again and again he would say, "We have to get this country moving again."

I found myself collecting little notes, just as he did. They showed a kind of cross-section of America, and ran from the most touching and unselfish, to the very humorous, to the merely self-seeking.

A man in a hospital in Madison, Wisconsin, dying of cancer, asked if the Senator would write him a few lines (he did); a man in Allentown, Pennsylvania, loaned the Senator a scarf to wear because it was cold (the Senator thanked him and sent it back); a polio patient painfully sent him her best wishes; a real estate agent left some brochures describing property he was sure would take the Senator's mind off his campaign; and there were requests by the hundreds for autographed pictures.

Also, whenever the Senator stopped in a town, people showered him with gifts. There were squirrels (stuffed), dolls, fruit, hats, pictures, books, and everything imaginable. I kept names and addresses, boxed up the gifts to be sent back to the office, and wrote thank-you notes while we continued on the campaign.

We were in the final week of the campaign. Each of us knew
181

exactly what to do, and we worked together in a smoothly operating team.

We went to California once again and then turned eastward to Ohio, Illinois, Virginia, and on November 5th New York City. The motorcade up Broadway was something I shall never forget. From the beginning of that ride to the end was one endless cheer, and we rode through a blizzard of confetti, streamers, and shredded newspapers. After a swing through the area around New York City, the Senator ended his campaign on home ground, in Boston.

Although the weather delayed our plane, the crowd in Boston was enormous. It took two hours for our motorcade to get from the airport to the center of the city. Why I didn't get off at my hotel when we went by I'll never know, but I stayed in the car until we reached the Garden, where the Senator was to speak at a rally. When I tried to get into the Garden I thought I was being torn limb from limb in the crush of supporters who wanted to get close enough to see or touch him. No matter how hard I pressed it was impossible for me to get an inch nearer to the door. I gave up and decided to take a taxi back to my hotel, but I might have been stuck in the center of a quicksand bed. In that mob, movement in any direction was almost impossible. Finally I shoved and wriggled my way to the street, where there was a jam of cars rivaling that of the bodies from which I had just escaped. Finding a cab was out of the question, so I slipped into the nearest restaurant, and, too tired to make any choice murmured, "A hamburger and a cup of coffee, please."

After eating I found a taxi that eventually struggled through the traffic to my hotel. The campaign was almost over. It was an experience few people ever have in a lifetime. I had missed Abe, but I had talked to him every night regardless of where I was and I had seen him several times during the last few weeks.

I had to get up early the next morning because I was flying with the Senator, Jackie, and some of the other members of his family over to Hyannis, where we would await the returns of the election. After phoning Abe, I sat and thought of my father and how hard he had worked for his country. I thought of the Senator and how hard he was working, and I recalled a letter from a young girl saying that she would be sixteen years old on November 8th and the only thing she really wanted for her birthday was to have the Senator elected President. Her last words were, "don't let me down."

CHAPTER 19

A Satisfying Moment

It was election day. I had breakfast in my room and then went down to the lobby of the hotel. The reporters who had been traveling with the Senator were standing around, bleary-eyed. Now that the trail was at its end, they looked as if they didn't quite know what to do with themselves.

During the campaign our luggage had to be outside the hotel door at least two or three hours before departure each day, sometimes as early as three o'clock in the morning. One of the reporters said to me, "When I get home again I will probably get up every morning and throw my luggage out the front door from force of habit."

The motorcade was about to begin. Jackie and the Senator came out of the hotel, got into their car, and we started to roll. There was just one stop before we reached the airport: the place where Jackie and the Senator were going to vote. The streets were lined with people—people with faces beaming. They were for him. The Senator was in a good mood, relaxed and rested. We stopped, and Jackie and the Senator went into a red brick building to vote. The photographers jumped out of cars and snapped pictures of them when they came out of the polling place a few minutes later. The Senator waved, brushed his hair to one side, grinned, and, walking behind Jackie, got into his car. We rode the rest of the trip at a leisurely pace. There was no reason to hurry. It was all over but the counting. It was a beautiful day—a little snappy, but the kind of weather that brought the voters out.

We pulled up at the airport, and I hurriedly got on *The Caroline* while the Senator walked around the enormous crowd shaking as many hands as he could. By the time he got on the plane I was at my desk opening some of the mail that had come into the hotel before we left. He stopped at my desk and went through some of the wires. He read one from a lady in Lawton, Oklahoma.

"Why are people calling you socialist, must have answer tonight, tomorrow election day, undecided."

"Tell her wholly untrue. This is the kind of thing used against Franklin Roosevelt." Then he added, "Oh, yes, wire Governor Herschel Loveless. 'Dear Herschel: Many thanks for your kind wire, and I hope that all goes well for you and that it will be possible for us to work together in the future as we have in the past. My very best to your wife.' "

He started to leave, then turned and said, "I want to send the following telegram to Senator Fulbright. 'Dear Bill: Regardless of the outcome today I want you to know how grateful I am to you for your help in the campaign. No one could have done more. Best regards.' " With that he walked back into the cabin to join Jackie and his sisters Eunice and Jean.

We landed at the lovely little town of Hyannis, Massachusetts, and the homefolks were out to greet the Kennedys. A big sign was stretched across the front of the airport: "Welcome Home." The Senator was pleased. As he stepped out the door of the airplane, the crowd moved in around him. He shook hands, recognized many who were there, asked them how they were, and then got into a convertible and drove off toward the cluster of homes owned by the Kennedy family.

We were told that we could do anything we wanted until

184

sometime during the afternoon. I checked into my room at the Yachtsman Motel. The air was invigorating and pleasant, and I lay down on top of the bed; before I knew it I had slipped off to sleep.

I was awakened by the telephone ringing. It was one of the girls at Bob's house. "We need you up here. The phones are ringing like mad and they are asking questions about the Senator that we can't answer." I told her I would be up there in a little while. First I wanted to get something to eat; this might be a long night with no time for eating.

Secret Service men were keeping an eye on the crowd gathering around the Kennedy compound and were prepared to take over on a moment's notice if he were elected President. The compound site was beautiful. The Ambassador's house was right on the harbor, to the right was Bob's house, and behind that the Senator's house. All three were white, and they seemed to glisten in the late autumn sun.

When I got to Bob's house, people were busily getting ready for the returns that night. Telephone men were installing phones all around a long table where girls from the campaign staff would take the calls and keep track of the returns. Each girl was responsible for three or four states. I was to answer all the calls that came in for the Senator, and refer the problem to Bob or one of the liaison men whenever possible. My telephone was in a room apart from the other girls.

Kennedys were coming in and going out all the time. Once I went over to the Ambassador's house to get something and found all of the grandchildren had been sent there to spend the night. Peter Lawford and Sarge Shriver were coming up the stairs from the recreation room where they had just taken a shower. All the family were dressed informally in the usual outfit: slacks, sport shirts, and sloppy straw hats. Even Mrs. Kennedy was dressed informally.

The Senator didn't show up during the afternoon. I thought he was probably resting for that evening. I was busy answering the phone, but every now and then I heard someone say, "Ken-

185

nedy got ten votes, Nixon two. Looks like a trend." Or, if the figures were in favor of Nixon, "It's a little early to tell yet."

The cooks were out in the kitchen making sandwiches by the dozens and the coffee was ready to brew. I thought, "Ethel always thinks of everything. We will have something to eat after all."

Then the girls who had worked on the campaign filed in. They were rested and all dressed up, ready to receive what they were sure would be good news.

Next the liaison men began to arrive. Bob was sauntering around the rooms, asking if everyone knew what they were supposed to do. Then he held a general briefing. Bob really knew how to get things organized.

The telephones representing the various states began ringing. The girls were busy jotting down figures, but everyone concentrated on the television. The girls themselves began to pay more attention to television than their own tabulations. Every now and then one of the liaison men would say to the girls, "Watch the phones and not the television." The tempo of incoming calls increased; the girls wrote furiously and gave the figures to the liaison men for their analysis. But all the time the television was much farther ahead than the figures the girls were getting.

More Kennedys with funny straw hats came through, looked at the television, and went out. Every now and then the networks switched to a California station where some commentator would tell what the Nixons were doing.

We were feeling great. Kennedy was piling up a big vote. At one time during the evening he held a lead of more than 1,500,000 votes over Nixon, but as the night wore on this high tide began to drop back.

Now the Senator came over from his house in slacks and sports shirt. I knew he would not be wearing one of those funny hats. He walked from room to room, speaking to first one person and then another. He stopped before the television. Once in a while one of the liaison men would make a call and then there would be a huddle over what had been learned.

Sandwiches and coffee kept coming out of the kitchen. It was nearly midnight and the earlier electoral college margin began to dwindle. The Senator walked around aimlessly. He was showing signs of increasing impatience. Bob was working feverishly trying to get the returns ahead of the television, but the telephone lines were jamming up and it was difficult to hear the party on the other end.

People were getting tired. All the Kennedys who had drifted out were coming back, and this time they stayed. The jokes and bantering died away as the tension grew. Soon no one was talking as we listened to the television commentator. During occasional flashes to Los Angeles the commentator said such things as, "Nixon is very optimistic. He is sure he will carry Pennsylvania." It was growing more and more obvious that two big states—California and Illinois—hung in the balance, and that whoever got both of them was almost certain to win.

The hands of the clock moved past midnight to one o'clock, to two o'clock, and still no decision in sight. The vote was shifting, teeter-tottering. It began to look as if this would go on and on until the last vote was counted. There was an atmosphere of uncertainty, almost nail-biting tension, in the room— but not gloom or defeat.

Finally the Senator stood up, took one last look at the television and said, "This will probably not be decided until morning. I think I will go over to the house and get some sleep." Turning to Bob he said, "Let me know if you hear anything." In his usual manner he turned and calmly went out the door.

Complete results from California, Michigan, and Illinois were still not in, and no one knew how long it was going to take. The equipment was idle and people stood around, too tired to do much else. Finally, near four o'clock, a few began drifting out. Soon more left. I couldn't see what good I was doing there, either, so I started to gather up all of my notes, pads, and pencils and put them into my briefcase, and said goodnight to those too tired or too discouraged to leave.

As I neared the outside door, Ted Sorensen, who was also

about to leave, said, "Do you have a ride down to the Yachts-man? If you'll wait while I go upstairs to get one of my brief-cases, you can ride down with me. My car is parked on the other side of the Senator's house."

A few minutes later we were walking across the back yard of Bob's house. We had to watch our step because the place was booby-trapped with Kennedy bicycles, wagons, and other little folks' equipment. There was a break in the hedge at the rear of the back yard and from there we walked across the Senator's lawn. Ted said, "I think the Senator was wise to go to bed; it will be hours before we know the outcome."

I was just agreeing with Ted when I looked over toward the Senator's house and saw through that window a sight I will never forget. There in his big easy chair, the light streaming over his shoulder, the Senator sat reading a book. Suddenly I was certain he was going to be our next President. I felt that he knew he was going to win. He was already getting ready for the next phase of his life.

I was sound asleep when the telephone awakened me the next morning. "The election. Now we'll have the answer," I thought as I grabbed for the receiver. But instead it was a re-porter asking, "What are the Senator's plans for this morning?"

The word "Senator" instead of "President" or "President-elect" sounded ominous. I told him as calmly as I could that I didn't know, I would check and see if I could find out.

It was now eight o'clock. I called out to the Senator's house and Provie answered. "They haven't called for their breakfasts yet," she said. "Do you want me to give you a ring when they do?" I told her I'd appreciate it, then reached over and flipped on the television.

I was amazed to discover that the outcome was still unde-termined. The Senator's total electoral vote from states ac-tually won was staying near 269. Illinois was crucial and still in doubt. I learned that Nixon had taken the lead there several times and the battle in that state had seesawed back and forth all night. Sometime in the early morning hours, we learned

188

later, Nixon had made an emotion-packed appearance in Los Angeles and conceded that, if the trend of voting continued, it would be a Kennedy victory—but we in Massachusetts knew nothing about that statement.

I decided to get dressed; they might want me to come out to the house to answer the phones. There was still no doubt in my mind the Senator would be elected, but I did wish it would be over. Around nine o'clock Provie phoned and said they were calling for their breakfasts. I headed for the compound.

I checked in at Bob's house to see what was going on. Everything was just as we had left it early in the morning. The equipment was still there, and the little note pads covered with figures were strewn all over the table. Several of the liaison men were out on the lawn.

"What's the latest?" I called out.

"No change."

Now it was almost noon. The Minnesota votes were nearing completion; that state had gone for the Senator. Then Illinois stayed in the win column for the Senator. The commentators were saying that Kennedy had won.

There was no jubilation when the announcement was made. There was a sudden air of seriousness. I think we all realized we had work to do. We were entering a new phase, and with Kennedy as the leader, we would begin moving again.

Soon the Senator appeared in the back yard. He was coming over from his house. He was dressed in the same casual clothes he had worn the night before. He walked through the door and everyone stood up. He paused for a moment while everyone congratulated him, then sat down. As far as he was concerned, things had not changed. He didn't start giving orders, he didn't boast about what he was going to do, he merely sat there discussing the election and the responsibilities he would now have.

But to us he was no longer merely a man or even a Senator. He was the President-elect. In the more than one hundred and seventy years our country had existed, there had been only

189

thirty-four others like him. He was someone people fifty or one hundred or one thousand years from now would read about and study when all the rest of us were erased from the memory of man. We all felt the difference, but it didn't affect him.

He said he wanted to go down to the Armory, the press headquarters, to make a statement, but first he wanted to wait for the wire from Nixon conceding the election. After a while he stood up and walked toward the door; everyone rose with him. He stopped, said a few more words, and they walked through the back yard and over to his house. Through the gap in the hedge I saw him catch Caroline up in his arms as she raced over to meet him. Someone later said she had, at Jackie's suggestion I am sure, greeted him as "Mr. President"—which pleased him greatly.

Ted Sorensen had discussed with the President-elect the wire received from President Eisenhower and some appointments that would be made effective next January. Ted began to dictate to me.

"Send this to President Eisenhower. He is at Augusta, Georgia. 'I am grateful for your most recent wire and your willingness to meet and work with me in order to effect an orderly transfer of executive responsibility. I am asking Clark Clifford of Washington to meet with General Persons as my representative in coordinating this effort. He will keep General Persons informed with respect to all further meetings between the present heads of the executive departments and representatives of the next administration. I look forward to meeting with you and again express my appreciation for your cooperation. Sincerely, President-elect John F. Kennedy.'"

Ted added, "When you have typed that go over to the house and check with him to see if this is what he wants to say."

I typed it up and then walked across the back yard and into the President-elect's living room. Caroline was coming down the stairs.

"Caroline, where is your daddy?"

She pointed upstairs.

Just then Jackie came down the stairs; when she saw me, she turned back and said, "Oh, Jack. Mrs. Lincoln is down here. . . . Hi, Mrs. Lincoln, how are you?"

"I am very happy."

"Thanks, Mrs. Lincoln." She took Caroline's hand and they went out into the yard.

I sat down and stared at his chair, the same chair that I had seen him sitting in early in the morning. He came down the stairs and greeted me.

"Ted dictated a wire to President Eisenhower," I said.

"Let me see it." He walked over to that chair and sat down. He asked me for a pen and started making some changes.

I saw him cross out the word "keep" and substitute "arrange with." Then he crossed out "informed with respect to" and wrote in "regarding." He also crossed out "further." The sentence now read, "He will arrange with General Persons regarding all meetings with the present heads of the executive departments and representatives of the next administration." Then as he was about to hand the paper to me, he took it back and crossed out the words "President-elect." He thanked me and started reading an article in a magazine.

I went back to Bob's house and gave the revised telegram to Ted. "Could you help me with some more dictation?" he asked. He dictated the Senator's announcement that, effective next January, he, Ted Sorensen, would serve as the Special Counsel to the President; Pierre Salinger would serve as Press Secretary to the President; and Andrew T. Hatcher would serve as Associate Press Secretary. Also, he had asked Allen Dulles to stay on as Director of the Central Intelligence Agency; he had asked J. Edgar Hoover to remain as Director of the Federal Bureau of Investigation; and he had asked James M. Landis, former Dean of the Harvard Law School, to undertake a study of the Federal regulatory agencies with a view to maximizing the effective dispatch of their business.

After I had typed this statement, the liaison men wanted to

read what Ted had written. They wanted more names added. Now that the election had been won, those around the Senator were jockeying for position. It seemed that two different factions had already developed: One composed of men who had worked with the Senator in Washington, the other of those who had worked during his campaigns. I only hoped I wouldn't get caught in the middle, or have to choose sides.

At approximately 12:30, he received a telegram from Vice President Nixon conceding the election and extending congratulations. President-elect Kennedy then announced that he would meet the press at the Massachusetts National Guard Armory at 1:45 P.M.

I hurried down to the Armory. The Secret Service had already taken over, and they escorted me right through the crowd and up near the steps of the platform. A woman in the crowd asked the Secret Service man who I was; when he told her, she said to me, "Could I have your picture? I'd like to take it home to my little girl." I was flabbergasted, but I told her to go right ahead.

Around 1:45 P.M. the President-elect and Mrs. Kennedy walked down the aisle. They walked slowly and with ease, as if nothing of great importance had happened. He joined his mother and father, his two brothers, and three sisters standing on the platform.

He stepped to the podium and began reading telegrams he had received from President Eisenhower and Vice President Nixon. Then, reading from a prepared statement he had dictated earlier, he said, "It is a satisfying moment to me. I want to express my appreciation to the citizens of this country and to Mr. Nixon personally." He went on: "The next four years will be difficult and challenging. There is general agreement by all our citizens that a supreme national effort is needed to move this country to safety through the 1960s. We need your help. All our energies will be devoted to the interests of the United States and the cause of freedom around the world."

Then, in a lighter note, he added, "My wife and I now prepare for a new administration—and a new baby." I glanced at Jackie; and she was glowing with happiness.

In reply to questions, Kennedy said he would have no statement on appointments in his administration before Thanksgiving.

One of the wire services aptly described the actions of the President-elect: "His manner all morning, and through the moment when he stood on the platform in the press headquarters, was a mixture of quiet satisfaction, humility, and seriousness."

While I went back to the Yachtsman to prepare for the flight to Washington and Abe, my mind flashed back to the moment eight years before when I had pinned my hopes on this man. With a satisfying feeling I said to myself, "My prediction came true!"

PART III

PART III

CHAPTER 20

A *Few New Faces*

THE next ten weeks were like an exciting, fast-paced ride
on a merry-go-round, with frequent stops in Palm Beach, Florida,
Washington, and New York City. At each stop, streams of people called on the President-elect: people seeking jobs in the
new administration, recommending someone else for a job, or
bringing an idea for his program.

It seemed that Senator Kennedy's weariness from the campaign vanished with the victory, and he plunged enthusiastically into planning for his administration, choosing a Cabinet
that would measure up to his high ideals, and mapping a program to carry out his campaign promises to get the country
moving again.

He remained in Massachusetts only a few days after the
election and then flew to his father's home in Palm Beach to
soak up sunshine, swim, and play golf between sessions of
work. His daily schedule was beginning to look like that of a
President; important names and topics were filling it. At his
father's home special security telephones were installed for his
use. They were connected with a communications system separate from the commercial telephone systems and he was to use
them throughout the time he was President. Wherever he went
as President, even to an embassy luncheon in Washington, one
of these special telephones was installed. It was easy to identify

because it was always white, and the operators who handled the calls on it were security personnel.

After the election I returned to Washington to get my files in order. Long ago I had decided the only way I could keep things at my fingertips was to do my own filing. When the Senator wanted something he wanted it right away, not ten minutes or five minutes later. If I filed it, I knew where it was.

I didn't get to work long, however, for Saturday he telephoned from Palm Beach asking me to come down there "right now." He needed someone at the house to answer the telephones. I must have hesitated, for he said, "Well, it will be all right if you come down on Monday."

The next Monday morning, after saying goodbye to Abe, I was flying south.

The sun was shining brightly when I landed at the airport. One of the Secret Service agents met me and drove me to the Ambassador's house, a large white Spanish villa with a red tile roof, facing the ocean. Evelyn Jones, the friendly and efficient housekeeper, greeted me and had my bags taken to the second-floor room that Eunice Kennedy Shriver usually occupied.

The beautiful room looked out over the waves rolling up and breaking on the brilliant white beach extending along the edge of the Ambassador's property.

Evelyn said the Senator and Torby Macdonald were out at the pool. She told me I could work in the little office where the Ambassador's secretary usually worked. I was getting set up in that office when Evelyn Jones came in and said the Senator would like to see me out beside the pool.

I had already seen the large dining room and caught just a glimpse of the living room on my arrival, but when I walked through them this time on my way to the pool, I was struck by the quiet beauty and good taste of the furnishings. Everything about the house was elegant and lovely. And the setting for the pool was equally beautiful. It was a tremendously large pool filled with azure-blue water, and in the background were graceful palm trees.

When the Senator saw me, he said, "Hello, Mrs. Lincoln, do you have anything for me?" I knew he would ask that, and I had brought along some mail. He seeemed happy to get it, and read it avidly.

There were memos from some of his staff members concerning people who were interested in working in the administration or might be persuaded to do so. One name mentioned was that of McGeorge Bundy, a Republican described as extremely gifted and "happy at Harvard" but perhaps willing to come to Washington if a suitable assignment could be found for him. There was also a memo stating that the Senator could soon expect an avalanche of invitations to visit South American countries. After reading this he turned to Torby and said, "They want me to come down to South America. I would like to make several trips down there."

After he had run through the mail and dictated replies, I returned to my office to type the letters. I was constantly interrupted by telephone calls from important people asking to speak to him. Each time I went all through that enormous house trying to locate him. Sometimes I would find him in the study reading the papers, or upstairs in his bedroom, or out in the "bull pen," an enclosed sunning area near the swimming pool.

It was the beginning of the pattern for our days in Palm Beach. After breakfast each day he would go through the mail and memos, return telephone calls, and see visitors until just before noon, when he would go for a swim. After lunch he would rest or take a nap in his room, then see more callers, and after a couple of hours play nine holes of golf. He was a great movie fan, and in the evenings after dinner he liked to watch a movie at home. They put up a large screen at the south end of the patio and had the projector set up at the north end. They placed chairs in a semicircle for those who wanted to watch the film, and it was delightful to sit out under the stars seeing the Hollywood stars on the screen. The Senator preferred pictures of adventure and history, with an occasional comedy. Some of the titles he called for during this period were *Cimmaron, Fanny, Where the Boys Are,* and *The Sundowners.*

His golfing companions were his father, old friends living nearby in Palm Beach, Senators and Congressmen who happened to be in Palm Beach or who came to see him, and friends who had helped him in the campaign. One afternoon he played golf with Governor Abraham Ribicoff of Connecticut and the former Republican Ambassador to Cuba, Earl E. T. Smith. Governor Ribicoff, one of his earliest supporters for the Presidency, spent a couple of hours with the Senator that day talking over the campaign and the new administration. They posed for a picture on the patio after their discussion, and I was sure that Ribicoff would have an important post in the administration.

The mail from Washington was flown down every morning. One day we received brochures on William Foster, Paul Nitze, and Roswell L. Gilpatric; the Senator was to consider them as possibilities for the new administration. Professor Walt W. Rostow of MIT was also mentioned in the memorandum sent down by Deidre Henderson, a pretty Massachusetts girl who had been working in the Senator's Boston office, serving as liaison between his staff and the Advisory Council, which had prepared position papers during the campaign. This Council had no permanent members. In 1952 he began asking individual Harvard professors for information, ideas, and research. And he continued to call upon them through the years that followed. Now he asked them for recommendations for administration policies, as well as to assist him in selecting qualified personnel.

During the days that followed, there was an almost ceaseless flow of résumés, memos, and names into the large file of people for consideration for positions. Not only was the Advisory Council making recommendations, the key men in the campaign were also serving as talent scouts for the President-elect, and members of Congress were supplying names, as were prominent Democrats all over the country.

Apparently one name planted with him about this time made a great impression, for he asked me to call one of the staff members in Washington to get him "all the information you can" on Dean Rusk, then President of the Rockefeller Foundation.

To those requesting appointments about a job in the new administration, he said he would see them after Thanksgiving. Another group asked for tickets to the Inaugural Ball two months away. To these he replied, "I'll get in touch with you as soon as I have some definite information."

He enjoyed reading what the newspapers and magazines had to say about him during this period, and gave a polite snort one day when he read he was going to plow up the putting green President Eisenhower had installed on the south lawn of the White House. "It will stay as long as I am there," he told me.

Although the Senator was not yet thinking about what he would wear to the Inauguration, his tailor was, and so were some of the planners of inaugural events. Rumors were flying that he planned to go hatless. He stopped them quickly with a statement that indicated he was looking forward to wearing his beloved top hat.

During the following week he began setting up task forces to make special recommendations in specific areas. He was determined to go into office well informed and prepared to make the decisions facing him. He wanted a report on Latin America. He wanted a report on the situation in Africa. He wanted a study of all State Department personnel in the field, and particularly how many spoke the language of the country to which they were assigned. He wanted more Negroes in the Foreign Service. He wanted a task force to study the Fulbright foreign study programs. He wanted a study of the United States Information Agency efforts. He wanted a study on allowances for overseas personnel. He wanted a study on the distribution of our agricultural surpluses abroad. And, he added in one asignment, "We should prepare to set up an Arms Research Institute."

In most cases he asked that the report be submitted to him by the end of the year so he would have twenty days in which to study it before he took office.

Jackie did not accompany the Senator on his trips to Palm Beach because she was awaiting the birth of her baby and wanted to be close to her doctor. He flew back to Washington again just before Thanksgiving to be with her. He telephoned me several times, the first time to tell me to be at the airport at ten P.M. for the trip back to Palm Beach. Later he asked me to bring along various memos and articles he had been reading at his house; and another time he asked me to bring along the mail and all the telephone calls he had received.

During the afternoon Abe took me to the Senator's house, where I gathered up the memos and papers he wanted to take back to Palm Beach. I put them in his black alligator briefcase —the one that had seen him through his Senate years, the campaign, and that he was going to take with him to the White House. He refused to discard it for a new one but when the seams ripped or the lock broke, he wanted them repaired. I did not see him at the house; he and Jackie had gone to Middleburg, Virginia, to look at a house they wanted to rent for the coming year so they could have a normal family life away from the hustle and bustle of the White House.

That night we were Palm Beach-bound again. I was glad I had stuffed his briefcase, for he kept calling for memos and other papers immediately after takeoff. He particularly wanted to discuss with Pierre Salinger an article he had torn from the *Washington Post* citing the need for streamlining the Civil Aeronautics Board.

It usually took approximately three hours to fly from Washington to Palm Beach when we did not have a tailwind. Everyone had settled down for the ride. A few minutes after takeoff a message came from the MATS radio room at National Airport asking the Senator to call Jackie at a given number. He immediately asked one of the Secret Service agents to call the number. Someone by the name of Kent Cooper answered and knew nothing about a call; the Senator felt there had been some mistake. A little while later he decided to take a nap, and so did the rest of us, unmindful of what was happening back in Washington.

That call had indeed been from Jackie; somehow the telephone number had got jumbled. She had also called Dr. John Walsh, her obstetrician, who immediately put in a call for an ambulance to pick her up at 10:35 P.M. She arrived at Georgetown Hospital at 10:50 for the birth of her baby.

It was not until we were within a few minutes of Palm Beach that a call came from the wire services for the Senator: "It's a boy!" The news had just been released by the hospital. Pierre went through the plane announcing that Jackie had just given birth to a boy.

A cannon could not have awakened the sleepy passengers more quickly. The Senator nervously paced the aisle and seemed unable to wait until the plane taxied up to the airport. He rushed to the telephone and called Dr. Walsh. As soon as he learned that Jackie and the baby were coming along nicely, he said, "We're going back."

It would take too long for the plane we came down on to refuel, so he decided to go back on the press plane that had followed us, a larger, faster plane. I thought I would stay in Palm Beach, but just as I started walking toward a car going into the city, someone shouted, "Mrs. Lincoln, Mrs. Lincoln." One of the girls on the staff rushed up to me and said, "The Senator wants you to return with him. Hurry, we are holding the plane for you." I raced back, found a seat, and was just about to sit down when I noticed the Senator in the compartment just ahead. I walked through the door, and found him just sitting there, looking ahead with a broad smile on his face.

"Congratulations on the birth of John Fitzgerald Kennedy, Jr."

He looked up at me with that twinkle in his eye that I knew so well and said, "Come to think of it, I might call him Abraham Lincoln."

As soon as our plane touched down at Washington's National Airport, he rushed off, with the press following, all on their way to the hospital to see the new heir and his mother.

I was still half asleep the next morning when the office called to tell me wires of congratulations were pouring in. "What should we do with them?" I told them I would come down right away. I rushed down to the office, but before I had a chance to look at the mail, the Senator called from his house. "What are you doing, Mrs. Lincoln? Why don't you come out here and answer the phone?" Then, after a pause, he added, "Also, bring the mail."

When I got to 3307 N Street I found Mary Gallagher, Mrs. Kennedy's personal secretary, going through Jackie's mail. She had a desk in the corner of the guest bedroom on the second floor, and I moved in with her. There was only one telephone—constantly ringing—and people were complaining that they could not reach the Senator.

The N Street house had an unlisted telephone number, but many of the Senator's aides had been given the number. Those who hadn't would call the Senate office and ask if they could talk to him. The office then called me to find out if they could give the number to them. If the Senator said yes, I gave it out. Soon the number became known to many people, and the need for additional telephones became urgent.

The telephone company promptly installed two more lines to the house and put in a buzzer system, which the Senator would not use. So, every time anyone called him I rushed down the flight of stairs to the living room, told him who was calling, and then rushed back up the stairs. By the time I got back someone else was on the line, and I would go through the same routine again.

While I was taking the Senator's calls on one telephone, Mary was busy on the other making arrangements for a birthday party for Caroline. Sunday was her third birthday, but she was going to have her party on Monday, and Mary was ordering balloons, paper hats, ice cream, cake, and even a clown.

Miss Shaw, Caroline's nurse, had taken her to the park that morning. On her way back to her room Caroline stopped off to see us. As soon as she spotted the typewriter she asked to type on it. She was so cute we couldn't refuse, and soon she was banging away at the keys. The next thing we knew it was broken and we had to call the typewriter repairman.

As a special birthday treat for Caroline, the Senator took her to mass with him at Holy Trinity Church in Georgetown. On the front page of *The Washington Post* Monday morning was a picture of their return from church. Caroline was strutting along the street, with the Senator in the background carrying her Raggedy Ann doll. He told me the next morning that taking her to church "was not the thing to do. She climbed over the pew, under the pew, and disturbed everyone around her." But he loved that picture and asked me to see if we could get the original and have it framed.

I had arrived at the house that Monday morning before the Senator got up. He had breakfast and read the papers in his bedroom, and on his way to the living room stopped by what I now called my office. "Mrs. Lincoln, will you tell everyone concerned that I want you to handle all of my appointments during this period. Also, I will probably go out to see Jackie around noon and again this evening." He reeled off in one-two-three fashion the things he wanted me to do. He started to go, then turned around and said, "And I would like to see Dean Acheson sometime this afternoon. Will you set it up? I will go to his house."

I knew from previous conversations that the Senator respected the former Secretary of State's judgment very much, and he was particularly anxious to get Acheson's views on a number of top appointments, including that of Secretary of State.

Caroline visited us again that morning, too. She was very excited about her party, and hopped around the room telling Mary and me all about it. Then she wanted to draw, so we gave her some paper and a pencil. She used first her left hand, then her right, but she seemed to favor the left. All she could do was to make circles, so she asked me to draw something. I am not much of an artist, but I drew what I thought was a cat.

"That's not a cat," she said.

"What's wrong with it?"

"He doesn't have whiskers. Where are his whiskers?" she asked indignantly.

I added some whiskers. Now it was a game.

"Draw another cat and let me put the whiskers on," she begged. When I did, she danced up and down with glee. This time she made the whiskers a little long but she made sure they were right on the cat's nose.

Most children tire of one thing quickly, but Caroline was still happily drawing whiskers when Miss Shaw came down to take her up to her pink bedroom for lunch. All the time I was drawing cats, I was also answering the telephone, running down to the living room to give messages to the Senator, and listening to Mary make last-minute arrangements for the birthday party.

The Senator went to the hospital to see Jackie, returned to lunch, and then went up to his bedroom to rest. I rushed down to the living room to pick up any papers he might have left by the telephone. He had been doodling on a legal-size yellow sheet, and I saw the letters HEW. He must have been talking to someone about the appointment for Secretary of Health, Education, and Welfare.

I had learned over the years to detect his mood and interest in a subject by the doodling. When he had a lot of doodles on his yellow legal paper, he was bored with the meeting. If there was a word or a name repeated over and over again, and circled or blocked, he was concentrating his attention on that problem.

Later that afternoon I had several messages for him by the time he sent word he had rested and was ready to make some calls. When I gave him little slips of paper stating that someone had called, the Senator always returned the call, no matter how many there were. This time there were so many he was on the telephone most of the afternoon. While he was talking politics, squeals and children's laughter seeped under our door from downstairs. The children were arriving for the party. Down the steps came little Caroline, looking like a little doll in her pink party dress. Her eyes sparkled with joy, although there was just a hint of timidness when she looked down the long stairs and saw so many children. But soon she was laughing with them at the antics of the clown.

Before the Senator left for his appointment with Dean Acheson, he went into the dining room to greet the children, and their squeals became louder. He went from one child to another, patting them on the head and asking their names. The mothers were there, too, and eagerly congratulated him on his new baby, who, he told them, was getting bigger every day.

Although I had been coming out to his house for just a short time, a pattern of activity had already become established. If he had a nine o'clock breakfast appointment, I arrived at 8:30. Then there was the constant coping with the telephone, typing schedules and important letters, my "drawing" sessions with Caroline, and breaks for lunch and coffee provided by Provie. There were countless messages. "Bob called and said he wanted to make an appointment for you to see Congressman George McGovern of South Dakota." "Congressman Stewart Udall called and said that your brother Ted thought you might like to see him." "Margaret Price, vice chairman of the Democratic National Committee, called and wants to know if she can see you on December 8th."

The messages were always the same, only the names were different, and most of the time they wanted to see him about an appointment in the administration. In most cases, the Senator had previously sent word that he wanted to talk to the person who called. He had asked Margaret Price, for example, to make a survey of major Presidential appointments of women to positions in government. On December 8th, she submitted her report; it contained not only a review of women in the Federal service at the present time, but also suggested areas for possible appointments, together with résumés of women to be considered for appointments.

Bob Kennedy had, indeed, talked with George McGovern about a post in the administration. The extremely capable Congressman had been a strong supporter of the Kennedy ticket, although he had been defeated in his own bid for reelection in a state where religion was considered a major issue.

Congressman Udall was also under consideration for a post. He had been a strong Kennedy supporter and was credited with throwing Arizona's support to the Senator. Ted Kennedy, who had been responsible for the campaign in the Western states, was aware of the big contribution Stewart Udall had made.

I kept a file on the people who were being considered for the various positions. In this file were the résumés and notations of each time they were brought out for consideration. In the beginning, the Senator assigned a staff member to get background information on each person suggested. When he had all the possible information, all those working on the recruiting would meet to review the qualifications. After the meeting, I gathered all this material and filed it away. Sometimes the Senator would tell me someone was going to call with a list of names for a certain post. I was to keep these names until he asked for them. Many times people called and dictated a statement to be attached to one of the résumés in the file.

Senator Kennedy had a fantastic memory; he was able to retain the names of individuals and positions for which they were being considered without referring to the files. The recruiters were many of the same small band of men who had threshed out the question of who should have the Vice Presidential nomination in Los Angeles. Bob Kennedy, Ted Kennedy, Sarge Shriver, Ted Sorensen, Larry O'Brien, Kenny O'Donnell, Ralph Dungan, Mike Feldman, Fred Holborn, and Dick Donahue held lively discussions in the living room of the Georgetown house. This same group met once in New York at the Carlyle

Hotel, and then they all gathered at Palm Beach to finish as much as they could before the Inauguration.

On December 1st, the President-elect announced his first Cabinet appointment. He stood in front of his red brick home in Georgetown and told the reporters and photographers who kept a vigil from the sidewalk that he was naming Governor Abraham Ribicoff of Connecticut to be Secretary of Health, Education, and Welfare. He had also selected Stewart Udall of Arizona as Secretary of the Interior, but he had not yet decided when he would announce it.

The next day we flew to Palm Beach, and Caroline and her nurse went with us. The weather was ideal when we arrived, but as soon as I stepped inside my hotel room the telephone began ringing, and I knew there would not be any time for me to sit in the sun. When people found they could not reach us at the N Street house, they called the office and learned we were in Palm Beach. The messages began piling up.

The next morning, December 3rd, I went out to the Ambassador's house. While I was waiting for the Senator to come out for breakfast, Caroline and Miss Shaw came by on their way to the beach.

"Let's draw a cat," Caroline said.

So we did some cat-drawing until the Senator came. He beamed when he saw Caroline and said, "Good morning, Buttons."

"Look, Daddy, Mrs. Lincoln is drawing a cat."

After we finished the mail, the Senator asked when Governor Luther Hodges of North Carolina would arrive and if everything was set up for the announcement concerning him. I assured him the press had been informed and that the Governor would be there some time before lunch.

Shortly after he arrived, the Senator and Governor Hodges went out on the patio where the Senator announced he was appointing him Secretary of Commerce.

Luther Hodges, although not well-known nationally, brought a lot of strength to the Cabinet. It was only the second appointment, but it inspired confidence in the way the President-elect was going about this difficult problem. Although no arch segregationist, Governor Hodges was a genuine Southerner, which helped gain support among Southerners suspicious of this Northern, "liberal," Irish Catholic who was about to become President. Hodges was a Protestant. He was mature, white-haired, and obviously a solid citizen of sixty-two. He was a businessman who understood the art of politics. As Secretary of Commerce his political and business skills could be put to very constructive work in helping to get the economy moving by expanding our foreign trade—something that particularly interested the Senator.

Monday night, December 5th, we returned to Washington. The Senator had an appointment with President Eisenhower at the White House at nine o'clock the next morning. He returned from that meeting in high spirits, and told us, "The one thing that the President seemed to take pride in was a button on his desk that he said would produce, if he pushed it, a helicopter in three minutes right below on the south lawn. He was so enthusiastic about it he did push the button and a helicopter actually did appear in three minutes." The soon-to-be President was learning fast about the power of his office.

That night we flew to New York. I loved the excitement of flying into an airport, hurrying from the plane, seeing the smiling faces trying to catch a glimpse of the Senator, and then going down the streets in a motorcade to our hotel.

This time it was the Carlyle Hotel, and what a delightful place it was! The Senator's suite was on the thirty-fourth floor, overlooking Central Park, and we could see the sparkling city spread out before us. In addition to the living room, the suite consisted of two bedrooms on a higher level, a dining room, and a study in the back of the living room. I took incoming calls in the study. My own suite was down on the eighth floor; it was so lovely I felt like "Queen for a Day."

The Senator had breakfast the next morning with Dag Hammarskjöld, Secretary General of the United Nations, and later he announced the appointment of Stewart Udall as Secretary of the Interior. I am sure he was glad to get that announcement over with, and be relieved of further pressure by others who had waged a campaign for the job.

On his way to breakfast he paused to give me my one-two-three-four instructions for the morning. "Remind me to talk to Sam Harris when he comes up here this noon about the blue suit and the black suit. Also, call Lem Billings and tell him I would like to have a gold PT boat tie clasp. Order me some white shirts, and then call Fred Coe and thank him for asking if I'd like to see the play *All the Way Home* while I am here in New York."

He had several other appointments and many telephone conversations before we returned to Washington that night, December 7th. The next morning at the N Street house he had a talk with Dean Rusk and asked him to become Secretary of State. Dean Acheson had recommended Rusk originally. There had been speculation in the newspapers that the post might go to Arkansas Senator J. William Fulbright, chairman of the Senate Foreign Relations Committee, but the Senator had already named one Southerner to his Cabinet.

The telephone rang constantly. I overheard him tell one caller, obviously a Stevenson supporter, "Yes, I know that Stevenson is essential for the success of the administration at the UN, and I am going to tell him that when I meet him this afternoon. I am also going to tell him that I have asked Dean Rusk to be Secretary of State."

The big interest now focused on the Secretary of Defense. He had offered the post to former Secretary of Defense Robert Lovett, but poor health would not permit him to accept. Lovett had suggested Robert McNamara, a registered Republican with independent voting habits, who had recently been elevated to the presidency of the Ford Motor Company. The Senator did not know Mr. McNamara, but he was also highly recommended by Sargent Shriver.

The evening of December 8th Sarge telephoned and said, "There's someone coming in to see about the Defense job. He'll be coming in the back way in an hour or so."

Soon there was a knock on the back door of the brick house in Georgetown. When I opened it, there stood a youngish man with glasses, wearing no hat although it was a very cold evening. As I let him in, I noticed how well dressed he was, and every strand of hair in place.

Sarge came right behind him, and the two chatted in the dining room until the Senator, who was talking with Senator Ralph Yarborough in the living room, was ready to see them. It was a short interview for such an important job. It couldn't have lasted more than half an hour, and then Mr. McNamara popped out again. It must have gone well, I thought, his hair is still in place. Later I heard Senator Kennedy say, "I think he is just the right man."

The Senator did not announce his selection of Robert McNamara as Secretary of Defense right away. He had some important family matters to take care of first.

It was homecoming day for Jackie and baby John. The Senator was going to the hospital for them at 10:30 that morning, and he was obviously very excited about it. Twice in between his early morning appointments he asked me to be sure to let him know well in advance when it was time for him to leave.

Jackie looked lovelier than ever when she arrived home with her new baby, but she hardly had time to look around before she was out again. She had an appointment at noon with Mrs. Eisenhower at the White House to discuss the problems of space and housekeeping at 1600 Pennsylvania Avenue. She wanted to take the mental picture with her to Palm Beach, where she would decide what rooms would be used for what. Although Mrs. Eisenhower offered a wheelchair to Jackie for going up and down the long corridors to see the layout of the rooms, she declined the courtesy.

Soon we were airborne for Palm Beach, where Jackie planned to stay until just before the Inauguration. Although I had filled the Senator's briefcase with reading material and papers, he didn't get much chance to work on this flight because the smallest passenger, baby John, was getting attention from everybody. However, there was one paper in his briefcase I was sure the Senator would study carefully. It pointed out why it would be a mistake for him to appoint his brother, Robert, as Attorney General.

When I went out to the Ambassador's house the next morning it looked as though Christmas had come early. One room on the second floor was piled high with gifts that had poured in from all over the country for the new baby. Every moment I could spare from the Senator's work, I was in that room unwrapping gifts and separating them into groups of wearing apparel, toys, and so on, putting the cards aside so that I could send a thank-you letter for each gift.

While I was doing this Jackie called and asked if I would come down and take some dictation for her. She was the most organized person I have ever met. She always knew exactly what she wanted and it didn't take her long to tell me what to say. She was very interested in an article Mary Van Rensselaer Thayer was doing on her for the *Ladies Home Journal,* and asked me to tell Mrs. Thayer she had some changes she wanted made and that she wanted to see the whole story before it went to press. She also asked me to find someone to take her dictation after I returned to Washington.

The Senator remained in Palm Beach until Monday night, December 12th, because he wanted to announce three appointments from his father's home: Dean Rusk as Secretary of State, Adlai Stevenson as United States Ambassador to the United Nations, and Chester Bowles as Assistant Secretary of State.

Back in Washington he faced a busy four-day schedule of appointments with what seemed like every Democratic member of Congress. He found time for his influenza immunization shot and for dinner one evening with his long-time friend, Charley Bartlett.

He also announced a series of appointments. First, Robert S.

McNamara as Secretary of Defense. Two days later he named Arthur Goldberg, the labor lawyer who had worked so faithfully with him in the Senate on labor legislation, as Secretary of Labor, and Minnesota Governor Orville Freeman as Secretary of Agriculture. Another day he named his brother Bob as Attorney General and C. Douglas Dillon to be Secretary of Treasury.

The day before he announced Bob's appointment, I ran across a draft of a press release on the subject that I thought expressed the way the Senator felt about the appointment, despite any criticism it might inspire.

"In looking for an Attorney General who must lead the fight for law enforcement, who must administer our laws without favor and with matchless integrity, I have turned to a man in whom I have found these qualities. I have every confidence that he will bring to his new position this same ability, this same energy, this same courage, this same independence of judgment, and this same integrity."

I knew that the Senator felt also that Bob had earned the appointment.

We returned to Palm Beach the evening of December 16th and the next morning he completed his Cabinet by naming J. Edward Day, a California insurance executive, as Postmaster General. Day had formerly been Stevenson's legal adviser.

During the weekend there were many telephone conversations about Massachusetts' Governor Foster Furcolo's appointment of someone to take the President-elect's seat in the Senate. I could tell the Senator wanted someone who would not run for reelection in case one of his brothers wanted to be the candidate for it in two years. Several names were mentioned: Howard Fitzpatrick, Professor James Burns, Professor Kenneth Galbraith, and Congressman Torbert Macdonald. Governor Furcolo didn't seem interested in any name being suggested.

Later I learned that the Governor, who had lost his bid for the Democratic renomination to that office, hoped to be appointed himself. He planned to resign before his term ended on January 4th, be succeeded by Massachusetts Secretary of State Joseph D. Ward (Lieutenant Governor Robert E. Murphy had recently been named to fill a vacancy on the Metropolitan District Commission), and then have Ward in turn appoint him to the Senate. Ward, however, wouldn't go along with the idea.

There was a long history of coolness between Senator Kennedy and Governor Furcolo. It had been increased when the Senator refused on a television broadcast to endorse Furcolo in his 1954 campaign for the Senate against Republican Leverett Saltonstall, for whom Senator Kennedy had great respect. Many people believed that this television incident might have been responsible for Furcolo's defeat. Now Furcolo, his own political career apparently at a dead end, was being asked by Senator Kennedy to appoint someone to a job he hoped to get himself.

I am sure Governor Furcolo's frustration was not calmed by the final choice: Benjamin A. Smith, Jr., a former Harvard classmate of the Senator. According to what I heard at the time, Furcolo at first flatly refused to appoint anyone. The Senator then pointed out that since the Governor's term expired on January 4th, it would be possible for Senator Kennedy to wait until after January 4th to resign, and he had no doubt that the incoming Governor—John Volpe, a Republican—would agree to Smith's serving.

Several days later, Furcolo reluctantly appointed Smith. The Governor did not appear in his own office for the swearing-in ceremony. Later, in his frustration, Furcolo bitterly attacked the appointment of McGeorge Bundy as special assistant to the President for National Security Affairs, calling it "completely incredible."

I flew back to Washington the day before Christmas to be with Abe and my mother on Christmas Day. We were getting ready to move to a new apartment and Abe was bringing his parents from Nebraska to Washington, renting adjoining apartments for us and for them. I managed, however, to persuade him to return to Palm Beach with me and stay until New Year's Eve. Then he flew back to Washington.

I was alone in Palm Beach on New Year's Eve, a good time for reflection. Except for the heavy blow of losing my father, it had been a good year, and in a way I hated to see it end. The next one would be full of new challenges. I wondered if I would be able to meet them and silently wished I had the Senator's eager confidence.

CHAPTER 21

A New Year

January 1, 1961, was a Sunday, and the streets of Palm Beach were almost deserted when I rode out to the Kennedy house on North Ocean Boulevard. Matilda, the cook, had been up since dawn, and there was, as usual, a pot of coffee waiting for me on the stove. I learned from Evelyn Jones, the housekeeper, that the Senator was coming out for breakfast in a few minutes, and I hurried into the library. When the maid brought his orange juice, I knew he was at the table. I took a couple of the more important letters in for him to read, but he was busy reading the morning papers, and I just slid them by his plate.

About five minutes later, Lem Billings, who was spending a few days with the Kennedys, came to the table. He had been the Senator's friend since their years together at Choate School. The Senator asked him if he was thrilled to be eating breakfast with the President of the United States. Billings said he had no feeling about it. Then I came in and he asked me, "Are you thrilled to be working for the President?"

"I am overjoyed."

"See there, she is thrilled and you, Lem, don't feel a thing." Then, with a twinkle in his eye, he said to Lem, "It is a privilege for you to be eating with the President."

He was soon to learn, however, the President had, in addition to the burdens of state, the everyday problems that everyone faces, such as gaining unwanted weight and finding a new home for the family cat. But on that day he seemed completely happy and carefree. His burdens and problems were in the future.

When Caroline came bounding in the Senator said, "Happy New Year there, Buttons." She smiled a response and then came running into the library, looking for me.

"Happy New Year, Caroline," I said.

"Hi."

She was dressed in a red outfit and I told her she looked like a redbird.

"No," she said. "I am a little red mousey."

The Senator and Lem Billings went to mass together and returned just before Senator Paul Douglas of Illinois arrived to discuss his bill to provide federal assistance to economically depressed areas of the country. They were going to have their picture taken together on the patio to get publicity for the bill, which Douglas was going to introduce the first day of Congress. Already the photographers and newsmen were gathered on the patio waiting for them, and I saw Jackie going out the back way, in a lavender linen suit and matching lavender scarf, on her way to the twelve o'clock mass.

After Senator Douglas left, Senator Kennedy came into the library through one door as Caroline came in through another. She ran to him, grabbed hold of his legs, and begged him to take her for a ride piggy-back. He picked her up, put her on his back, and away they went into the living room. She was laughing and talking all the way. Soon he was back with her and he asked Miss Shaw to take her down.

After Jackie returned from mass the Senator went into her room to talk to her before he left for the Seminole Country Club for lunch with Chris Dunphy, a Palm Beach friend, and for a round of golf in the afternoon.

Since it was a holiday and Sunday, too, I left shortly after he did and returned to my hotel, put on a sun suit, and sat on my balcony soaking up the sunshine.

It was back to work early for both of us the next day, however. He answered three telephone calls—from Dean Rusk, Congressman "Topper" Thompson, and Mr. John Fell—before he sat down to breakfast. By this time his coffee was cold and he asked for more. He heard Evelyn Jones ask if she should awaken Lem Billings, and he answered, "Call him. I don't want anyone sleeping while I am awake."

He and Lem were going to the Orange Bowl football game in Miami. Before they left he dictated several things for me to put on his "reminder" list. "Do something about Charles Merriwether; check on appointment of a fellow from Connecticut by the name of John Macy as chairman of the Civil Service Commission; I would like to talk to Kenny [O'Donnell] about (1) Godfrey T. McHugh for Air Force Aide; (2) Senator John Sparkman's son-in-law for Naval Aide; and how about an Army Aide?"

After he left for the football game, I returned to my hotel room and turned on the television to see him sitting in the sun enjoying the game.

Two days later we flew to New York. The President-elect didn't regret leaving the warmth of the sunny South for the frigid North. He was anxious to meet with the people he had been talking to over the telephone. I could tell from his telephone conversations that he was eager for new ideas, new thoughts, new approaches to these problems. He was always looking forward, never backward.

He had a stream of callers in his suite at the Carlyle Hotel the next day. Just before lunch Pierre Salinger came into the den where I was working and waited for the Senator to come out from his appointment in the living room. When he did, Pierre said, "What I have to tell you I think I should tell you privately."

The President shook his head and said, "You don't need to be afraid to talk in front of Mrs. Lincoln. She has heard every-

218

thing." I suppose it was important to Pierre at the time, but I don't remember now what it was they discussed.

That night we flew back to Washington, and the Senator met at his Georgetown house with Dean Rusk. Then he came up to my office with a personal problem. "I understand that Charley, the dog, insists on biting Tom Kitten so I think we should take Tom Kitten away. (Tom and Charley had been staying out in Merrywood, the Auchincloss home.) Could Abe take care of Tom Kitten over the weekend in your apartment?"

"He would be delighted to do it, but our cat, Sputnik, doesn't like other cats and Tom would not be happy there."

"I'll check with one of the neighbors who may have room for him."

I was glad to get home again. Abe had done a tremendous job of moving everything from our old apartment to the new one. I didn't get a chance to enjoy the new setting for very long, though, before flying to New York to join the Senator. Mrs. Eleanor Roosevelt was to be his breakfast guest the next morning. Shortly after I arrived, Abba Schwartz called to check on last-minute arrangements. He wanted me to be sure Mrs. Roosevelt had tea with lemon for breakfast.

The Senator had a full day of appointments, and that night we were on our way to Palm Beach again. I had settled down for a fairly relaxing trip when suddenly the President called, "Mrs. Lincoln, come in here and bring your pad." I scurried into his compartment and he said, "I am going to dictate some thoughts that I have for my Inaugural address." He dictated and dictated and dictated. Then he said, "Will you type that up and have it ready by the time we land?"

"Yes, I will."

I went back to my desk and for the rest of the trip I typed. I was busy typing words, but I could tell this was not an ordinary speech. In that dictation, in its original form, was that now-famous line: "Ask not what your country is going to do for you, ask what you can do for your country—my fellow citizens of the world."

219

While we were taxiing up to the airport in Palm Beach, I took the last page out of my typewriter. When I went in to his cabin to make sure that all of his papers were in his briefcase, I had the speech draft with me. He looked at me, grinned, and said, "Oh, I see you have it done."

I was very thankful the President did not have a schedule for the next morning, because I wanted to go down on Worth Avenue and get a dress for the Inaugural Ball. It was one time I was really going to splurge; I might never get to another ball like this one. I found a lovely green dress and then went to a nearby shoe store to have a pair of slippers tinted to match.

Ted Reardon, the Senator's liaison with the Inaugural Committee, was sending messages almost daily for the Senator's decision on details about the ceremony and events. I sent him the replies. One day I wrote: "The Kennedys decided that it would be better for all of the children to be together in the place you have reserved for them in the Treasury Department. Otherwise, they thought it might look like kiddies day at the circus in the box."

Robert Frost had been invited to read one of his poems at the Inaugural ceremony. When I arrived at the house the next morning, the Senator immediately asked me to "be sure to get the wire from Robert Frost in our permanent files."

While he was eating breakfast, Jackie came out to see him and said she wanted to see him in her bedroom. As soon as he finished, he went through the living room and into her bedroom. In a little while I had to take him a message that Douglas Dillon wanted to talk to him. He came to the door and said he would talk to Dillon, but he did not want to be disturbed for a while. He did not like to ask Jackie to share their moments together with his public responsibilities and demands.

It was Saturday; Lyndon Johnson was coming for an eleven o'clock appointment and lunch afterward. He had sent word that he wanted to have Congressman and Mrs. Frank Boykin of Alabama and Congressman and Mrs. Mendel Rivers of South Carolina, as well as Mrs. Johnson, with them while they lunched.

When Senator Kennedy learned that Mrs. Johnson was coming, he invited the Johnsons to stay at the house.

The maids were running around like barnyard chickens at feeding time, changing bedrooms and getting the lunch ready. The Johnsons arrived at eleven and their guests shortly after them. It was well after 2:30 before the luncheon was over. The Senator and Mr. Johnson planned to join Natalie Cushing and her husband for a round of golf at three, and there was not much time to spare. As soon as they left, I returned to my hotel. The Johnsons left the next morning.

The following morning the Senator was in a very good mood. He was dictating a letter when he looked into the mirror, stopped dictating, and exclaimed, "My God! Look at that fat face. If I don't lose five pounds this week I might have to call off the Inauguration." He looked so unhappy as he pulled at his cheeks I could hardly keep from laughing out loud. Then he proceeded to prance up and down the room, dictating sentences and striking half of them out.

He looked out the window and saw Caroline.

"Buttons, what time are we going swimming?" She evidently didn't remember, so he said again, "I can't remember when we were supposed to go swimming."

She answered with the first number that came into her head.

"Eight o'clock."

"All right, I'll be there."

He finished dictating and tried on a hat someone had sent him.

"Now this hat fits. What are we going to do about my hat?" I reminded him that he had his Overseer hat but some hat men were going to meet with him in New York in a few days. Then he settled down to telephone calls and his appointments for the day.

The next day we were flying to Washington, but I had several things to take care of before we left. One was to make a dental appointment for the Senator to get his teeth cleaned, another was to make sure that the Fitzgerald family Bible was on its way. The Senator had told me that was the Bible he wanted to use in taking his oath. And Evelyn Jones had handed me a note that read, "Please call someone's attention to the fact one pair of Mr. Jack's black shoes needs tapping (hole in sole)." This is interesting, I thought; Adlai isn't the only one with that problem.

The Senator had several appointments in his Georgetown house after we arrived in Washington, and then we flew on to New York. I heard him talking to his doctor on the telephone about his weight. The doctor said it was natural for him to gain because of the let-up of his strenuous campaign activities and eating regular meals now. That seemed to satisfy the Senator—he turned to me and said, "I'll have my usual breakfast."

He also asked me to call Bill Walton, the Georgetown artist who had served as his liaison man for New York state during the campaign, and tell him he would like to use his house in Georgetown the next day for appointments; Jackie was going to be busy at the N Street house with dressmakers. After I got permission from Walton, I had to call all his appointments and give them the address.

We flew back to Washington that afternoon. Ted Sorensen was waiting for the Senator to review his Inaugural speech once again. The Senator was planning to stop by a reception and buffet honoring the Vice President-elect and Mrs. Johnson at the Statler-Hilton, and then he was going to pick up Jackie and attend a private dinner party. The Inaugural festivities were beginning.

I went straight home to Abe and the new apartment. It was good to be there.

CHAPTER 22

The Inauguration

I stepped outside the door and discovered it was snowing. The Senator had finished his day of appointments at Bill Walton's home, and I was on my way to a four o'clock appointment with the hairdresser. After that I was going by his N Street house to pick up some things, then head home to dress for the Inaugural Gala.

I didn't think the snow would amount to much by Nebraska standards, so I told my driver to come back to the hairdresser's to pick me up in an hour and a half. When I stepped outside again, the street was jammed with cars at a virtual standstill in the snow. My driver was not among them, but I spotted Muggsie. He had been sent to pick up Jean Louis, the hairdresser who had been out earlier in the day to set Jackie's hair and was going back to comb it for tonight's Gala. I decided to ride with them.

Off we started for N Street. For each foot forward it seemed we had to stand still ten or fifteen minutes. Muggsie was working hard but not getting anywhere, and after two hours of spinning and turning the hairdresser said he was going to walk back to his shop, but we continued on. Finally, after more than four hours covering a distance that would ordinarily take fifteen minutes, we got to the Senator's house.

I telephoned Abe and learned he was marooned in Congressman Macdonald's office. He said it looked so bad he was going to stay there. Someone had brought him a sandwich and some coffee, and he planned to sleep on a cot in the Congressman's office. "So," he said, "I guess you have no choice but to stay where you are, because we could never get out to the apartment, dress, and get to the Armory in time to see the Gala."

I looked out the window; it was like staring into a pillowcase. The snow was coming down in large hunks. I hated to miss the Gala, with the performances of all those Hollywood stars Peter Lawford had rounded up. But Abe was right. I had no choice but to stay where I was.

Mary Gallagher had also been caught by the snow, and we resigned ourselves to having Provie give us some dinner and fixing up some beds for us to sleep on. Every time the front door opened and someone came in, he would stamp his feet on the rug by the door and say, "This is the worst snow we have ever had, and I can't see any end to it." Out in front of the house, photographers and newsmen moved around like living snowmen. They were waiting to see the President and Jackie leave. First they were going to a reception at the Philip Graham home, then a concert at Constitution Hall, and then out to the National Guard Armory, all the way across town, for the Gala.

He came into the bedroom where we were eating our dinner and asked, "Aren't you ladies going to the Gala?" I guess we must have looked pretty sad as we told him we couldn't get to our homes to dress, for as he turned to leave he said, "There's always a bright side. At least you will be here in the morning." We both said, "Have a good time, Mr. President," and he left.

Jackie came downstairs looking radiant in her elegant long dress and coat of white silk. They opened the front door and looked up into the klieg lights and flashbulbs awaiting their appearance.

Before I turned out the light to go to sleep I read the Inaugural speech that the President was going to give the next day. It was his reading copy, and I was guarding it with my life. I wondered where I could put it and then decided it would stay right on my bed beside me.

I was awakened about eight o'clock by a rustling outside my door. Then I heard a knock and the President's voice.

"Mrs. Lincoln, can I have the reading copy of my Inauguration speech?"

I jumped out of bed, grabbed the speech, opened the door, and handed it to him.

"Did you have a good time last night?"

"Yes, we got home around four o'clock."

He looked as if he had slept at least ten hours.

Provie brought me my breakfast after I had dressed. While I was eating, the President was in the bathroom next to my bedroom, taking a bath, and reading his Inaugural speech out loud. I thought, the entire world will be listening to him give that address at noon today, but here I am getting a private preview.

When he left the bathroom, he hollered, "Tell Provie that I want my breakfast served in the living room." In his bedroom, he was still reading his speech. He continued to read it aloud as he walked down to the living room, and in between bites of his breakfast. The speech meant a lot to him, and he wanted it to be exactly right in sense and sound.

After breakfast he returned the speech to me and got ready for church. Bill Walton came by to go with him.

During the time the President was at church, Pierre Salinger was up in my little corner office making phone calls about where his children were going to sit during the parade. Soon the President was back from church.

He was dressing for the Inaugural ceremony when a comic-strip emergency developed. He couldn't find the right collar.

"Call my father and see if he has one I can wear."

I called the house where his father was staying and was told, "If you can send someone over he can have one of his collars."

Muggsie went over. He had just returned from my apartment, where he picked up the President's precious top hat.

Muggsie came back with the collar, but another emergency. It didn't fit. We dug through all of his old collars and finally came up with one that seemed to work. It was really an ordeal getting him ready, but after he was dressed, he certainly looked like a President.

"Now where is my speech?"

225

I told him I had given it to the Secret Service, and they
ould see he had it at the right time. I had also told the Secret
ervice to see that the speech was picked up after he left the
platform in front of the Capitol.

Jackie came down the stairs looking very beautiful in a beige
coat and hat with black accessories. While they were waiting
to go out to their car, I asked Andrew Hatcher, the assistant
Press Secretary, to save space for me in one of the cars going
to the White House. He put me in with the photographers.

While the President and Mrs. Kennedy were inside the White
House visiting with President and Mrs. Eisenhower, I went
inside and met Ann Whitman, President Eisenhower's secretary,
and asked the Secret Service if I could leave my briefcase there.
Then I rushed out to find a ride to the Capitol. This time Andy
Hatcher put me in a car with some newsmen, including Hugh
Sidey of *Time* magazine and Sandy Vanocur of NBC.

When we got to the Capitol, one of the newsmen took me
under his wing and saw that I got up to the rotunda. Then he
left me to shift for myself. I scooted to a roped-off place and
found myself standing in front of the door that the President
would soon come through to go down to the platform. I spied
an empty space a little way up on the steps, right behind Esther
Peterson and her husband, and I got that. Esther was a former
labor leader who had worked with the President in 1958 and
1959. I was glad to find someone I knew—I had left my ticket
back home in the dresser drawer.

The ceremony itself had an extra measure of excitement.
Richard Cardinal Cushing made a seemingly endless invoca-
tion while the podium smoldered from a short circuit. Robert
Frost was unable to see the poem he had written for the occasion because of the bright sun shining on the white paper, and
he recited one from memory. Marion Anderson sang beautifully.

The President looked so slight sitting there—too slight, almost,
for the heavy weight he would have to carry by day and by
night. And then it was time for him to speak. As he walked to
the podium, a hush swept over the great crowd. He stood for a

moment without hat or topcoat in the bitter cold and what seemed slightness was shown for what it really was: a kind of metallic keenness. He was like a bright sword poised there, and his words began to fall with swordstrokes upon us, cutting away our doubts, slashing through the bonds that were holding us down and making us dull. The strokes cut away, one after the other, and each one bit through the heavy dust of the past: "... symbolizing an end as well as a beginning...." But the main, solid, unforgettable feeling shared, I am sure, by all who heard, or saw, or read of that Inaugural, was that America possessed a leader and that he had found a way to make the steel of English cut us free.

After the ceremony, while the President and Mrs. Kennedy were having lunch in the old Supreme Court Chamber in the Capitol, I went over to the new House Office Building to meet Abe. We had some hot coffee while we waited for a car from the White House to drive us to the President's reviewing stand to watch the Inaugural Parade. It was bitter cold but we sat for an hour and a half alternately watching the Parade and the President. Then we returned to the White House, and I picked up my briefcase and asked for a car to drive us home. The usher told us to go down to the Diplomatic Reception Room, where a car would be waiting for us.

As we walked through this great white building where so much history had been made, I couldn't realize that we had finally made it. It seemed like a fairy tale. Here I was, a country girl from the plains of Nebraska going to work tomorrow for the President of the United States, as his personal secretary.

I was up early the next morning and eager to go to work. No one had explained to me where I was supposed to go or when I was supposed to be in the office, but it seemed natural to show up at my regular time.

Abe began my day perfectly. "Evelyn, I'd be proud to drive you to work this morning."

We got into our red 1951 car, already a veteran of many

227

miles, and down Sixteenth Street we went. The snow was still piled high along the sides of the street, and it was a clear, crisp, bright day. We drove up to the northwest gate at the White House, and the guard, unfamiliar with the new people coming to work for the President, took my word that I was the President's secretary and Abe was my husband. We drove through the gate to the door of the West Wing. As Abe left me he said, "I'll call you later."

I had never been in the West Wing and had no idea where the President's office was located. The guard, after looking me over very suspiciously, took me down a hall, past the press office, into another hall. Then he opened a door and said, "I guess this will be your office." I put my briefcase down and looked to the east; two white-curtained doors opened onto a portico that overlooked what was called the Rose Garden. I walked over to another door. This must be the Cabinet room, I thought as I turned the knob, and it was. I turned around and walked south, opened the door, and there it was—the President's office. It was oval-shaped with many slightly curved windows. When I walked over to look out at the other side of the lawn, I noticed that the bottom portion of the glass was at least an inch thick but perfectly transparent. Must be bullet-proof, I thought.

I was somewhat disappointed in the color scheme of the room. The walls were painted the same light green I had seen in so many government buildings and there were green draperies and beige curtains at the windows. On the floor was a green oval rug with the Presidential seal in the center. Everything else was green except the furniture, which was mostly brown except for a cerise-colored sofa against the southeast wall.

The President's desk was massive and almost covered with black telephones. There must have been at least eight of them. I wondered what he would do if they all rang at once.

Then I returned for a closer look at my own office. I opened another door and found a washroom and closet space. My office was also painted government green and two desks stood facing each other directly in front of the doors to the Rose Garden. To the east side of each desk was a two-drawer file cabinet. Another desk was against the south wall, and two four-drawer file cabinets were against the north wall.

I was just getting ready to rearrange my office when I heard footsteps in the President's office. I looked up to see him walking toward me.

"Good morning, Mrs. Lincoln, is there any mail?"

"As soon as it arrives, I'll bring it in to you," I replied, unable to hide a smile—things hadn't changed much.

He asked me how I liked my office, then went back into his office, sat down at the desk, and looked at all the buzzers lining both sides of the desk and the battery of telephones.

"I don't like them. Too cluttered. And this desk is too big." He thought there should be an arrangement of chairs near the fireplace, opposite his desk, and as I suspected, he wanted the cerise sofa changed.

While he was thinking about ways to make his office reflect the JFK taste, I was rearranging mine. I had only to tell the supply officer what I wanted and it was done promptly. I had the metal desks exchanged for wooden ones and mine turned so that I faced the President's office door.

Soon other members of the White House staff were finding their way to the offices in which they would work. I had two extra desks, and two of the girls came into my office until desks could be provided for them elsewhere. One of them, Janet Des Rosiers, who had been Ambassador Kennedy's secretary for twelve years prior to serving as the stewardess on *The Caroline* during the campaign, didn't stay many weeks, however. An old arm injury began giving her trouble, and she took a leave of absence. After her recovery she did not return to the office, but asked for a position with the American Embassy in Paris. The President was delighted to recommend her to Ambassador James Gavin.

The other girl who shared my office was Priscilla Wear—

229

"Fiddle." She also had worked during the campaign. Priscilla was a delightful person to have around and very helpful to me in handling all the requests that came in the mail. She was young, attractive, and easy-going. She was always threatening to learn shorthand, but working at the White House didn't leave many spare hours. However, her typing was excellent. She stayed until the fall of 1962, when she, too, wanted to go to Paris; and from that time on I was alone in my office.

On that first day the press was very anxious to get in to see the President. For about ten minutes they were brought in to take some pictures and just look. The President posed at his desk with the American flag and the Presidential flag in the background.

After the photographers and reporters left, he came out and gave me his first dictation as President: tell Larry O'Brien that he would like to have the legislative leaders meet with him at nine A.M. next Tuesday, January 24th. Then he said, "There should be a staff meeting of Ted Sorensen, Ralph Dungan, Larry O'Brien, Ted Reardon, Fred Dutton, and Kenny O'Donnell on Monday." As he turned to leave he said, "Oh, yes, be sure to have plenty of my cigars over here in case I might ask you for one."

He hurried out for a meeting he had arranged with President Truman. They entered the President's office, and Mr. Truman walked around, fully enjoying his first visit to the White House since he had left it in 1953. Then I saw them pass my doors, out on the portico on their way over to the Mansion. I thought, What a wonderful spot for my office. I can see the President in his office, I can see him when he leaves the Mansion to come over to the office, and he has to walk through my office to get to the Cabinet room.

When the President returned after bidding Mr. Truman goodbye on the north portico, he noticed that I had the reading copy of his Inaugural address on my desk.

"I read the other day that one of the former Presidents was offered $75,000 for his Inaugural address. Mrs. Lincoln, give me a pen so I can sign mine." After he signed it, he added, "Here, keep this $75,000 for me."

Chicago's Mayor Richard Daley and Mrs. Daley were waiting in the Cabinet room with their six children to shake hands with the President and have their picture taken with him. They were the first family to see President Kennedy and they were clearly delighted about it. He went into the Cabinet room and soon came out, followed by the Daleys. He stopped by my desk and introduced them to me. After they had their pictures taken and departed, the President went to the Democratic National Committee offices to thank the workers for their help during the campaign.

As soon as he left, the painters moved in and began changing the government-green walls to a soft off-white. And I went to work getting my materials out of the bags and boxes I had been shipping from place to place during all those months.

The swearing-in ceremony for the Cabinet members was scheduled in the East Room at four o'clock, and after that the President was going to the Alfalfa Club dinner.

When he arrived at his office on Monday morning he was delighted with the new wall color. I added to the good beginning by having some mail for him. In one of the letters, a schoolteacher sent him a quotation from Lincoln, which she felt summed up his own philosophy: "I am not bound to win, but I am bound to be true. I am not bound to succeed, but I am bound to live up to what light I have. I must stand with anybody that stands right, stand with him while he is right, and part with him when he goes wrong."

He was starting the day with a full schedule. Some of the items were new to me—there was a meeting that morning to discuss the Laos situation. I was going to have to get used to dealing with problems I had never known before.

I learned right away that one of my duties would be to rush into his office as soon as he left for any reason, clear the papers from his desk, take them to my office, and see that everything of a security nature was locked in the files.

From the very first day I left the door to my office open so that people going by could drop in. The door between my office and the President's office was also open quite a bit of the time, just as it had been when he was a Senator.

And he continued his Senate habit of coming out to my desk between appointments to look at the mail I kept in a box on the corner of the desk. He stood there with the letters, dictating answers as he read them.

One day he said, "Rather than you coming in with messages, and me coming out here to give you messages, maybe we can put an instrument on our desks that we can talk into." I said I would check into it, and I did. Soon we had "squawk" boxes on our desks, but the first time he used it his voice came through so strongly they heard him down the hall. He never tried it again. The boxes stood on the desks gathering dust.

Toward the end of the day the President called me into his office and asked me if the fireplace worked. He was standing by his desk, deep in conversation with Walter Heller, Chairman of the Economic Advisers. There was snow on the ground and it was cold.

"Why don't you light the fire?" he said. I crumpled some paper, stuffed it under the logs, and put a match to it.

Almost immediately the room was filled with smoke. Maintenance men began running into my office shouting, "Where's the fire?" Sam "Mitch" Mitchell, one of the assistants who had custody of the President's office, rushed in saying, "Oh, my land, what has happened?" Newspapermen, who had been dozing in the leather chairs out in the reception room, came to life with a rush. The telephone started to ring. All the doors and windows were open. People were running in and out. Mitch came out and said to me severely, "Do you know that the damper in that fireplace wasn't open?"

The President had never stopped talking. Before the smoke cleared, he and Chairman Heller were back in the middle of his office, still discussing the growth of the economy.

He decided to hold his first press conference as President on Wednesday, January 25th. He wanted briefing material sent to his bedroom the day before so he might read it before he retired. That began the custom of preparing an envelope of reading material to be placed in his bedroom before I left every evening.

His schedule for the day of the press conference was fairly light, but staff members were coming and going all day long with memos and briefing material. At 5:30 he stood up from his desk, asked me for a hair brush, brushed his hair, grabbed a few papers from his desk, and went out the door on his way to the State Department Auditorium. Four hundred eighteen newsmen were waiting for him.

When he stepped on that platform before the microphones, he was calm and sure of himself, and he began to read from the papers he had taken from the desk. I watched it on television in my office.

"I have several announcements to make. First, I have a statement about the Geneva negotiations for an atomic test ban. These negotiations, as you know, are scheduled to begin early in February. They are of great importance and we will need more time to prepare a clear American position, so we are consulting with other governments, and we are asking to have it put off until late March."

When the half hour was just about over, he was asked: "Mr. President, on a related subject, without being morbid, have you given any consideration to the problem which President Eisenhower resolved with his Vice President, that is, the problem of succession in case of injury, illness, or some incapacitation? Have you thought of some agreement with the Vice President, such as your predecessor had, or some other?"

"Yes—well, I haven't developed that at this present time, though I do think that President Eisenhower's decision was a good one, and I think it would be a good precedent. Nothing has been done on it as yet, but I think it would be a good matter we could proceed on."

Then one of the reporters said, "Thank you, Mr. President," and the conference was over.

The next morning he was to hold his first Cabinet meeting. The first thing he said when he arrived at the office was, "Is the Cabinet waiting for me?"

I told him the meeting was not until ten o'clock.

"Do you have anything for me?"

I gave him a message that Congressman Frank Thompson had called and was anxious to talk to him. He returned the call promptly, and then said, "I wonder if you would get a couple of cold tablets from the doctor. I feel a little cold coming on."

I spoke to the doctor—a Navy physician assigned to the White House—and he wanted to see the President. He looked at his throat and nose and told me he would send a couple of pills for me to give him.

In the meantime the President had asked me to get him a cup of coffee. I opened the door with the coffee and the pills. Dr. Jerome Wiesner, who later become his adviser on science, and Pierre Salinger were in with him. I handed him the two pills and he stuffed them into his pocket rather hastily, giving me the impression that perhaps I shouldn't have given them to him with anyone else in the room. I put the coffee down and went out thinking, He's got to realize everyone knows even Presidents catch colds.

Soon the Attorney General came into my office, and I told him that the President had tried to get him earlier and maybe he should go in to see him. When he opened the door, I noticed that Dr. Wiesner and Pierre were no longer there, and I went in to remind him about the two pills in his pocket. He took a little sip of coffee and swallowed them.

When he and the Attorney General came out of his office, it was almost time for the Cabinet meeting to begin. He said to his brother, "Why don't you go through the other door." The President waited until the Attorney General entered the Cabinet room from the hall door, and then he walked into the

234

room from my office. As he entered they all stood, and his first Cabinet meeting began.

They must have had many problems to discuss because they were in the Cabinet Room for almost two and a half hours.

The President was so busy that day I had to remind him about lunch, and it was nearly 1:30 before he left for the Mansion. While he walked over he conferred with his naval aide, whom he had asked to find some suitable marine pictures for the walls of his office.

The President was due to leave for a briefing at the CIA at 2:20. Although it had snowed all morning and the streets were beginning to jam with traffic, he and Mr. Bundy headed for the CIA over in Virginia. He stayed there until five o'clock. When he returned, Professor Walt W. Rostow was waiting to see him.

He called me into his office. I was sure he was going to ask me to light the fire, but he said, "Perhaps we could have some tea." In a few minutes a tray arrived from the kitchen, and they settled down for a talk that lasted until almost six o'clock. Kenny O'Donnell had some nominations for him to sign, and Ted Sorensen had some questions concerning the upcoming State of the Union message. Then he dictated some letters. It was almost eight when he headed for the Mansion.

The President was certainly touching all bases. The next day he had lunch with Treasury Secretary Douglas Dillon; Labor Secretary Arthur Goldberg; Health, Education, and Welfare Secretary Abraham Ribicoff; Commerce Secretary Luther Hodges; and Congressman Wilbur Mills of Arkansas, chairman of the House Ways and Means Committee. About 3:30 I sent a note to his bedroom asking if he wanted to see Bill Walton, who had come to discuss pictures to be hung in the President's office.

He sent word back he would be right over, and he was—in less than five minutes.

The two Air Force officers freed by the Russians were coming for tea with the Kennedys later that afternoon. Someone called to ask the President, "Where should Mrs. Kennedy go for the meeting with the Air Force men?"

"Tell her I'll be up to her room to pick her up and that we'll go down together to the front door to meet them."

A few minutes later a guard called from the front gate to advise that the men and their families had arrived. We stalled them for about ten minutes to give the President time to get there to welcome them.

The President returned to the office, and from then until about 7:30 he talked to staff members or he dictated letters. Finally, Mrs. Kennedy called over to say his dinner guests had arrived; he said he would be right over. Lem Billings was one of the guests; he planned to stay overnight at the White House. He had been sitting in my office waiting for the President to finish his business so they could go over to the Mansion together.

The next day was Saturday. In the afternoon Mrs. Kennedy came over to the office to look at the pictures that had been chosen for the President's office.

"Mrs. Lincoln, will you have them remove those curtains at the window? They keep the scenery out, and the view is so beautiful."

I had the curtains removed. She was right.

Colonel McHugh, the President's Air Force Aide, was waiting impatiently in my office one afternoon with some papers for the President to sign. The President's door was closed. Finally, Colonel McHugh said, "I'm going to open the door just a little, and see if the President is alone." As he did, the President opened it quickly from the other side, and McHugh almost fell into his arms. He flushed red and apologized, but the President thought it extremely funny, and chuckled as he signed the papers.

CHAPTER 23

Getting Adjusted

For the next few weeks both the President and Mrs. Kennedy were so busy with newsmaking activity in the White House it looked as though they were competing for space on the front pages of the nation's newspapers.

On January 30th, the President delivered his first State of the Union address before a joint session of Congress—a speech that ranked in importance with his Inaugural Address. While he was walking over to his office that morning, I could see he was in a good mood and eager to get going on the speech. It was a brisk, cold morning, but, as usual, he walked without overcoat or hat.

There were some last-minute changes to be made in his reading copy and the two copies he signed for filing with the House and the Senate, and then he began reading the speech aloud in his office. At eleven o'clock, he telephoned his father in Palm Beach to tell him to be sure to watch him on television. His father had been present for the Inauguration but had returned to Palm Beach immediately after the festivities.

Mrs. Kennedy rode to the Capitol with the President. When she walked into the family gallery in the House of Representatives and took her seat in the front row, the members of both houses, already in their seats below, rose to give her a standing ovation. As the President walked down the aisle to the rostrum, scores of hands were outstretched from both sides to shake his as he went by.

His speech met with one round of applause after another; the Congress listened intently as his New England accent resounded within those historic walls.

One passage, summing up his appraisal of the state of the union, seemed to strike an especially responsive chord:

237

"Life in 1961 will not be easy. Wishing it, predicting it, even asking for it, will not make it so. There will be further setbacks before the tide is turned. But turn it we must. The hopes of all mankind rest upon us; not simply upon those of us in this chamber, but upon the peasant in Laos, the fisherman in Nigeria, the exile in Cuba, the spirit that moved every man and nation who shares our hopes for freedom and the future. And in the final analysis, they rest most of all upon the pride and perseverance of our fellow citizens of the great Republic."

After the address, the President and Mrs. Kennedy went to the Foreign Relations Committee room to attend a luncheon given by his former colleagues on the Committee and their wives. They returned to the White House a little after three o'clock, and for the next three hours the President had one appointment after another.

My little office was beginning to become a meeting place of the staff members. The President would come out between appointments to look at the mail and give me reminders, and anyone willing to wait for him could get in a few quick questions.

The President was very quietly launching a campaign to pave the way for passage of his program in Congress in the months to come. He had a list of the birthdays of every member of the Congress, and he sent each a hand-delivered letter on his birthday. One morning he asked me to tell Ted Reardon to read the *Congressional Record* every day and prepare a letter of congratulations and appreciation whenever a Representative or Senator commented favorably on a Presidential proposal or issued a favorable committee report.

"For example," he said, "tell him we should send a letter of thanks, or rather of high regard, to Senator Kerr of Oklahoma for the report he did on water, indicating that we are following along. That way all the members of Congress will feel that we are watching their work. And tell him I want to sign all these letters."

Occasionally the President would receive a gift of cigars. If they were not his brand, I would put them in a humidor on top of the small refrigerator in my office.

When I dropped those cigars in the humidor, it was like putting seed in a bird feeder. "I see that the boss got some cigars," Muggsie would say, slipping some in his pocket. If the President asked me to get Pierre, on his way out Pierre was sure to stop by the humidor. Naval Aide Captain Shepard always paced the floor while waiting in my office. He couldn't pass by the humidor without taking a peek. Nor could Andy Hatcher. There were many other samplers. The humidor, like my candy dish, served a useful purpose. It helped make for camaraderie, and to ease the tensions that hovered around that all-important threshold.

The Rules Committee of the House of Representatives acts as a clearing-house for all legislation. A conservative band of Republicans and Southern Democrats on that Committee could pigeonhole any legislation they wished. The President threw his support behind Speaker Rayburn's move to enlarge the committee membership from twelve to fifteen, putting this band in the minority.

Nearly every afternoon while the battle was going on, the President made personal telephone calls to influential members of the House on both sides of the aisle, enlisting their support for the expansion of membership on the Rules Committee. The sharp controversy was reflected in the final vote: 217 to 212. The change was made.

One morning the President said to me, "Tell McB ... Mc-Bundy ... (He too was having difficulty with McGeorge Bundy's name) that I would like a copy of any memoranda, minutes, notes, and such which he might make for our files. Tell him it is my understanding that the files of the National Security Council, as part of a statutory organization, do not automatically become a part of the White House files. When I leave the White House it would be helpful in reconstructing the record of the Administration to have that material in our files."

239

Whenever he dictated a message like this, I sent it as a memo from me, saying, "The President asked me to tell you. . . ." In this way I would have a record in my own files for any necessary follow-up. This was the procedure he had followed during his six years in the Senate. It was not uncommon for him to give me messages to be sent to Cabinet officers, government officials, staff members, members of his family and friends.

He also preferred to have letters to Cabinet officers and other government officials delivered by hand, rather than through the usual channels. At first I received frantic calls saying I was not supposed to send letters directly; I replied that the President had asked me to do it that way. He wanted action, and he had found this way he could get it.

Mrs. Kennedy was making news in her own way. She had found a dust-covered desk in the White House basement that she thought the President would want to use. It was made of timbers from the British ship *H.M.S. Resolute,* which had been wrecked off the shores of North America, and had been presented to President Andrew Jackson by Queen Victoria. It had not been used since Franklin D. Roosevelt sat by it for his fireside chats to the nation. The President was very pleased with the desk, but discovered a problem—his knees hit the middle drawer. We had carpenters raise the desk on a base.

He had only two buzzers installed on the desk, one on the east side for my office, and one on the west side for Kenny O'Donnell, his appointments secretary. The multitude of telephones were replaced by a single instrument with buttons. I was glad to see that. Once I had picked up one of the telephones and seconds later what seemed like an entire regiment rushed up the stairs. Later I learned I had picked up the "alert" telephone that President Eisenhower had used.

Mrs. Kennedy, who had helped arrange the furniture in his office, was also busy in the private family quarters on the second floor. A family kitchen, a butler's pantry, and a spacious dining room were installed in what had once been Margaret Truman's bedroom. Food would no longer have to be carried from the kitchen two floors below. She had also redecorated the rooms for Caroline and John. Caroline's was pale pink with a white canopied bed, and John's was white with blue trim. He was going to share his room with his nurse, Maud Shaw.

Mrs. Kennedy also announced the creation of a Fine Arts Committee for the White House to restore and preserve its historic furnishings and particularly to accept or purchase those White House pieces that had got into private hands.

The President was proud of and interested in this project—and so was the nation. The number of visitors to the Mansion increased greatly. In 1961 the total topped the one million mark some time in August.

On a snowy Saturday in February, Caroline and John came up from Florida to move into the White House. They had remained in Palm Beach throughout the Inauguration, and their return had been postponed while Mrs. Kennedy was having their rooms redecorated. Naturally the President and Mrs. Kennedy were eager to see the children and went out to the airport to meet them. Mr. Robert Redmond, the White House gardener, made a snowman to welcome the children. Caroline insisted on running out to touch it.

The following Monday morning Caroline began a practice that was to continue as long as she lived in the White House. From my window I saw her walking with the President along the colonnade from the Mansion to his office. Almost every morning after that she walked with her father to work. It was a highlight of her day.

That first morning he brought her into my office. Right away she asked, "Where is some paper, Mrs. Lincoln? Draw something." Then she saw the candy dish on the table at the side of my desk, and wanted to know why I had candy there. I told her I thought maybe the people working at the White House would enjoy it.

"But," I added in a whisper, "it really is so when you come over, you can have some candy."

Mrs. Kennedy was determined that Caroline should have as

normal a childhood as possible while she lived in the White House. To keep her from being isolated from other children and too much in the company of adults, she organized a play group for her, which met at the White House three times a week from 9:30 A.M. to 11:30 A.M. The group consisted of twelve children and their mothers. For days carpenters hammered away in the solarium on the third floor of the Mansion, converting it into a room for the children. They also built a playhouse under one of the trees on the south lawn, near the putting green where President Eisenhower used to spend his free moments relaxing. Caroline was delighted with both her play group and her playhouse.

Several weeks after the Inauguration, the Kennedys decided to sell the house in Georgetown; a buyer was found for it almost immediately. One Friday before going to Glen Ora, the estate they had leased near Middleburg, Virginia, Mrs. Kennedy came by my office to sign the papers selling the Georgetown house.

As she looked them over, I said, "So many wonderful memories were in that house."

She looked at me wistfully and said, "If you say the word, I won't sign these."

I laughed and she signed them. The President had already signed them, and I put the papers in an envelope for Clark Clifford, their attorney.

On Saturday the President followed her to Glen Ora, where they spent a quiet weekend. He never took any members of the staff with him when he went there for the weekend, only George Thomas, the valet, and Provie. In the little town of Middleburg it was not easy to accommodate the essential people —Secret Service agents and communications and transportation aides. There simply wasn't room for staff.

On his weekends at Glen Ora the President found time for the reading he felt essential to satisfy his thirst for knowledge. He read more than half a dozen newspapers daily; he could do it in little more than the time it took other people to read one

242

thoroughly. And he was not unmoved by the kind things written about him.

One evening before he left the office he asked me to make sure he thanked Ruth Montgomery for an article she had written for the New York *Journal American*. It said in part:

"This ordinarily blasé capital is fascinated by the novelty of having a President who reads the newspapers. . . . At least twice during his first ten days as President—probably the busiest period of his life—he has demonstrated that he not only skims the headlines but pours over the fine print as well. The first proof occurred when he read in a local paper that the White House had slammed the door on special tours for the constituents of Congressmen, and that GOP Representative Robert R. Barry of New York had protested. Barry's explosion was relatively mild compared with JFK's reaction. Throwing down the paper, he sent for Press Secretary Pierre Salinger and read the riot act to him and everyone else on the staff who had anything to do with the decision. As a former Congressman as well as a reporter, he needed no one to tell him the public relations value of doing little favors for constituents. The VIP tours were promptly reinstated."

The article concluded: "The current reaction to Kennedy's Cabinet appointments, his Inaugural address, State of the Union message and general conduct has been so lopsidedly favorable that he would probably win a run-off election today by a landslide. Approximately one eighth of the proverbial "honeymoon" period is now gone, and die-hard Republicans are still waiting for the first real Kennedy blooper. It is not yet in sight."

The VIP tour was set aside for friends of Congressmen, Senators, Cabinet officers, or members of the official staff. It started at 8:15 A.M. and was over before the public tour started at ten o'clock. When the matter was brought to his attention, the President immediately wanted to know how the tours were handled. He wanted them arranged so as to take care of as many people as possible, and he periodically asked how many

243

had been accommodated on a given day. He wanted this tour to be something special.

When I went through the papers sent over from the President's bedroom on Valentine's Day, I found among the official letters and memos a Valentine from Caroline to her daddy. She had signed it by printing her name in large letters. She must have given it to him before he went in to breakfast with the legislative leaders. I sent the Valentine back, knowing Mrs. Kennedy would like to keep it.

I began to look forward to Caroline's visits every morning. The first thing she would ask was, "Do you have anything for me, Mrs. Lincoln?" Then we scrambled through the top drawer of my desk to see what she could take home with her. It didn't make any difference to Caroline what it was, just so she had something. I began to pick up inexpensive novelties at the drugstore. She seemed to get so much pleasure out of taking something back to show her "Mommy."

One thing more had been added to her visits. She wanted to type her name on the typewriter. "Which one is the C?" she would ask. She could hardly wait until she got to the *e*, so she could run and show her daddy what she had done.

One morning President Truman was one of her daddy's callers. When he came in, the President closed the door between our offices, and Caroline and I went right on typing and drawing houses. In a short time the door opened and the President and Mr. Truman came over to my desk. Caroline never liked to have anyone notice her. When her father said, "Caroline, this is President Truman," she scooted under my desk. The President calmly went on talking to Mr. Truman, who tried to coax her out by saying, "I have a grandson about your age." But it was plain that nothing was going to get her to budge.

When the President and Mr. Truman returned to his office, Caroline came out of hiding.

"Who was that?"

I told her it was President Truman and that at one time her daddy's office had been his office.

After a moment she said, "Oh."

On George Washington's birthday the President took a two-hour golf holiday before returning for a series of late appointments. The following Saturday he was on the links again at the Burning Tree Country Club in nearby Bethesda, where President Eisenhower had often played. It was about the only exercise he got except his daily dips in the White House swimming pool and an occasional stroll around the south lawn, and there was little time for that.

The President's schedule seemed to grow daily. People who couldn't get on his appointment list through the regular channels began seeking other avenues of access. Many times the President would say to me in the morning, "Mr. So-and-so is coming to see me at twelve and I told him that he could come in through your office. Will you put him in the Cabinet room and let me know when he is there." Often his friends would call me and ask if they could see him. When I checked with him, he would say, "Yes, tell them to come through your office."

This caused other members of his staff to think I was trying to be the appointment secretary, but I felt that I was working for the President—and answering only to him—and if he wanted me to do things like that I was not going to tell him I could not do it. They would say to me: "Well, the President would never turn down anyone." I thought he certainly knew whom he wanted to see and whom he didn't want to see.

Once back in 1960 Abe came by the N Street house to pick me up, and I asked him to come in as I was going to be busy for a little while longer. While I was finishing up the last things, Abe chatted with the President-elect about various matters, and mentioned that he would love to become a part of the administration if there were a place for him. Mr. Kennedy seemed pleased, and asked me to remind him of this after he was inaugurated.

Not long after the Inauguration Abe was called to the Veterans Administration to interview General John S. Gleason, Jr., the newly appointed Administrator, about the job of legislative liaison between the administration and Congress. He was accepted for the position and told to report for duty with the VA on February 20th.

Although Abe was reluctant to leave Congressman Macdonald, he was pleased to be a part of the "New Frontier." Work at the Veterans Administration started at eight o'clock in the morning, and I began arriving at the White House at eight so that we could ride to work together. I was happy to have this extra hour to get my work organized before other staff members arrived and the telephones started to ring.

Abe's work kept him at his desk long after the 4:30 P.M. closing time of the Veterans Administration, and he always checked with me to find out when I would be leaving. If I thought it would be soon, he would come over and we would ride home together.

The President was always delighted to see Abe whenever he came to wait for me, and often asked, "Is Abe going to stop by tonight?" He would ask his opinion, not only concerning the problems of the VA, but also on current issues and seemed to enjoy talking with him.

During these days the President made every effort to strengthen his ties with Congress, especially its leaders. On St. Patrick's Day he went to the annual party given by Congressman Michael J. Kirwan of Ohio at the National Press Club. He then returned to the White House for the private party he and Mrs. Kennedy gave in honor of her sister, Lee Radziwill, and her husband, who were visiting them from London.

The next morning the President appeared in the office with a patch over his eye. I never asked what happened, but someone told me he had hit his eyebrow on the edge of a table while scuffling with the children. That morning he had a meeting in the Cabinet room, and afterward he and Mrs. Kennedy were to attend a State Department ceremony celebrating the one hundredth anniversary of the unification of Italy. I took a note

246

to him in the Cabinet room when it came time for him to leave, and Caroline followed me in. To her, the note was not sufficient. She said loudly and clearly, "Mommy wants you." In about two minutes he came out and left for the ceremony. Caroline stayed around and talked to me.

Mrs. Kennedy made headlines again when she began searching for new chefs for the White House. One day two appeared: René Verdon, a Frenchman who had previously been chef at the Carlyle Hotel in New York, and Julius Spessot, an Italian. Both were very friendly and happy to be working at the White House, although they found it quite different from their formal hotel work. Soon stories began to be told about the great improvement in the food served at White House dinners. The two chefs often visited my office, walking over from the Mansion wearing their tall white hats.

While the President was getting settled in his new job and life in the White House, members of his staff were making their own adjustments. The titles had been given and the lines of responsibility drawn, and everything seemed to be going well on the "New Frontier."

At the top of the list and closest to the President was Ted Sorensen, his special counsel. Ever since he had joined the staff back in 1953, it was obvious that his work for John F. Kennedy took precedence over everything else, and he understood that he would serve neither Kennedy's interests nor his own by trying to get into the limelight. He was rarely seen or heard outside the White House. He stayed in the background where his brain and energies were at work day and night in behalf of John Kennedy.

Ted was far more than a ghostwriter for the President, although his speeches and other writings were excellent. He was really more shadow than ghost—shadow in the sense that he was never very far from Kennedy during the twelve years they worked together. He wrote the famous "Bailey Report" (named after Connecticut Democratic leader John Bailey, later Democratic National Chairman, who sent it to Democratic leaders

247

around the country), which almost succeeded in getting the Vice Presidential nomination for Senator Kennedy in 1956, and which persuaded many that his Catholicism would be more of an asset than a liability in 1960.

Ted traveled throughout the country with Senator Kennedy in the four-year campaign between 1956 and 1960, working out plans to win the Democratic nomination. I once overheard the President say, "I want to keep Ted with me wherever I go in this campaign. You need someone whom you can trust implicitly."

As their relationship grew stronger, there seemed to be a kind of unspoken communication between them. Often Ted would start to work on something with little more than a nod from the Senator. Ted moved even closer to John F. Kennedy after he became President. As crisis after crisis broke against the White House, Ted was called upon for advice, ideas, and words. The words were almost always pure gold. The creation of a Kennedy speech was always a joint effort, with Ted and the President drawing upon each other's ideas, but many of the most effective and memorable phrases were Ted's contribution. He was like a younger brother to the President, and, outside of his brother Bob, there was no one the President trusted or relied upon more.

When President Kennedy announced that Harvard historian Arthur Schlesinger, Jr., would join the White House staff as his special assistant, you could almost hear the teeth of conservatives grinding throughout the country. To them, Schlesinger embodied everything they mistrusted about the Democratic party. He was a book-writing egghead, a too-brilliant professor, and the man who helped found the Americans for Democratic Action.

Schlesinger is a strongly partisan man, and his phrase-making for Adlai Stevenson's speeches did nothing to reduce Republican dislike or suspicion. (He referred, for example, to right-wing Republicans as men ". . . who have had to be dragged, screaming and kicking into the twentieth century.") When he entered the White House, many built up a picture of a bewildered President being rapidly led down dark and devious paths, paths that turned ever more leftward, by what they viewed as a radical Harvard Svengali.

They did not know that no one had ever led the President anywhere he had not already decided to go. In addition, his relationship with Schlesinger was never that close. He admired Schlesinger's brilliant mind, his enormous store of information, and his ability to turn a phrase, and he benefited from Schlesinger's many friendships with people in the academic world who could come up with new ideas; but Schlesinger was never more than an ally and assistant. The President understood that he supported him only because he felt that, as President, Kennedy was in the best position to further his own liberal ideas. He knew that Schlesinger would have preferred to be working for "President" Adlai Stevenson.

McGeorge Bundy, special assistant to the President on matters of national security, was a quiet, intelligent man who gained in stature by his painstaking devotion to his complicated job. He was a scholar and a stickler for details. His handwriting was so small you almost needed a magnifying glass to read it, and his Cabinet room doodles—squares filled with minute and precisely drawn horizontal and vertical lines—showed the steadiness of his hand. He never talked to the President without being fully informed on the problems at hand, and the President had high regard for his views and recommendations.

Pierre Salinger, the President's press secretary, was a short, stocky man in his middle thirties who was always weight-conscious, and gave the solid appearance of having everything under control. He was strong-willed and outspoken, but he soon learned after he moved into the White House that the President made the decisions. He was ever mindful of the rights of the press, and I felt he treated them exceedingly well.

And then there was the group the press liked to call the "Irish Mafia." One member was Dave Powers, a special assistant to the President, who handled a multitude of chores and still kept the President smiling. A jolly Irishman, his favorite saying was, "Hi, Pal." Dave with a wealth of stories, kept up a line of chatter that the President enjoyed. Dave did an outstanding job in helping relieve the tension during critical moments. He was also an ardent baseball fan and could quote batting averages at a second's notice.

Kenneth "Kenny" O'Donnell, special assistant to the President, handled his appointments and fought a daily battle to say "no" nicely to the dozens who wanted to see the President when there was not enough time to work them in. He was a straight-faced Irishman who rarely smiled—a trait he perhaps acquired working on the Senate Rackets Committee. Kenny was thin and wiry, and his heels never seemed to touch the ground.

Ralph Dungan, special assistant to the President, also handled a multitude of details, including personnel matters. He was a hard-working Irishman who could always be found at his desk, coat off, working on huge stacks of papers. He was pleasant and easy-going, and also a little plump.

Lawrence O'Brien, known to everyone at the White House as "Larry," was special assistant to the President on legislative matters. A stocky Irishman who walked on his heels instead of his toes, he worked long and hard to win support in Congress for the President's legislative proposals.

CHAPTER 24

Visitors and a Crisis

Things were bustling around the White House. We were flying south to Key West with the President for a meeting with Prime Minister Harold Macmillan. What a thrill to be going there in the President's official party. This was a new phase of activity, but when we were around the President we learned to take new challenges in stride.

It was the first time since the Inauguration that the President was to meet with a leader of one of the Big Four nations. He wanted to welcome him to the United States personally and to tell him how much he was looking forward to his visit in Washington. The meeting was short, but extremely friendly.

As we flew back to Washington that Sunday evening I looked over the President's schedule for the week; he was going to be busy. There were many briefing sessions scheduled in preparation for the Prime Minister's visit. Also, Andrei A. Gromyko, Minister of Foreign Affairs of the Soviet Union, was coming in on Monday.

The President and Mr. Gromyko met with the Russian Ambassador, Adlai Stevenson, Chester Bowles, Charles Bohlen, and Foy Kohler for about twenty minutes, and then the President and he walked out to the Rose Garden and sat on a bench where they continued their discussion. They didn't release a statement on what was discussed, but they did pose for pictures before Mr. Gromyko left.

It was a warm cloudy day when the Prime Minister arrived, and the President's welcome was as warm as the temperature outside. The two men, both tall and slender, posed for pictures in the office, then came out, walked past my desk and into the Cabinet room, where they were to begin their conference with representatives of both the governments. As they walked the length of my office, I busied myself with my work, but I stole a glance at the young President walking with head erect beside the graying, older Macmillan.

The meeting lasted until time for them to go over to the Mansion for lunch, but before they left they walked onto the portico and posed for more pictures. They met again in the afternoon in the Cabinet room, and then Mrs. Kennedy asked the President if he could come over to the Mansion and meet Lady Dorothy Macmillan, who was having tea there. He returned a little while later and stopped by my office to look at the mail. While he was going through it he said, almost in a whisper and without raising his head, "I think it would be nice if you would stand when a dignitary walks through your office." Then he went on reading and soon left for the day.

I thought he might have come back to the office just to tell me this, so I found myself thinking maybe now he was President he wanted me to stand when *he* entered the room. The next morning I said to Priscilla Wear, "Let's stand when he comes into the office." And we did.

With a puzzled expression on his face, he said, "Why are you standing?"

"A dignitary just walked in."

He chuckled and waved us to sit down. But from that time on I always stood when he brought anyone of unusual importance through my office, Robert Frost, for example. I know he was pleased because he never failed to stop at my desk and say to whomever he was with, "This is my secretary, Mrs. Lincoln."

That afternoon the President and the Prime Minister had lunch aboard the *Honey Fitz,* a ninety-six-foot yacht that was named the *Barbara Anne* during the Eisenhower administration. The new name, painted in golden letters on the stern, honored the President's grandfather, John (Honey Fitz) Fitzgerald. It was one of three yachts available for the President's use.

When Joseph Cronin, president of the American Baseball League, arrived one day to present the President with a season pass to the baseball games and invite him to throw out the first ball on opening day, I knew that spring had arrived. To prepare for the opening game, one Saturday afternoon he and Ted Reardon got a couple of gloves and went into the garden outside my office and tossed the ball back and forth. It reminded me of the times he and Ted used to toss that little rubber statue around in the office.

The President came back from the opening game with a ball that had been signed by all of the players. This ball was on my desk when Bob Healy, a newspaper reporter from Massachusetts and a good friend of the President, brought his family in to meet him. While talking to the Healys, the President picked up the ball and gave it to one of the Healy boys. He couldn't have given him anything that pleased him more.

West German Chancellor Konrad Adenauer was the next visiting dignitary, and I remembered to stand when the President brought him through my office. I was delighted that I was given the opportunity to shake his hand, and as they walked out of my office, I was struck with the thought that here together was the past and the present, the old and the young, and they seemed completely at ease with each other.

April 12th was an exceedingly busy day for the President. After entertaining the Chancellor at luncheon, he was to have a press conference in the auditorium of the State Department, and there was a full schedule of meetings with staff members after that. It was close to eight o'clock before he called it a day and headed for the Mansion.

The next day the President and Mrs. Kennedy went to the Pan American Union Building to participate in a session of the Council of the Organization of American States. When they returned they walked around the south grounds of the White House to discuss what could be done to beautify them.

The day the President's first crisis in office broke was a beautiful Monday in April with the temperature in the high 50s. He had returned from a restful weekend at Glen Ora, where he played golf with Jackie, Steve and Jean Smith, and Lem Billings. It was the morning the first state visitors arrived. (Macmillan and Adenauer had been termed "unofficial" visitors.) The President and Mrs. Kennedy gave a state luncheon for Prime Minister and Mrs. Constantino Caramanlis of Greece. Between appointments during the afternoon, the President strolled around the south lawn deep in thought, but he did not voice his concern.

Throughout the day there had been news reports of an anti-Castro revolution in Cuba, and for days the news had hinted that infantry and artillery units were being trained for this revolution by United States experts. Secretary of State Dean Rusk called a news conference that morning to express the sympathy of the American people for those who struck against Castroism in Cuba. But he added, "There is not and will not be any intervention there by United States forces."

The next night, the President and Mrs. Kennedy were giving a reception for members of Congress, and I rushed home to get dressed because they had invited me and Abe also.

For some reason—I did not immediately learn why—there seemed to be a sudden rush of activity at the end of the day, and the President did not leave his office until nearly eight o'clock. The reception was to begin at ten.

Abe and I got to the White House at 9:45 and stopped off at my office to leave our coats. Then we walked out through the French doors and down the portico toward the Mansion. The lights were burning brightly in Mrs. Kennedy's room, and I could imagine she was getting ready to greet the members of Congress. While we walked into the long hall and up the stairs to the floor where the state rooms were located, we could hear the Marine Band in the big foyer tuning up. Quite a few guests had already arrived, the ladies in long dresses and the men in white tie.

The Kennedys were going to establish a precedent tonight. They were not going to stand in one room and let the people file by and shake hands with them. Instead, they were going to move from room to room among the guests and leave the huge East Room free for dancing. The state rooms were packed with people, who seemed to follow the Kennedys wherever they went. Finally, Mrs. Kennedy went upstairs, and the President remained talking to first one Senator, then another. Abe and I tried dancing, but the floor was too crowded and we gave up. When we left the Mansion to return to my office, we noticed the lights were on in the President's office. I thought perhaps he was talking to some of the Congressmen. The door to his office was closed and I sat down at my desk to rest my feet for a moment. When I started to get up, Abe said, "No, let's wait a while. The President might want you."

A member of the staff came out of his office and said the

anti-Castro revolution in Cuba and invasion from the Bay of Pigs had failed. When he came through the door, I saw the President sitting at his desk deep in discussion. Another staff member came out, and this time I could see the President pacing the floor. He saw me at my desk and sent word that I did not need to stay, he would see me in the morning.

Soon after I arrived at the office the next morning one of the aides came in and said he hoped he had not disturbed my desk, but he had used my telephone to make several calls the night before. He said it was close to three o'clock before the meeting in the President's office broke up. I thought, the Prime Minister of Greece is still here and will be in to see the President at ten.

Despite the strain he must have been under, the President looked rested when he came to the office, and he greeted the Prime Minister warmly. They conferred for about an hour in the Cabinet room, and then I looked out my door and saw them walking slowly in the sunny garden.

After the appointments on his schedule had been taken care of that morning, the President and members of his staff discussed the Cuban situation. For three hours he held discussions, first in his office and then in the Cabinet room. There were so many ideas and proposals and reports on the Bay of Pigs incident that he had only fifteen minutes to dress for the dinner he and Mrs. Kennedy were to attend at the Greek Embassy given in their honor by the Prime Minister and Mrs. Caramanlis.

The next day the President was noticeably disturbed by what had happened in Cuba. He was no longer able to conceal his concern, although he had made cordial farewells to the Prime Minister of Greece. The President decided to explain what had happened in Cuba in his address the next day before the American Society of Newspaper Editors. At his news conference the following day he took full responsibility, saying, "There is an old saying that victory has one hundred fathers and defeat is an orphan."

But the President was eager to get the answers to why the disaster had happened and make sure it did not happen again.

He asked his brother Bob to look into what went wrong and to find out how so much bad advice could have been given.

Although I am unaware of the details of his investigation, I do know that the Attorney General spent hundreds of hours talking to the CIA and military people and reading documents. I am sure he asked sharp, tough questions; his experience as a Senate investigator had taught him how to get clear, correct answers.

This is the kind of service the President needed badly, not only about the Bay of Pigs, but on many other problems as well. Bob could move around government agencies and talk to subordinates, ask them questions, and pick their brains. The President was not able to do this. He could not call in a man working in a Pentagon office and ask him what he really thought of a policy of the Secretary of Defense. But Bob could—and did.

That was why the President appointed his brother to the Cabinet in the first place. He needed what his brother could offer him—absolute loyalty, dedication to the same views, a powerful drive to get things accomplished, experience with the very rough side of politics. One of those who most vigorously opposed the idea of Robert Francis Kennedy as Attorney General was Robert Francis Kennedy. He felt his appointment would be an embarrassment and a liability to his brother. That he thought of his brother first is typical of the real Robert Kennedy, but it is a side of his nature not many know.

After he accepted the job, he carried heavy burdens for his brother, in his own job in the Justice Department and in every major crisis that came up: Ole Miss; the Dutch-Indonesian conflict over West New Guinea; Russian missiles in Cuba; Brazil's financial crisis; Cuban prisoner ransom; the steel-price furor; and dozens of other problems, large and small. No one telephoned the President more often than his brother Bob, and it was a rare day when he did not see him at least once. But Bob always came on appointment made through Kenny O'Donnell's office. Neither he nor the President wanted it to appear that he had greater access to the President than any other Cabinet officer.

In the months following the tragedy of the Bay of Pigs, Bob Kennedy was to help raise $3,000,000 in cash and $53,000,000 in food and drugs as ransom price for the release of the prisoners held by the Castro regime.

After the Bay of Pigs disaster, the stream of visitors to the White House continued. The President flew to Andrews Air Force Base to welcome Dr. Sukarno, President of the Republic of Indonesia, and they came by motorcade together to the White House. The President towered over the President of Indonesia as they walked from his office into the Cabinet room, where they were in conference for nearly two hours.

Another afternoon New York's Governor Nelson Rockefeller and His Royal Highness Prince Bernhard of the Netherlands were on the calling list. The President took Governor Rocke-feller for a walk around the south grounds, and, after the Gov-ernor left, he went out walking again with Prince Bernhard.

On the day the President received an honorary degree from George Washington University, he and Mrs. Kennedy also went to MATS Terminal at National Airport and welcomed the Presi-dent of the Tunisian Republic, Habib Bourguiba, and Mrs. Bourguiba for a state visit.

It was a beautiful day, and the red roses Mrs. Kennedy gave Mrs. Bourguiba shone in the sunlight. The President of Tunisia was a short man but he stood erect by the side of President Kennedy. There were no conferences between the two Presi-dents that day, but the Kennedys gave a state dinner that night in honor of the visitors, who stayed in Blair House, across Penn-sylvania Avenue from the White House.

May 5th was the day astronaut Alan Shepard was to be launched into space from Cape Canaveral. I had the television in my office on, and the President paused to glance at it as he rushed into the Cabinet room for a meeting of the National Security Council. When the countdown started and Commander Shepard was off in the rocket, I rushed into the Cabinet room with a little card and handed it to the President. Before I could turn around, he had announced that Shepard was on his way, and my office was quickly filled with the men from the Security Council meeting. The President watched with his arms folded. The Attorney General looked grim-faced and transfixed. Also watching were Paul Nitze, Secretary McNamara, Secretary Rusk, Arthur Schlesinger, Ted Sorensen, General Maxwell Taylor, now the President's military adviser, and others.

As they were watching, Mrs. Kennedy walked by my door, and the President rushed out and called to her, "Commander Shepard has been launched into space. Come in and watch this." She joined the group of spectators gathered around my television set.

All that morning the communications unit had been working to set up a telephone so that the President could speak to Commander Alan Shepard when they brought him aboard the aircraft carrier. That telephone was set up in my office, and later I heard the President speak to him.

"Hello, Commander," he said. "I want to congratulate you very much. We watched you on television, of course, and we are awfully pleased and proud of what you did."

CHAPTER 25

Journeys Abroad

The President and Mrs. Kennedy were going to Canada on May 16th on their first state visit outside of the United States. I was not quite aware of how much work was involved in one of these visits, but we spent weeks preparing for it. One of my duties was to get together the autographed and framed photographs of the President that would be presented as gifts to all the Canadian officials he met. The photograph to be given the Governor-General of Canada was placed in a silver frame with the Presidential seal hand-engraved at the top. Other members of the official Canadian staff would receive autographed pictures in leather frames, and lesser officials would receive photographs mounted on cardboard and placed in white envelopes.

On May 11th, I started putting small stacks of photographs on the President's desk for him to autograph them whenever he had time between his other duties.

Always before a state visit or a trip anywhere by the President, a team consisting of a man from transportation, one or two Secret Service agents, and a man from the press office, went to the area the President would be visiting and inspected every route he would take. They investigated possible hotel accommodations for the staff and members of the press, and accommodations for the President. They returned with their report, which was studied carefully. Then a more explicit plan was drawn. From this plan of operation, another team went to the area to set up communications, arrange hotel accommodations, set up security stations, and make sure that all security precautions had been made to assure the safety of the President. Every parade route, every ceremony was timed down to the last minute so that the President could keep on schedule.

Wherever the President went—abroad, to Palm Beach, or Palm Springs—he was always easily accessible by telephone or telephone-radio through the White House communications system, and so were members of his staff traveling on official White House business. The story is told of one staff member who picked up his telephone and asked the operator to get Pierre Salinger for him. When Pierre came on the line, the staff member asked him please to step into his office. Pierre replied he could hardly do that—he was in a plane then circling to land at Orly Field in Paris.

During the entire campaign the President had stressed the need to start rebuilding the prestige of the United States abroad, and he was eager to participate personally in this effort. He went to Palm Beach for a few days before the trip to Canada, and on his return to Washington spent one full day in intense study preparing for his visit to our northern neighbor. He was going to Canada to receive an honorary degree and at the same time confer with Canadian leaders. The trip had been discussed during Canadian Prime Minister John G. Diefenbaker's visit to the White House in February.

The President wanted to talk to him about Canada joining the Organization of American States as evidence of establishing collective action in the Western Hemisphere. He was also interested in discussing the possibility of the Prime Minister designating an observer to attend the meeting of the Inter-American Economic and Social Council in Uruguay in July. He thought this would bolster the Alliance for Progress program in Latin America.

I shall never forget a sentence the President dictated to me for a speech to the Canadian Parliament to be delivered in the House of Commons chamber on May 17th. "This trip," he said, "is more than a consultation—more than a good-will visit. It is an act of faith—faith in your country, in your leaders—faith in the capacity of two great neighbors to meet their common problems—and faith in the cause of freedom, in which we are so intimately associated."

Shortly after the President and Mrs. Kennedy landed in Ottawa they were escorted to the Government House, where Prime Minister Diefenbaker called upon them. He invited them to a tree-planting ceremony on the grounds of Government House at 6:30 that evening. They were escorted to the spot where they were to plant a tree in commemoration of their visit, and, instead of merely turning over a speck of dirt with the ceremonial shovel, the President did what anyone who knew him could have expected—he lifted a symbolic shovelful of dirt. In doing so he strained a disc in his back. He was in pain during the entire visit, and although there was some mention in the press of the fact that he seemed to have injured himself, he went about the other activities with hardly anyone knowing about it.

The President and Mrs. Kennedy arrived back at the White House on May 18th just before noon. He got out of the helicopter and walked to the Mansion with Mrs. Kennedy, then turned around and came over to the office. He looked tired. He came out to my desk, picked up a copy of *The New Republic,* read a few pages, and said, "Mrs. Lincoln, would you get me a copy of *Jobs and Growth* by Leon Keyserling?" Then he said, "I believe I will go over for lunch." He looked almost exhausted, and, even more surprising to me, acted somewhat cranky. He came back to the office again at 3:30, met with several members of the staff, and then went back to the Mansion for another in a series of late afternoon coffees he was having for members of Congress as a part of his legislative liaison program.

The next few days were busy ones—so busy the President didn't have much time to think about his aching back. Staff members were busy preparing memos for his trip to Europe, where he would confer with French President Charles de Gaulle and later with Soviet Premier Nikita Khrushchev in Vienna, although this encounter had not been publicly announced.

On May 23, 1961 he spent three hours in the Cabinet room with his advisers on foreign affairs, discussing various matters in preparation for the meeting with de Gaulle. Before he left that night, he gave me a list of reminders that showed he had a lot of other matters on his mind: One, get a report on what progress had been made on the Alliance for Progress; two, get an up-to-date report on what we are doing about the Dominican Republic; three, speak to John Bailey about the Democratic Committee; four, ask Kenny O'Donnell to find out what the results of the Kraft poll were in New Jersey; and five, look into the list of guests for the White House dinners.

Another day Princess Grace of Monaco and her husband were guests of President and Mrs. Kennedy at a small luncheon in the White House, and afterward they took a stroll together on the south lawn.

Before the President left for his European visits, he addressed a joint session of Congress, telling what the people would have to do in order to strengthen the country. On May 27th, he spoke at a birthday dinner in his honor at the National Guard Armory sponsored by the Democratic National Committee to raise funds for the party. Then he flew to Hyannis to spend Sunday and his birthday, May 29th, at his home there. On the evening of his birthday, he flew to Boston and attended another big birthday party given by the Democrats in that area. The next evening we were to take off for Paris.

I went home early from the office on the 30th to finish my packing, and Abe and I left the apartment at 5:30 P.M. to go to Andrews Air Force Base. I was sorry Abe was not going along, but that was the only cloud on my horizon. I was excited about my first trip to Europe, and I promised Abe someday we would go together.

The plane flew first to New York to pick up the President, who was there that evening to speak at the Eleanor Roosevelt Cancer Foundation dinner. The President arrived at the plane ahead of Mrs. Kennedy who was flying up from Washington. When he came down the aisle he stopped at my seat and said, "Hello, Mrs. Lincoln, glad to see you."

If I thought the briefings and preparations for his visit to Canada had been intense, I found they were even greater for his meetings with General de Gaulle and Khrushchev.

The President had arranged to have six teams study six different problems to be discussed with the French President. These topics were NATO, political matters, Africa, Latin America, Southeast Asia, and China. Each group was given thirty minutes in which to report their findings to President Kennedy. He also called on several friends who either knew General de Gaulle, or had friends who knew him, to give their opinions on how the meeting would go. In that way he did not rely solely on the briefings prepared by the State Department.

All of us except the President and Mrs. Kennedy, who had bunk beds in their compartment, were going to sleep in our seats during the overnight flight across the Atlantic. I took a sleeping pill and was deep in sleep in almost no time at all. The next morning I awakened relaxed in time for breakfast before our 10:30 A.M. landing at Orly Field.

The airport was jammed with people. It was beautifully decorated with the national colors of France, and when the President and Mrs. Kennedy stepped out on the ramp and started down the steps, the band played "The Star-Spangled Banner." After they had been greeted by President and Mme de Gaulle, the band played "The Marseillaise." It was a beautiful, sunny day and, strange as it may seem, my first impression of Europe as seen from the Paris airport was that it looked just like any American airport we had visited during the campaign.

The President looked proud and happy as he walked by the side of President de Gaulle reviewing the guard of honor during the arrival ceremonies. The French President was about an inch taller than Kennedy, and wore a double-breasted suit while Kennedy wore his usual two-button suit and a pin-striped tie. Mme de Gaulle was half a head shorter than Mrs. Kennedy, and pleasingly plump, but a pretty woman.

I didn't wait to see the entire welcoming ceremonies but raced to find car number twelve, to which I had been assigned for the motorcade into the city. Soon the long line of cars was moving, snaking through the crowds that had gathered on both sides of the street. And they were enthusiastically shouting, "Ken-a-dee, Ken-a-dee," and "Zack-ee, Zack-ee."

President and Mrs. Kennedy were staying at the Quai d'Orsay, the headquarters of the French Foreign Ministry, and so was I. It was a large, impressive building with many arches and surrounded by a high iron fence. At the entrance two officers on beautiful horses guarded the gate. I was told I was going to be in room number nine and that I would have an office on the second floor. As I walked along the halls of this historic old building, I was impressed with the beautiful tapestry and paintings.

My office was one of the main rooms on the first floor, located near the dining room. I was then taken up a flight of stairs and into room nine, a beautiful blue room of immense proportions. On the dresser was a huge bottle of Chanel No. 5 perfume as a gift of welcome.

The Kennedys had the lavish royal suite that had been used in the thirties by the King and Queen of England. The view was glorious. From one window they looked out across the Seine toward the Champs Elysées or back toward the golden dome of Les Invalides.

I stayed in my room long enough to freshen my makeup and then rushed back down to my office. Some of the embassy staff were on their way to lunch and asked me to join them. President Kennedy was holding his first private meeting with General de Gaulle at the Elysée Palace, and so I was free to accept. It was most interesting listening to the foreign service officers tell of their experiences in Paris, but a two-hour lunch was not in my schedule. I excused myself and went back to the office to find the telephone ringing madly. Other members of our staff, who were staying at a hotel down the street, called to ask questions about adjustments in the schedule arranged for President and Mrs. Kennedy.

There was plenty of work for me to do. I spent many hours in that office taking dictation from various of the President's advisers for the meetings with General de Gaulle and notes concerning the meetings themselves. From this dictation I could easily see that things were progressing satisfactorily. The Berlin situation was the first problem the two Presidents discussed, and then they moved to Laos and Latin America. I gave the President a memo reminding him that he also wanted to discuss with General de Gaulle the sending of an observer to the Organization of American States meeting in Uruguay in July.

That afternoon, the President accompanied President de Gaulle to the Tomb of the Unknown Soldier. Despite a pouring rain, the streets were lined with people, and the President repeatedly rose to his feet and waved to them. Both he and General de Gaulle were soaking wet by the time they reached the

Arc de Triomphe. When President Kennedy got back to his suite, he was dripping. He asked me to get a towel and rub his head. I could tell he was in a good mood and thought that his meeting with General de Gaulle was going along smoothly. Also, he was proud of Mrs. Kennedy, who had thoroughly charmed the French people. She had studied at the Sorbonne in 1950, and seemed to have a natural rapport with the Paris citizens.

That first day in Paris was climaxed by a formal state dinner in the Elysée Palace with one hundred and fifty guests, followed by a reception attended by fifteen hundred guests. I had dinner with a friend and then went to my room to rest until time to dress for the ten P.M. reception. I had invited my friend to go with me to the reception, and her husband drove us to the Palace. It was surrounded by a mammoth traffic jam of guests arriving for the reception and swarms of sightseers.

When we finally reached the door, the attendant asked, "Your name, Madam?"

"Mrs. Lincoln."

In a big, resounding voice he announced, "Madame Lincoln."

The President, dressed in white tie and tails and standing next to General de Gaulle in full dress uniform, began to laugh when he heard my introduction, and I was so amused I hardly knew what I said to General de Gaulle when I shook his hand. Mrs. Kennedy, in a sophisticated sheath, looked like a portrait as she stood in line and later moved through the elegance of the Palace.

My friend and I wandered through the crowded room admiring the tapestries and paintings until almost midnight, when her husband was to pick us up. When I got back to the Quai d'Orsay, a maid asked me as I passed through on my way upstairs if I would like something to eat. I told her I would like a cup of coffee, and soon she brought me a pot of coffee, a little toast, and an apple.

The next day was even more impressive, glittering, and busy than the one before. The President and General de Gaulle held three hours and twenty minutes of private meetings, and

I was busy most of the time taking dictation of memoranda from first one staff member and then another for the President. I managed to steal a little time away to visit one of the French dress shops to buy a Paris-designed dress. One of the Secret Service agents took me downtown, and I told the saleswoman, who spoke English fluently, that I wore a size ten.

"Madame, we do not go by sizes," she told me. "You pick out a dress you like and our dressmaker will alter it to fit you."

I found a size fourteen, a lovely shade of lilac, and she promised to have it altered to fit me before we left the next day for Vienna—and she did.

That evening President and Mrs. Kennedy were guests of honor at a dinner given by General and Mme de Gaulle in the beautiful Hall of Mirrors at the Palace of Versailles. The dinner was to be followed by a ballet performance in the Louis XV Theater located in the Palace.

The dinner was set for eight o'clock and because I was going in the President's motorcade, I was dressed and in my car at 7:30. Mrs. Kennedy's hairdresser had combed my hair and I felt rather chic. When the President and Mrs. Kennedy appeared at the door of the Quai d'Orsay, they were a picture of grace and beauty. Mrs. Kennedy had a new upswept hairdo with a tiara ornament on top. The President was dressed in white tie and tails and in his right hand was a hat. When they arrived at the Escalier de la Reine at eight o'clock, they were greeted by General and Mme de Gaulle and escorted to a small room decorated especially for the occasion with brocade and paintings depicting the history of the United States. Here the President and Mrs. Kennedy were asked to sign the Golden Book. From this room, they went to the Salle des Gardes de la Reine, where presentations were to be made. I went directly from the car to this room, and I was enchanted by the beauty of the Palace.

I then went to the Hall of Mirrors to be seated at the table that extended the length of the extremely long hall. I was seated near the end of the table, but I had a clear view of the room and most of the guests. Despite the pomp and splendor of the dinner, to which the cream of French society had been invited, one could not forget the history of this fabulous building—a monument to French genius, so costly to build it almost bankrupted the country and so expensive to maintain it took a millionaire to do what the French government could not afford.

It was a natural setting for a man like General de Gaulle. He has an instinct for the grand gesture, and for President and Mrs. Kennedy he had used Versailles in a way that would have made Louis XIV very proud.

We all had box seats for the ballet following the dinner. After the performance, we were taken on a drive through the garden behind the Palace; lights flooded the foliage and the fountains, whose dancing waters added a soft musical note. When we returned to the Quai d'Orsay, I was too excited to sleep.

While the President was conferring with General de Gaulle, Mrs. Kennedy had become the sensation of Paris. She took a ride over the city, visited a child-care center and the Jeu de Paume Museum, followed everywhere by cheering crowds.

The next day the President opened his address to the press with this remark: "I do not think it altogether inappropriate to introduce myself. I am the man who accompanied Jacqueline Kennedy to Paris, and I have enjoyed it."

On the last day I, too, took time for a quick ride through Paris with my friend, she drove me out to the American PX. I was amazed by the scarcity of traffic lights and the every-man-for-himself policy among drivers.

The two Presidents finished their talks and exchanged gifts. President Kennedy presented autographed photographs I had been carrying around for days for him to sign in spare moments. There were many drafts and redrafts of a joint communiqué released at the termination of their final meeting:

"The conversation which has just taken place allowed the President of France and the President of the United States to know each other and to set forth fully the respective position of the two countries, taking into account the interests and responsibilities incumbent upon each of them. Thus the talks have made an essential contribution to the development of relations between France and the United States. The deep solidarity which binds the two nations together in the tradition of Franco-American friendship remain the basis of these relations."

As soon as the plane was airborne from Orly Field, headed for Vienna, President Kennedy called me into his cabin and dictated a letter to be hand-delivered to General de Gaulle.

"As I leave France may I express again for Mrs. Kennedy and myself our deep thanks to you and Mme de Gaulle for all that you did to make our visit to France fruitful and happy. We shall always remember the warmth of greeting which France offered us, and the high level of understanding which you and I reached in our conversations will be a source of new encouragement and strength to me and I hope to our common efforts for peace and liberty."

It was an hour and fifty minute flight from Orly Field to Schwechat Airport, Vienna, and the President spent the rest of the time discussing his meeting with Khrushchev with the men who were accompanying him.

It was Saturday and raining when we arrived in Vienna. Austria's President, Dr. Adolph Schaerf, greeted President Kennedy at the airport. He wore an overcoat, but Kennedy was coatless as he descended the steps of the airplane, and they stood side by side while the national anthems were played. In the background at the airport were various signs: "Lift the Iron Curtain" and "Give him hell Jack."

President and Mrs. Kennedy went to Hofburg Palace to make a courtesy call on President Schaerf before they went to the United States Embassy, where they would stay during their visit in Vienna. The crowds along the streets to the Palace were just as big as the ones in Paris, but they were different. They were more restrained and serious. When we waved at them, they waved back, but not with the same enthusiasm that was displayed in Paris.

I got out of the car when we arrived at Hofburg Palace and looked at the grounds. They were exquisite and neatly kept. The President's visit there was very brief, and soon we were on our way to the Embassy.

At the Embassy we set up an office in the hall on the second floor. By this time there were quite a few people working on material to be used by the President in his talks with Khrushchev. Among them were Secretary of State Dean Rusk; McGeorge Bundy; the American Ambassador to the Soviet Union, Llewellyn E. Thompson; a former Ambassador to Russia, Charles "Chip" Bohlen; Foy Kohler; and Paul Nitze. The President deeply hoped his talks with Khrushchev would bring about a meeting of minds on the Berlin Wall situation, the test ban, and many other areas of disagreement.

The President had been at the Embassy only about ten minutes when we heard that Khrushchev was approaching the Embassy, and the President went out front to greet him. The short, stocky Soviet leader wore a gray suit with a gray-figured tie and three medals, two above the pocket on the left and one on the right lapel. President Kennedy extended his hand warmly, and as Khrushchev grasped it there was a trace of a smile. The two men smiled again when they posed for pictures on the steps.

As they walked from the door through the hall past the stairs, where the President paused to introduce me and other members of his staff, I noticed that Khrushchev's heavy step seemed to shake the rafters. We had been told he had an unusual ability to project the force of his personality, and I certainly believed it.

They talked for five hours, and when the President came back up the stairs he was fidgety. He said he wanted to rest, but he didn't rest. Then he wanted one of his cigars, and after much searching we were able to find them. He did lie down for a short time. Mrs. Kennedy was getting ready to attend the dinner being given by President Schaerf at Schönbrunn Palace that night for President Kennedy and Chairman Khrushchev.

The hairdresser was busy setting her hair while Provie was getting her clothes in readiness.

Several times I had to go into their living quarters to get some papers the President had been reading for the men who were working in the office. One time I found the President pacing the floor, deep in thought.

"How did it go?" I asked.

"Not too well."

Before I left for my room at the Bristol Hotel to get ready for the dinner, I went in again and gave the President some memos I had been working on. This time he was dressed in formal clothes and had regained his composure. When I left the room he said, "I'll see you at the dinner."

I dressed quickly at the hotel and one of the drivers assigned to the official party called for me to drive me to Schönbrunn Palace.

The Palace was ablaze with lights as we drove past the honor guard and up to the main entrance. I felt I was back in Paris at Versailles. This building, which contained fourteen hundred rooms, had the same great balanced sweep, and the lovely, immaculate gardens were divided into formal sections by wide white pebble walks laid out geometrically. The rooms in this Palace seemed more spacious, the stairways wider than at Versailles, and the room where the dinner was held was twice as large as the Hall of Mirrors.

President Kennedy and Chairman Khrushchev and their wives went first to a smaller room where they talked briefly. At dinner, the guests of honor sat at a long table facing the windows and the other guests were at small tables that seated eight or ten. I was at a table to the left of the long table, and could see the honored guests very plainly. It was easy to see that Mrs. Kennedy, stately and beautiful in a long white gown, had deeply impressed the Soviet Premier; he was all smiles when he talked to her through an interpreter.

The next morning, Sunday, the President and Mrs. Kennedy were up early because they wanted to leave the Embassy at

8:30 to attend mass. After the mass, the President went to the Soviet Embassy for a meeting with Khrushchev at 10:15, and Mrs. Kennedy returned to the American Embassy. The meeting between the President and Premier lasted until one o'clock when they went in to a luncheon given by Khrushchev and attended by the President and his advisers. It lasted until 3:15 P.M.

I waited at the American Embassy for their return. I shall never forget the look on the President's face when he came up the steps. As he rounded the curve for the flight directly in front of my desk, he was deep in thought. Then he looked up and saw me. He shook his head as if to say it had been tough going.

"When do we take off for the airport?" I told him at 4:35.

"Are we ready to leave?"

By that time several members of his official party had caught up with him. The President said, "He wouldn't budge, would he?"

One of the men answered, "He has built up this tremendous image of being immovable, but I think you penetrated, and back of this cold reserve, I have a feeling he respected you and was beginning to think he could not bluff you."

Then they went into one of the rooms to discuss the joint communiqué to be issued just before we left.

At 4:15 I was packed and ready to go. I went down to the car in the motorcade to which I was assigned. Agents were busy checking the cars, transportation men were loading bags for a speedy takeoff for the plane prior to the President's arrival, and the armed Austrian guards were in evidence everywhere.

Soon Ambassador and Mrs. Matthews and President and Mrs. Kennedy appeared at the door, and said their goodbyes. Down the steep grades we went, through the iron gates and onto the streets of Vienna. People had gathered to see the young President, and this time they smiled and waved as though they were happy that he had come.

It was about 7:30 P.M. when we arrived in London. Once

again thousands lined the streets. I noticed the girls were all very beautiful and gay, but still not so gay as the crowds in Paris.

My first job in London was to get the President to autograph some pictures he was presenting to Queen Elizabeth at a dinner at Buckingham Palace the next evening. I knew it was out of the question that night, but I checked the schedule for the next day to see when I could get the pictures to him.

The President and Mrs. Kennedy were staying at her sister's house. The next morning at eleven o'clock he was going to confer with Prime Minister Macmillan at No. 10 Downing Street and return to the Radziwill home around three o'clock. Then the Kennedys were to participate at the christening of the Radziwills' daughter at 4:30. I decided the best time for me to get him to autograph the pictures was between three and four o'clock.

That afternoon at the Radziwill home people were running here and there. Things were in a state of high excitement because everyone was getting ready for the reception that would follow the christening. The house was small but attractive. On the second floor I found Provie getting Mrs. Kennedy's things ready for the reception and also for the dinner that night at Buckingham Palace.

"Where is the President?" I asked Provie. She asked me to follow her. We found him in his bathrobe sitting on the edge of the bed. He looked up and nodded. I told him about the picture. I had a ballpoint pen, but it didn't work. I put my things down and went to look for Provie. We found a pen and ink and back to the President I went.

When I came into the room, he was going through the papers I had brought along; among these papers was the little book in which I was writing my diary.

"Are you planning on writing a book?"

"Not necessarily," I said. "I thought this might be helpful to you when you write your memoirs."

He seemed to like my answer, and then asked me for the

272

picture he was to autograph. He inscribed it, "With esteem and warm regards." While he was autographing the picture I sat and looked at him. He seemed completely alone. I didn't know it then, but I was to see him many, many more times sitting alone with only his thoughts.

I delivered the picture to the Chief of Protocol, Angier Biddle Duke, who saw that it was placed in Buckingham Palace for presentation to the Queen. Then I went to the American Embassy to type up some dictation the President had given me on the plane trip from Vienna. After I finished my typing, McGeorge Bundy, who was in the next room, gave me some dictation on the meetings with Khrushchev and Macmillan, and I stayed there until I had finished, because I was not going to the dinner at Buckingham Palace. I had dinner at the Coq d'Or with a friend who had telephoned me shortly after I checked in at my hotel.

The dinner at Buckingham Palace was a small one. Mrs. Kennedy wore a straight formal dress; the Queen had on a bouffant dress and her crown jewels. Mrs. Kennedy still had her hair in an upswept style, but this time she wore the ornament on the right side. The President and Prince Philip, Duke of Edinburgh, wore dinner jackets. It was a very impressive dinner, I learned, done in all the pomp and splendor of the royal setting.

After the dinner we were leaving for Washington. Soon, too soon, I was on the plane and we were off the ground.

I sat back in my seat, drifting into that half-dazed state that seems to be the body's defense against the boredom of long plane rides, particularly when the strain has passed, anticipation is satisfied, and the course turns homeward. Inside the cabin of *Air Force One,* sounds were muted. One by one the exhausted group, who had spent weeks preparing for the trip and had often worked eighteen hours a day in Paris, Vienna, London, and in between, nodded into sleep. We were going to stop in Goose Bay, Labrador, to refuel, and then wing on to Washington.

Our trip to Europe was over. It seemed days had passed since the President had said a pre-midnight goodbye to congenitally sad-looking Prime Minister Macmillan at the London airport. My mind wandered idly over the highlights of the trip— the motorcade through Paris and the million people cheering the President and Mrs. Kennedy; the plumed Garde Républicaine saluting the President with sabers drawn; the brilliant state dinner and ballet at the Palace of Versailles; luncheon in the Vienna woods with Molotov sitting at the next table looking like a glum frog behind his steel glasses; my introduction to Khrushchev, whose smile was somehow both genuine and terrifying. I smiled when I recalled the President's comment on the gold bathtub in his Quai d'Orsay suite, and Mrs. Kennedy's silver one. "It may seem funny to us, but maybe it's a better use for gold than locking it up in Fort Knox." Visions of the whirlwind six days gradually faded, and I too slipped into sleep.

Then I found the steward gently shaking me. "Mrs. Lincoln, the President would like to see you."

I brushed myself off and, wide awake, moved quickly forward to his cabin. He asked me to remove his papers and documents; he was going to try to get some sleep. As I started to clear the table, I noticed a little slip of paper on the floor. I picked it up and placed it with the other papers.

Back in my seat, going through the papers to be sure those dealing with classified matters were properly secured, I came across this little slip of paper. On it he had written a few lines. The words were curious, and the language almost poetic:

"I know there is a God—and I see a storm coming;
If he has a place for me, I believe that I am ready."

That was all there was. A few words he had no doubt scribbled for one of his speeches. He had often used this little quotation, he had made, but this time the words bothered me. I knew from his remarks that he feared he had failed to make Khrushchev see the dangers of miscalculating America's determination.

"I told him that we enjoyed living well," he said, "that we were not weak, and that twice in recent history very sad and dangerous miscalculations were made about our willingness to fight for our beliefs, but he didn't waver."

I knew he was deeply discouraged about Khrushchev's stubbornness and that he saw waiting for him at the end of this flight not only the growing crisis in civil rights and in domestic reforms, but also Laos, Cuba, the Dominican Republic, Vietnam, and—most serious—Berlin, over which he and the Russian leader had totally disagreed.

"I see a storm coming" was no idle phrase.

We arrived in Washington at 8:30 A.M., glad to be back on American soil. Mrs. Kennedy had remained in London because she and her sister were going to spend a few days vacationing at Athens.

The weather was in the 80s when we arrived. We went directly to the White House to take up where we had left off a few days before. The President was going to report to the nation at seven o'clock that evening on his trip. He and his staff worked on it all day. It was a speech filled with warnings of things to come.

"But I found this meeting with Chairman Khrushchev, as somber as it was, to be immensely useful. I had read his speeches and of his policies. . . . But I bear the responsibility of the Presidency of the United States, and it is my duty to make decisions that no adviser and no ally can make for me. It is my obligation and responsibility to see that these decisions are as informed as possible, that they are based on as much direct, first-hand knowledge as possible. I therefore thought it was of immense importance that I know Mr. Khrushchev, that I gain as much insight and understanding as I could on his present and future policies. At the same time, I wanted to make certain Mr. Khrushchev knew this country and its policies, that he understood our strength and our determination, and that he knew that we desired peace with all nations of every kind."

He then called upon the American people to support his efforts to build our defenses in this everlasting struggle for peace.

Then the President plunged into his regular duties. He gave the graduation address at the United States Naval Academy, after seeing a group of seniors from Tomak High School, Tomak, Wisconsin. That evening he spoke to the National Capital Big Brothers dinner in honor of Edward H. Foley, the man who had been chairman of the Inaugural Committee. Before he left for that dinner, he received word that Mrs. Kennedy and her sister had arrived safely in Athens.

The next day the President was obviously having difficulty with his back. During his trip to Europe, he had often been in pain, but he had never stopped. On Thursday afternoon he left for Palm Beach, where he stayed for several days trying to get rid of the gnawing pain. He returned to Washington on June 12th, three days before Mrs. Kennedy arrived home from Greece.

CHAPTER 26

A Parade of Visitors

The last day of June was Friday, and with it came the realization that Caroline would not be coming over to my office again for several months. The President and his family were leaving for Hyannis Port, and although he would be back on Monday, Mrs. Kennedy and the children would remain there for the summer. I would miss Caroline's daily visits and her constant cheerfulness.

The President loved the Cape, and he seized every possible

chance to go out on the family boat, *The Marlin*. Over the Fourth of July weekend, he spent four days sailing on Lewis Bay. When he returned to Washington on the 5th, he looked tan and happy.

I did not go with him to Hyannis the following weekend, and when he came into the office the next Monday morning he asked me to have a dictaphone placed on his desk in the cabin of *Air Force One* so he could dictate while flying back from Hyannis on Monday mornings. The weekends I did not go with him he used the dictaphone, and the weekends I did travel with him, he dictated the reminders to me either on the plane or at his house on Saturday.

I remember one morning Chairman Walter Heller and Secretary of the Treasury Douglas Dillon were having a lively discussion in my office about the gross national product. Budget Director Dave Bell stood silently listening. The President came out, listened for a while, and said, "I would like memos on this subject from you three to read at the Cape this weekend."

Soon calls came from their offices. "What time is he leaving? What is the deadline for getting this memo into the briefcase?" It was getting down to the wire. Two memos arrived by messenger. The chopper was waiting on the lawn to take the President to the airport. The briefcase was packed and ready to be closed when Chairman Heller himself burst through my door. I could see the tension drain from his face as I placed his memo in the briefcase. That was the way people had to work with the President.

Mrs. Kennedy returned with him one Monday morning because they were going to entertain Mohammed Ayub Khan, the President of Pakistan, and his daughter at a state dinner. They had decided to do something a little different and have the affair outdoors at Mt. Vernon, the home of George Washington. It was a beautiful setting, with the tables arranged on a platform beneath a turquoise tent and gold-colored tablecloths and turquoise seat covers adding to the colorful scene. Many of us at the White House held our breath all day for fear bad weather would spoil all Mrs. Kennedy's plans. Fortunately our fears were needless, and the evening was perfect.

Guests were transported down the Potomac River on boats and had a choice of walking or riding in limousines from the dock up the hill to the lawn and house. After the dinner the guests assembled on another part of the lawn and heard a concert under the stars by the National Symphony Orchestra. It was a memorable evening, and Mrs. Kennedy was lovely in a long white gown with a wide pale green belt. Ayub Khan's daughter was also in white.

After a strenuous week of entertaining and being entertained in return, the President and Mrs. Kennedy were glad to board *Air Force One* that Friday afternoon and head back to the Cape for a few days of rest.

A few weeks later General Douglas MacArthur came to the White House for lunch. He had just returned from an historic visit to the Philippines, and the President wanted to hear about his trip. The tall, erect General was a forceful man in spite of his age, and the President enjoyed talking with him.

During the summer the situation in Berlin had not been improving. There had been high-level meetings nearly every day to discuss the situation, and one day the President decided it was time to tell the people just what was happening. He and members of his staff began working on a speech. He read it and made suggestions. Then it was rewritten, and finally they thought they had it right. The President was to make the television address at ten P.M., and when he went over to the Mansion for dinner and a little rest he took the reading copy of his speech with him.

He usually liked to undress, take a bath, and have his dinner brought to him on a tray in his bedroom. He did so on this evening, and while he was eating and reading he had a new thought. He called me and said, "Will you take this down. I want to add it to the speech I am giving tonight." He began dictating words that I sensed were coming straight from his heart.

"Finally, I would like to say a personal word. When I ran for President of the United States I knew that we faced serious challenges in the Sixties, but I could not realize, nor could any man who does not bear this responsibility, know how heavy and constant would be its burdens.

"The United States relied for its security in the late Forties on the fact that it alone had the atomic bomb and the means of delivery. Even in the early Fifties when the Soviet Union began to develop its own thermonuclear capacity we still had a clear lead in the means of delivery, but in the very recent years the Soviet Union has developed its own nuclear stockpile and has also developed the capacity in planes and missiles to deliver bombs against our country itself. This means that if the United States and the Soviet Union become engaged in a struggle in which these missiles are used then it could mean the destruction of both of our people and our country.

"What makes this so somber is the fact that the Soviet Union is attempting in a most forceful way to assert its power and this brings them into collision with us in those areas, such as Berlin, where we have long-standing commitments. Three times in my lifetime our country and Europe have been involved in wars and on both sides in each case serious misjudgments were made which brought about great devastation. Now, however, any misjudgments on either side about the intentions of the other, more devastation could be rained in several hours than we have seen in all the wars in our history. As President and Commander-in-Chief, therefore, and as Americans you and I together move through serious days. I shall bear the responsibility of the Presidency under our Constitution for the next three and one half years. I am sure you know that I shall do the very best I can for our country and our cause.

"Like you, I have a family which I wish to see grow up in a country at peace and in a world where freedom endures.

"I know that sometimes you get impatient and wish we could make some immediate action that would end our perils, but there is no easy and quick solution. We are opposed by a system which has organized a billion people and which knows that if the United

279

States falters their victory is imminent. Therefore, we must look to long days ahead, which if we are courageous and persevering can bring us what we all desire. I ask therefore in these days for your suggestions and advice. I ask your criticisms when you think we are wrong, but above all, my fellow citizens, I want you to realize that I love this country and shall do my best to protect it. I need your good will and support and above all your prayers."

Then he said, "Will you type this up and give it to me when I come over."

Bedlam always prevailed in my office when they set up the equipment to broadcast one of the President's speeches, and this was no exception. I didn't go home for dinner, and it was a good thing, with the dictation he gave me.

About 9:30 he came over to his office to test the lighting and the height of the chair behind the desk. Then he came out to my office and asked for his dictation. He took it into the Cabinet room, he sat at his place at the table, and read and revised his speech. Several staff members went in to talk to him, and when it was just about time to go before the cameras, he came into my office and asked for a hair brush. He went into my washroom and brushed his hair, then walked into his office and took his place behind his desk. I turned on the television in my office to hear him.

After it was over, he thanked the television men and radio announcer, came through my office, and returned to the Mansion.

As the summer slipped into fall, the Berlin situation and Russia's hostility hung like a cloud over everything. One day the President issued a warning to the Soviets when he replied to charges made by the Soviet government concerning West Berlin.

". . . What must be taken seriously by the whole world, however, is the scarcely veiled threat of aggression against the Allied air routes to and from West Berlin. The United States must serve a solemn warning to the Soviet Union that any interference by the Soviet government or its East German regime with free access to West Berlin would be an aggressive act for the consequences of which the Soviet government would bear full responsibility."

On September 19th, President and Mrs. Kennedy went to MATS Terminal at National Airport to participate in the red-carpet welcome extended to President and Mrs. Manuel Prado of Peru, who arrived for a three-day state visit. Mrs. Kennedy, wearing a pink coat, handed a bouquet of red roses to Mrs. Prado. That night at a state dinner in honor of the Prados, President Kennedy said of the Peruvian leader: "I do not know anyone in the free world, with the possible exception of General de Gaulle, who played a leading role in the Second World War, who was a more active figure in mobilizing the republics of this hemisphere in the fighting against Fascism, and who now bears this great responsibility, almost twenty years later. . . . You have been a leader in the fight against Communism, and you are where you began: a defender of your country's stature, a defender of the cause in which we all believe."

The next Monday the President addressed the United Nations. He was determined that this speech, laying down the position and policy of the United States in the world situation, be properly delivered. He had made marginal notations: "slow," "deep", "quietly," and "very quietly and slow." He had also underlined the words he wanted to emphasize. After the speech, he attended a luncheon at the Waldorf-Astoria with the Latin American delegations to the United Nations, and Mrs. Kennedy returned to the Carlyle Hotel.

There were several messages for him that afternoon, but I did not tell him about them until the next day when we were at Newport. The President and Mrs. Kennedy were staying at Hammersmith Farm, her mother's summer home, and I stayed in the Navy's B.O.Q. (Bachelor Officers' Quarters). I told him that his brother Ted had asked if Peter Princi could be sworn in as Collector of the Port in a ceremony in Newport, and that the secretary of Krishna Menon, India's aggressive, anti-American Minister of Defense, had asked if Menon could see the President.

The President said yes to the first request but to the second, said, "Let's wait on that one."

A couple of days later I told him that he had an appointment with Krishna Menon in Washington the next Wednesday. He gave me a strange look and said, "Did you do that?"

"Yes, I was told by Captain Shepard that you wanted me to. I can call and tell them that I loused it up and that you had not told me to make the appointment."

"No, I will see him."

Naturally, I was worried that I had done something to blow up relations between the United States and India, and I promised myself then and there that never again would I rely on what an aide told me. Only one person could give me instructions—the President.

When we returned to Washington, the parade of state visitors began again. Never in history had a President seen so many foreign leaders in so short a time, but President Kennedy was eager to talk with them and let them know his position and get to know them and their views. Early in the week he welcomed El Ferik Ibrahim Abboud, President of the Supreme Council for the Armed Forces of the Republic of the Sudan, and he and Mrs. Kennedy gave a state dinner in his honor. Toward the end of the week, he met with Andrei Gromyko, Minister of Foreign Affairs of the USSR.

These were followed by President Urbo Kekkonen of Finland and Mrs. Kekkonen, who were honored at a state luncheon, and then the President of the Republic of Liberia, William V. S. Tubman, a jolly, pleasant man who greeted me warmly when the President brought him by my desk.

Early in November former President Harry S. Truman was an overnight guest at the White House, and a dinner was given in his honor. Invitations were sent to people who had been closely associated with President Truman, and during the entertainment after the dinner, he was asked to play the piano, which he did.

Often a late afternoon meeting in the Cabinet room would run long, and many of those attending would be going on to dinner at one of the Embassies. First one, then another would call his wife and ask her to bring his white tie to his office so he could dress there. One day McGeorge Bundy said to Secretary Rusk, "You know, I've been away from home so much lately, my wife is bringing the whole family to my office so that we can have dinner together for a change."

Pierre Salinger often brought his evening clothes to the office in the morning, and it was not uncommon for him to finish his day's work in formal attire. But Pierre liked the simple life, too. Several mornings I've heard him tell Andy Hatcher or Jerry Wiesner about the cook-out in his back yard the night before. "I can really cook a mean steak, with all the trimmings, and you should see me with my chef's hat and apron on," he said modestly.

On November 13th, Governor Luis Muñoz-Marin of Puerto Rico visited Washington, and President and Mrs. Kennedy held a state dinner in his honor.

The next visiting dignitary was the President of the Republic of Senegal, Leopold Sedar Senghor, who looked a lot like Tubman. His visit came on the day the White House announced that Mrs. Kennedy was going to pay a two-week visit to India and Pakistan. She would be the guest of Prime Minister Jawaharlal Nehru in India, and of President Ayub Khan in Pakistan.

The following Monday, the President and Mrs. Kennedy flew to Newport, after a weekend in Hyannis, to welcome Prime Minister Nehru and his daughter, Mrs. Indira Gandhi. I had never seen the Prime Minister, and was surprised to find that he was so tiny when he showed up at the office the next morning. He was short and thin and wore white leggings, black shoes, a short coat, and a white cap resembling the ones worn by army privates. And he never took the cap off. That night the

283

Kennedys gave a state dinner in honor of the Prime Minister. For this he wore black leggings instead of white ones, but he continued to wear the white cap. He was very friendly, and I think the President enjoyed having him as a guest.

Friday night, while getting ready to go to the Mansion, the President asked me for his schedule of the next day. I told him he had a meeting at 9:30 and was then going to speak at the annual Veterans Day ceremony at Arlington Cemetery at eleven.

For some months Abe had been asking me about the invitation General John S. Gleason of the Veterans Administration had sent the President, asking him to speak at the Veterans Day ceremonies. The first time I mentioned it to the President, he said, "What am I doing that day?"

"You don't have any appointments."

"Oh, I might do it."

I brought the subject up again several weeks later while he was signing the mail one evening.

"If you are sure that I don't have anything else on that day, I will do it."

He still didn't have any appointments, and I put it on his schedule. I could hardly wait to get home that night to tell Abe the good news; it meant a lot to him and to the Veterans Administration to have the President speak on this occasion.

When he came into the office on the morning of November 11th and looked at his schedule, he said, "I see that I am going to speak at Arlington Cemetery this morning."

"Yes, Mr. President."

"Who got me into this?" He didn't seem to want to go.

"I did, Mr. President."

He looked out the window; I think he was hoping for rain, but the sun was shining brightly.

"Do I have anything to say?"

I handed him some remarks one of the staff members had written hurriedly.

"All right, let me know when I am supposed to go."

After he left, I watched the ceremony on television and saw him walk past the Tomb of the Unknowns and up to the stage facing the Amphitheatre. He was surprised, I am sure, to see so many people gathered there. He spoke with deep feeling from notes he had scribbled on the back of an envelope, and it seemed to me he put extra heart into it.

When he came back he walked straight to my desk.

"Thank you, Mr. President. It was great."

"It was a fine ceremony. I'm glad I went."

CHAPTER 27

Sunshine and Sadness

President Kennedy scheduled two more visits outside the country during his first year in office. He and Mrs. Kennedy were going to Caracas, Venezuela, and Bogotá, Colombia, on December 16th and 17th. And he was going to Bermuda before Christmas to confer with British Prime Minister Harold Macmillan.

Before leaving for the South American trip, he flew to Palm Beach for a few days of rest and then returned to Washington for an early Christmas Party in the East Room for White House employees. The Mansion staff had been bustling around for days getting ready for the holiday season and the party. A huge tree, as tall as the ceiling, had been placed in the center of the Blue Room. It was called the "Nutcracker Suite" Christmas tree because the decorations were little toys and objects reminiscent of the *Nutcracker Suite.*

It was a busy afternoon for me, but just before the party ended I ran over to the Mansion to chat with the other latecomers. I was very happy with the Christmas gift from the

Kennedys: a picture of the White House taken from the fence, showing the south lawn and the ducks swimming in the pool around the fountain.

The next morning, December 15th, we were airborne, en route to South America. Our first stop was San Juan, Puerto Rico. The plane touched down about four o'clock in the afternoon. It had been raining and the air was humid. Governor Luis Muñoz-Marin and Mrs. Muñoz-Marin were there to greet President and Mrs. Kennedy, and then the motorcade snaked its way through the crowds of cheering people who had come out to extend an enthusiastic greeting.

Most of the staff and I were staying at the magnificent San Juan Intercontinental Hotel, and my windows overlooked the beautiful fifteen-hundred-foot private ocean beach and the brilliant blue water beyond. I didn't have long to take in the beauty, however. I quickly unpacked my things—supply boxes filled with paper, pencils, ink, typewriter ribbons, carbon paper, and other supplies—and got together the things I wanted to take to the President, who was staying at the Governor's Mansion.

Once there, I had to wait some time before I was able to see the President. He greeted me with "It is beautiful here, isn't it?"—then began dictating. He sent a message to Adlai Stevenson at the United Nations, praising his skill and leadership on the Chinese representation issue that had just been voted upon. He also dictated a letter to Dean Warner Lawson of Howard University, Washington, D.C., thanking him and the Howard University Choir for the performance they had given at the Christmas party for White House employees.

We left early the next morning for Caracas, Venezuela. We had been told this was one place where we might have trouble. Former Vice President Richard M. Nixon's visit there a few years earlier had been a near fiasco. However, the efficient Secret Service had worked very hard for weeks to insure proper law enforcement for the President's visit.

We landed at Maiquetia Airport, and while President and

Mrs. Kennedy were being welcomed by President and Mrs. Romulo Betancourt, I went to the motorcade and got into the car assigned to me. Dr. George Burkley, the White House physician who accompanied the President in all his travels, soon joined me. Evidently the driver, who was Venezuelan, got his signals crossed. Before we knew what was happening, we were being driven down the route of the motorcade ahead of the President.

The people lining the streets didn't know whether to wave or not—they weren't sure who we were. We noticed the crowd was being held back by soldiers armed with guns, but the people appeared to be very friendly. We were taken directly to the Hotel Tamanaco, where we were staying. The President and Mrs. Kennedy went first to an Inter-American Development Loan Rural Housing project, where the President cut a white and gold cord to inaugurate the Alliance for Progress project and therewith changed the name of the project from El Frio to Aldea Alianza.

The President and Mrs. Kennedy were staying at Los Nuñez, President Betancourt's house. Their schedule was completely filled for most of the afternoon, and I took the opportunity to sit on the patio at my hotel, built on a hill overlooking the city in the valley below, and admire the view.

Toward evening I went out to Los Nuñez to make sure the President had everything he needed for his talks with the Venezuelan President.

We left Caracas the next morning for Bogotá, where once again the President and Mrs. Kennedy left the motorcade and went to dedicate housing and school projects before going to the San Carlos Palace, the home of President and Mrs. Alberto Lleras Camargo.

This city was something to behold. The streets were even narrower than those in Caracas or even in Philadelphia, and sprinkled among the older architecture were some modern buildings.

Each day we were away from Washington I received a pouch

of mail from the White House with letters and telegrams to be brought to the attention of the President. Often the mail arrived ahead of us. Sometimes we also found telephone messages waiting for us.

I had a batch of letters and telephone messages for the President, and I decided to go out to the Palace in the hope I might have a few minutes with him. That began one of the most interesting trips I have ever taken. We wound around in among the alleys and streets, and it seemed we could not drive a block without being stopped by the police. "You can't go through here," they said. But after seeing my credentials, they waved me through. After several experiences of the sort, we finally pulled up to an old, old building fenced in by a high black steel fence, and from there the Secret Service waved me through. The place was a maze of corridors, halls, and little alcoves. I was thinking that someone could easily get lost in there and not be found for years, when I heard laughter coming from the top of a marble staircase.

I climbed the staircase and saw signs of life, especially around a bar that had been set up. I asked someone where the President was and was told he was expected shortly, and I sat down in one of the empty rooms. It did not remain empty for long. In came President Kennedy and the President of Colombia with members of their staffs to start a conference.

President Kennedy saw me and motioned for me to stay where I was. They began discussing problems between the two countries. I took some notes because I did not know what was expected of me. When they had finished—after what seemed like hours—one of the members of President Kennedy's staff asked me to take some dictation and type it up right away. Finding that no typewriter was available, he decided to wait until he got back to the hotel to dictate to his own secretary.

I spent the rest of the afternoon shopping for Christmas presents, and that night, at midnight, we left for Washington. President and Mrs. Kennedy boarded the plane in their evening clothes after the state dinner given in their honor at the San Carlos Palace.

Mrs. Kennedy was not planning to return to Washington with us, and so we landed in Palm Beach. The President and Mrs. Kennedy and the children were going to spend Christmas in a house they had leased from Michael Paul. The President had picked up a slight cold during the trip, and he spent the day in the sun beside the swimming pool.

The next morning, the President's father and John rode out with him to the airport. I noticed that Ambassador Kennedy's face seemed flushed and he was a little unsure of his steps when he carried John in his arms. He and John were standing in the sunlight smiling when the plane doors closed and the engines started.

Only a few hours after we arrived in Washington, there was a telephone call from the Ambassador's house in Palm Beach saying that after seeing the President off, the Ambassador had gone to the golf course, where he had been taken ill. He was then in bed in his house. A little later another call came—this one directly to the President—telling him his father had been taken to St. Mary's Hospital and that his condition was serious. Soon the President was on his way to the airport to return to Palm Beach.

I didn't go on back to Florida, because I knew that I had to get things in order if we were going to make the scheduled trip to Bermuda on the 21st for the President's meeting with Prime Minister Macmillan. Several times the next day, I talked with the President on the telephone. He said his father had suffered a stroke and was in serious condition. He added that the doctors had assured him there was nothing he could do, and he was going to make the trip to Bermuda as planned.

We were all saddened by his father's illness, not only because it grieved the President but also because we had grown fond of the Ambassador.

It was a beautiful day in Bermuda when we landed. I was assigned to car number four in the motorcade, and we made our way up the hill to Government House, where the Prime Minister and President Kennedy were to stay. Major General Sir Julian Gascoigne, the Governor of Bermuda, was host. After I had unpacked my briefcase in an office assigned to me in Government House, I went down to the Bermudiana Hotel, where I was to stay. It seemed that hotels were getting more plush at each stop. This time my room overlooked the harbor, and the sun was just setting over the deep azure water.

The meetings were to begin at 9:45 the next morning, and about 9:30 the President came into my office. I could see that he looked tired. I didn't say anything about it, but learned later that they didn't have heat in the bedroom in which he slept, and, since it was a little colder than usual, he had a hard time getting to sleep.

During one of the breaks in the meetings Pierre Salinger came in with some cashmere sweaters he had bought. The President, just like any other tourist, wanted some sweaters for Mrs. Kennedy and Caroline and asked me to go down and get some like those Pierre had. "And," he added, "you might get one for me in a red shade." When I got back, he was so pleased with the red sweater he asked me to go back and get another one.

The Governor of Bermuda was host at a buffet luncheon. Before the final conference, they went out on the lawn for a tree-planting ceremony, but this time the President did not wield a spade as he had in Canada. Then he took off for the airport.

As soon as we were airborne, the President dictated a wire to the Governor.

"I want to express my great appreciation to you and your wife for your kindness to us during the past two days. You made us feel very much at home and your hospitality was most helpful in making our meeting such a success. I send you both my very best wishes for a very Merry Christmas."

Back in Palm Beach, the President autographed bound copies of his Inaugural address as gifts for close friends and members of his staff. When he autographed mine he said, "Will you see that Provie gets a raise in salary? And don't tell her about it. I want to tell her myself just before Christmas." He wanted to make it a happy holiday for others, but his own Christmas was saddened by the illness of his father, who remained on the serious list.

I flew back to Washington to spend Christmas with my family, and then went back to Palm Beach because the President was going to remain there until after the New Year.

PART IV

CHAPTER 28

The Kennedy Touch

PRESIDENT and Mrs. Kennedy had not been in the White House twenty-four hours before they were discussing changes they would like to make. They were concerned not only with their own comfort and convenience and acute sense of beauty; they also wanted to make the White House a national shrine of historical interest to all Americans.

At the end of their first year in the Executive Mansion, it bore the Kennedy touch inside and out. The interest they had created in the White House was reflected in the number of tourists who lined up daily for a tour of the state rooms.

Mrs. Kennedy felt the key to what the White House should represent to the nation was the historical nature of the Mansion, which had come a long way since Abigail Adams, the first President's wife to live there, had complained about its barn-like, unfurnished vastness.

Mrs. Kennedy wanted to remove everything that was second-rate and replace it with genuine antiques that either had belonged to the Presidents or were of their periods.

"Everything that is here," she said, "should have a reason for being here." And she began her expeditions into the dark cellar storerooms of the White House, coming up with all sorts of forgotten treasures, including "some old junk" that turned out to be President Monroe's gold and silver flatware, made to his order in France in 1817.

It was immediately obvious to Mrs. Kennedy that it would not be possible for her to do the restoration alone. A White House Historical Association was formed to help locate antique furniture of historic value and raise donations to purchase the pieces, if necessary. She persuaded Congress to pass a law making donations to the White House collection tax-deductible, and soon lovely things began to arrive.

The Secretary of the Treasury and Mrs. C. Douglas Dillon gave a whole room full of American Empire furniture, including a sofa that once belonged to Dolly Madison. A rare portrait of Benjamin Franklin worth $165,000 was given by Walter Annenberg, a Philadelphia publisher, and was hung over the mantle in the Green Room. Eighteenth Century French furniture valued at $100,000 was donated by Mr. and Mrs. John Loeb of New York. People all over the country sent things large and small, authentic and phony, valuable and worthless. Each gift was carefully screened by experts, and accepted or returned. Mrs. John N. Pearce was employed as full-time curator for the White House. Gradually the Presidential Mansion took on a new, more historic look.

The Green Room, to the rear of the first floor of the Mansion, was the first one completely refurnished by Mrs. Kennedy's White House Historical Association. It soon became a fashionable, Federal parlor in which President Jefferson or John Adams would have been right at home. Abigail Adams, I am sure, would have loved Mrs. Kennedy's choice of the "Adams style" Axminster carpet, the moss-green watered silk walls with matching draperies, the Empire mantelpiece, and the early American Sheraton, Chippendale, and Hepplewhite furnishings.

Her own favorite, I was told, was the Red Room, which she furnished as an Empire parlor of the period around 1820. Situated on the opposite side of the south portico from the Green Room, this room has a bright fuchsia silk wall covering with a gold-scroll border, and the furnishings used the same color and design. In this room the furniture donated by the Dillons was placed. The Blue Room reflected the President

Monroe period, and to the Diplomatic Reception Room, on the ground floor beneath the Blue Room, which had been partly restored by the Eisenhowers, Mrs. Kennedy added a lovely, bright panoramic wallpaper made in Alsace in 1830.

Another room that greatly benefited from Mrs. Kennedy's touch was the state dining room, which was decorated in white and gold instead of the previous somber green.

Although the restoration was Mrs. Kennedy's project, the President himself was keenly interested in every step. Many times when Mrs. Kennedy or Mrs. Pearce, the curator, came across something they thought would interest the President, they would rush it over to my office, or call and tell me about it, and ask me to check with the President to see what he thought.

The President and Mrs. Kennedy spent many, many hours at night going over the various plans and acquisitions, and he was particularly pleased with her television presentation of a Tour of the White House, which was telecast on February 14, 1962. The next morning he was as anxious to learn what everyone thought of her presentation as he was to get the responses to his own television appearances. The actual filming of the tour took place on January 15th, and the President made a final statement in the Treaty Room, which was restored as a conference room with furnishings of the Ulysses S. Grant period and with framed treaties on the walls.

One day the President received a letter from columnist David Lawrence concerning a typewriter that had been in the White House during President Wilson's administration—the typewriter on which President Wilson had typed his Fourteen Points and other important statements. It had recently been at the American Red Cross, but because of its historical significance, Mr. Lawrence thought it would be a valuable asset to the collection of articles in the White House, and he presented it in a ceremony in the President's office. In accepting it, the President drew laughs when he commented, "My wife has collected everything and this is my—this is the only thing I have produced. . . ."

He was proud of it, and after the donors left, I put it in my office until he could decide where he wanted to keep it. One day he said, "Why don't we put it in the Fish Room?" And there it remained—displayed for his visitors to see.

The President had his own project for beautification of the White House: the garden just outside his office in the West Wing. Morning after morning as he walked along the portico on his way from the Mansion to his office, he passed the barren plot of ground commonly called the Rose Garden. Only a few rose trees and some rows of hedge were planted there.

One morning he came into my office and wanted to know if the gardeners could consider planting flowers along the walkway. He asked me to have one of the gardeners come over to talk to him about it, and then he learned there was no money available for the type of garden in which he was interested. Mrs. Paul Mellon of Upperville, Virginia, a good friend of the Kennedys, learned of the President's dream for a flower garden and offered to supply trees, shrubs, and flowers necessary to make this garden a beautiful one. The blueprints were drawn and accepted.

Before the actual planting was begun, the President designed the new steps that led from the top of the walk down to the garden. The top step was built as a platform from which he could talk to groups gathered at the west end of the garden. There was also a place to set up microphones on the top step.

It was in the early spring of 1962 that the garden renovation began. First the area was cleared of all vegetation. Then four full-grown magnolia trees were brought in to be planted in the corners of the rectangular garden. After they were planted, it seemed as if they had always been there. The President watched each development with interest.

"What I want is blooming flowers on the three sides, and especially along the portico where I receive groups," he said.

"And I would like to look at those flowers as I walk from the Mansion to my office. And I would like them changed from season to season."

Sometimes Mrs. Mellon was in the garden supervising the planting. When the President saw her, he would hurry out to talk with her. He was eager for the blossoms to appear, although he had no preferences among flowers. He liked them all. He asked only that as soon as one kind of flower faded away, another kind be planted in its place so there would always be an array of color and profusion of blooms.

After the flowers had been put in the border of the new geometric pattern of Speaker Sam rose bushes, rows of grass were planted in the center of the rectangle. At the east end, on a patio of Pennsylvania flagstone, was an arrangement of chairs. Sometimes the President would take his callers there for their conferences.

At first it took the grass a little while to take hold, and the President became impatient. It was not uncommon for him to come into my office in the mornings and say, "Mrs. Lincoln, do you see that brown spot out there on the lawn? Will you tell them to have that fixed?" Sometimes when there was to be a meeting in the garden, the gardeners would spray the grass with a green substance to make sure that none of the brown spots showed.

The President loved this garden so much that he would take guests, even heads of state, for walks out on the grass. I would watch him coming around the corner from the Mansion, enjoying every minute of the walk as he surveyed his garden.

Several times he called from his office, "Mrs. Lincoln, get Macaroni out of my garden." I would rush out and chase Caroline's pony out of his garden. It was not long before Macaroni was forbidden the freedom of the White House lawn.

Oftentimes when Caroline and John were playing on the lawn, he would walk out on the portico and into the garden and clap his hands twice. Caroline, more fleet of foot, would arrive first, running as fast as she could, excited and out of breath. Little John would follow, in the care of Miss Shaw.

Right after the Cuban missile crisis, the President dictated a letter to Mrs. Mellon to let her know how much he appreciated the garden she had made possible. "I need not tell you that your garden has been our brightest spot in the somber surroundings of the last few days," he said.

The Kennedy touch soon became evident in yet another area: the entertaining in the White House. The most celebrated social event of the Kennedy Administration was the dinner President and Mrs. Kennedy gave to honor the forty-nine Nobel Prize winners. Many of America's greatest intellectuals gathered for an event that culminated in the first public reading of an unpublished work by the late Ernest Hemingway. The President was very grateful to Fredric March for the reading, and dictated a letter to him the next morning. He also had copies of pictures taken at the dinner sent to each winner with a letter he signed personally.

In addition to the Nobel winners, one hundred and twenty-four other scientists, writers, editors, and educators were invited. The guest list included seven Pulitzer Prize-winning writers, including the President himself, and two politically controversial scientists, Dr. Linus C. Pauling and Dr. J. Robert Oppenheimer. The President described the dinner to his guests as "probably the greatest concentration of talent and genius in this house, except for those times when Jefferson ate alone."

Being a scholar himself, he sincerely appreciated the companionship and the challenge of such outstanding minds. The event proved so enjoyable to all the notables that the dinner lasted longer than had been planned.

The Kennedys introduced theater in the royal tradition to the White House. Early in October of their second year in residence there, scenes from *Macbeth* and four other Shakespearean plays were presented on a specially built stage in the East Room following a state dinner in honor of President Ibrahim Abboud of the Sudan.

A month later Pablo Casals, who had last appeared at the White House for Theodore Roosevelt and had sworn never to perform in any country that recognized Spain's Franco, gave a much-celebrated concert in the East Room following a state dinner. In inviting the famed cellist to appear, the President had written, "We feel that your performance as one of the world's greatest artists would lend distinction to the entertainment of our invited guests."

Another evening, following a state dinner for the Grand Duchess Charlotte of Luxembourg, the poetry and music of Elizabethan England echoed from a three-tiered platform with a red velvet backdrop. In time the stage, which could be dismantled and stored when not in use, was used for presenting ballerinas and bassos, sopranos and symphonies.

The Kennedys also had a platform erected on the south lawn, where various groups performed. One chilly spring day in 1962, the Greater Boston Youth Symphony Orchestra, played there for an audience of children. President and Mrs. Kennedy went out to meet the children and to listen to some of the concert. The President returned to his office, before the concert was over, but he told them he was going to leave his office door open so that he could hear the music. Although it became quite cold in both his office and mine, he would not let me close the door as long as the orchestra played.

CHAPTER 29

Crisis in Steel

On the afternoon of April 10, 1962, it was quiet in the west wing of the White House. The President and Mrs. Kennedy were giving their annual reception for members of Congress at 9:30 that night, and I wanted to go home early to dress for the event. I had attended the Congressional reception they had given the year before, and I recalled it was the day of the crisis over the attempted invasion at the Bay of Pigs. Thank heaven we don't have anything like that in the making today, I thought.

There was only one more appointment on the President's schedule for the afternoon, a visit by Roger Blough, chairman of the board of the United States Steel Corporation. The President wanted to know if there had been any indication what Mr. Blough wanted to discuss, but no one seemed to know. On March 31st a new wage contract had been settled between the industry and the unions, and the President had issued a statement saying it was a forward-looking and responsible agreement. The Administration had urged the United Steelworkers of America to soften its wage demands in those negotiations, and the formal settlement had been signed before Mr. Blough asked for an appointment to see the President.

With the thought that Mr. Blough's call might have something to do with union-management relations, the President had asked Secretary of Labor Arthur Goldberg to stand by.

Mr. Blough arrived about twenty minutes before six and I asked him to wait in the Cabinet room. The President was in his office, and I told him Mr. Blough was waiting. About ten minutes later the President came out to my office, walked into the Cabinet room, greeted Mr. Blough, and took him into his office. They were discussing little pleasantries as they passed my desk. Mr. Blough's dark-rimmed glasses made him look like a serious-minded man who had done a lot of reading in his day, and he didn't seem very friendly. He clutched a black briefcase in his arm. They entered the President's office and the President closed the door. I was thinking that he would probably be in there for only ten minutes when I got a sharp buzz. When I stepped into the office, the President said sternly, "Get Arthur Goldberg on the line."

In a few seconds I rushed to the door, stuck my head in, and said, "He's on, Mr. President."

"Can you come over here right now?" the President asked.

302

"I am leaving right now."

It took the Secretary about ten minutes to get to the office. The three men were in the President's office for at least thirty minutes, and then the President and Mr. Blough came into my office. I could tell the President was not satisfied with the conference, and, although he bade him goodbye in a fairly pleasant tone, as soon as Mr. Blough left, he hurried back into his office to confer again with Secretary Goldberg.

After Mr. Goldberg left, the President asked McGeorge Bundy, Walter Heller, Ted Sorensen, and James Tobin to come to his office. The conference lasted until seven o'clock. When it broke up I learned that Mr. Blough had handed the President a copy of a statement that had been given to the press for release at seven o'clock in which United States Steel announced a six-dollar-per-ton price increase.

The President came out to my office, and he was furious. He walked up and down the length of the office. "This is uncalled-for," he said. "It's a doublecross on the part of U.S. Steel." He paced back and forth a little longer, then seemed to collect himself. "I'll see you in the morning. I'm going over to the pool before I eat supper."

It was eight o'clock when I got home. Abe was already dressed in his dinner jacket. I dressed hurriedly, and we were on our way back to the White House and the Congressional reception.

The President and Mrs. Kennedy came down the stairs, were followed by the Congressional leaders and their wives. Mrs. Kennedy wore a beautiful white dress. The reception was even more informal than the one the year before, and the President gave no indication he was thinking of the bombshell that hit his office only a few hours earlier. He was smiling and shaking hands with everyone he met.

He was up early the next morning, however, and held a meeting to discuss the situation. After his conference with Roger Blough and Arthur Goldberg, he had called Secretary of the Treasury Douglas Dillon and Senator Estes Kefauver, chairman of the Senate Antitrust subcommittee, and told them what had happened. Senator Kefauver had immediately issued a statement saying, "From the information now available, the price increase proposed by U.S. Steel is shocking and irresponsible." He had ordered the staff of the subcommittee to begin an immediate inquiry into the matter. The wheels were rolling.

While the President was consulting the various government personnel involved, he had to carry on with his official duties. At twelve noon, he went with Mrs. Kennedy to the MATS Terminal to welcome the Shah of Iran and Empress Farah, who were arriving on a state visit. He didn't get back to his office until after one o'clock. He stayed about an hour making more calls on the steel matter and then went to the pool for a quick swim on his way to the Mansion for lunch.

That afternoon at 3:30 he held a press conference, and began by saying, "Some time ago I asked each American to consider what he would do for his country. . . . In the last twenty-four hours we had their answer." This was the clue to the line he was to take in the steel price increase: an appeal to public interest and patriotism. He went on:

"Simultaneous and identical actions of United States Steel and other leading steel corporations, increasing steel prices by some six dollars a ton, constitute a wholly unjustifiable and irresponsible defiance of the public interest. In this serious hour in our nation's history, when we are confronted with grave crises in Berlin and Southeast Asia, when we are devoting our energies to economic recovery and stability, when we are asking Reservists to leave their homes and families for months on end and servicemen to risk their lives—and four were killed in the last two days in Vietnam—and asking union members to hold down their wage requests; at a time when restraint and sacrifice are being asked of every citizen, the American people will find it hard, as I do, to accept a situation in which a tiny handful of steel executives whose pursuit of private power and profit exceeds their sense of public responsibility can show such utter contempt for the interests of one hundred eighty-five million Americans. . . ."

304

When the President returned to his office, I gave him a note reading: "Congressman Albert [of Oklahoma, the Democratic Whip in the House of Representatives] called; said that Representative Celler [of New York, chairman of the House Judiciary Committee] has issued a statement that his staff will begin an immediate investigation of the steel-price raise."

More members of the House and Senate began calling to tell the President they were in accord with his statements issued to the press.

That night he and Mrs. Kennedy gave a state dinner honoring the Shah of Iran and the Empress Farah. The President's sense of humor showed in his remarks following the dinner. In a toast that complimented both Mrs. Kennedy and the Empress, he said, "Ladies and Gentlemen: I know that you all join with me in welcoming our distinguished guests to the United States. His Highness and I have a 'burden' that we carry in common—we both paid state visits to Paris last year, and from all accounts we might both as well have stayed at home."

Negotiations between Secretary of Labor Goldberg and representatives of United States Steel continued during April 11th and 12th. Then on the morning of April 13th, over the press wire came the story that Joseph L. Block, chairman of Inland Steel Company, had said his company would not raise its steel price. I took the bulletin in to the President. He smiled as he read it and showed it to the Attorney General, who was in his office at the time. The press had asked to make photographs of me handing the bulletin to the President, and he agreed.

At two o'clock he left for lunch in the Mansion. He had not been gone fifteen minutes when Edgar Kaiser called him. I asked him to hold a minute while I checked with the President, and he told me to switch the call to him. Then he switched Mr. Kaiser back to my telephone, and the latter dictated the following statement:

"Edgar F. Kaiser, chairman of the board, Kaiser Steel Corporation, today announced that his company will not raise its mill prices at this time. The company has recently completed a $225,000,000 expansion program doubling its capacity to serve the country and the growing West. As a result the company has incurred heavy fixed charges which may require some mill price adjustments in the future, but not at this time."

About 3:30 that afternoon, Bethlehem Steel rescinded its prices, and at 5:28 P.M. we received a press bulletin saying United States Steel had pulled back the price increase that began the three-day crisis.

During the entire time this issue was under consideration, the President acted with the same cool, calm determination he always showed in time of stress. He got all the facts, weighed every angle, and called on the people who had influence in the situation. He demonstrated his ability to turn from one subject to another and then come back to the first problem with renewed effort. Between appointments, he would sit at his desk writing little notes, or ask me to call someone to get a quick answer on a point that was causing him some concern.

His actions were never jerky. He never banged the desk, waved his arms, or raised his voice in a shrill shout. Instead, he would sit crouched at his desk, push his hair to one side, stand up, turn around and stare out the window, sit down, pick up the telephone and place a call, then hang up the receiver to wait for the operator to contact the party. The operator would call me when the party was on the line, and I would tell the President his call was ready. Sometimes he was so anxious to talk to the party he still had his hand on the receiver waiting for me to give him the word.

The President had flown to Norfolk, Virginia, to go aboard the USS Northampton when the news of United States Steel's capitulation arrived, but he was confident it was coming before he left the White House at 2:30. He held no hard feelings toward Mr. Blough for the trouble his action had caused. Several days later Mr. Blough was in Washington and asked to see the President. He said to tell him to stop by around six o'clock.

When they came into my office following their conversation in the President's office, they were on exceedingly good terms.

The President spent the Easter holidays in Palm Beach with Mrs. Kennedy, Caroline, and John-John, and I flew down with them. Every morning at 10:15, I would meet with the President on the patio of the Michael Paul home, where they stayed, and go over the messages and mail that had been flown down from the White House.

We returned to Washington on Friday just in time to welcome Prime Minister Harold Macmillan, and on that day the President held a meeting in his office to discuss his brother Teddy's campaign for the Senate in Massachusetts. The decision that Teddy would seek the seat formerly held by the President had already been made; this meeting was merely to give him advice on the organization of his campaign. President Kennedy did not feel that those of his staff members who were from Massachusetts should take any part in his campaign.

Political rumor had it that the President had hoped Teddy would not run because of the potential embarrassment to his program, and that his father had demanded the President's support, saying, in effect, "You've had your turn, now it's time for him [Ted] to have his."

From my observation of the relationship between the three brothers, and from conversations I heard in the White House, I knew that there was nothing to that. First, the President knew that if he did a good job, people would support him whether there were three or thirty-three Kennedys in government; and that if he did a bad job, it wouldn't help if he sent every Kennedy in the country packing back to Ireland.

Also, the President knew the people of Massachusetts would decide who they wanted to represent them in the Senate, and the more outside pressure exerted against Teddy, the more likely he would be to get support in the state, where it counted.

As for the President knuckling under to his father and reluc-

307

tantly supporting his brother, that also was not true. He was always close to Teddy and his younger brother adored him. During the terrible period when the back operations almost cost the President his life, Teddy did everything he could to cheer him up. When he left the hospital after the operation, two people went with him to Palm Beach, his wife and Teddy. When he went sailing in the Mediterranean after his disappointment at losing the Vice Presidential nomination in 1956, his sailing companion was Teddy. Never was there between the President and Teddy the kind of aggressive rivalry that had existed between the President and his brother Joe. There was no question at any time of the President being upset by his brother's plans.

The next day, in the corner of my office, General McHugh and President Kennedy were going over plans for a new 707 Boeing *Air Force One*. The President drew a little picture, and said to General McHugh, "Now, this is the way I want it."

A few days later, General McHugh came over with a new set of plans. The President selected one. "But I don't want orange paint on it," he said.

"But, sir," protested General McHugh, "all planes have some orange paint. It's the color most easily seen from other planes."

"I know all that," President Kennedy said, "but I think it spoils the looks of the plane. I am confident that the personnel charged with the responsibility of keeping the air lanes free will do their jobs."

"Yes, sir," said General McHugh.

The President spent most of his weekends during the spring of 1962 at Glen Ora, the country estate near Middleburg, Virginia, and he always came back refreshed and eager to get to work. However, there were some days he was edgy, and since he shared his problems only with those who could help solve them, I did not always learn the cause of his edgy disposition.

One such day the Russian Ambassador Dobrynin brought a Russian astronaut to the White House to meet the President, who had Colonel John Glenn there to represent our efforts and achievements in space. After spending a few minutes with these men, the President went to the White House to preside at a luncheon in honor of Dr. Alfons Gorbach, Chancellor of Austria. They were to meet again in the afternoon, but before that the President was scheduled to meet in the Rose Garden with a group from Miss Porter's School, which Mrs. Kennedy had attended. When he went out to greet them, however, they were not there. When he returned from the Mansion after lunch, he was not in a very good humor. Later in the day he even bawled out a member of his staff and a newspaper reporter with whom he was generally very friendly.

I didn't ask him what was wrong, but shortly afterwards he called me into his office. He dictated two letters to people he had reprimanded, apologizing for his action. As I gathered up my papers to leave the room, he said, "Would you type those letters before you leave?"

I typed the letters and brought them in for him to sign. Then he went to the Mansion. I was closing up my desk and locking the files when the telephone rang. It was the President.

"Mrs. Lincoln, would you see that those letters go out to-night?"

I assured him I would, marveling that he could be so tough and so sensitive about others at the same time.

All spring the President had greeted one foreign visitor after another, and now he was going to make a visit himself. The envelope of reading material I sent him at night included brief-ing papers on Mexico, for at the end of the month he was going to Mexico City.

Takeoff time was 9:30 A.M. on Friday from the south lawn of the White House. I arrived there at my usual time of eight o'clock, checked my briefcase to make sure I had everything I would need, and hurriedly looked at the morning mail to see if there was anything else I should put into my bag. People who were going with us by helicopter to the airport were beginning to congregate in my office. Soon we could see the choppers in the distance rapidly moving toward the south lawn. I never liked to be on the lawn while they were landing because the downblast from the propellers almost sent people sailing through the air. I was always amused to watch men standing nearby when the helicopter landed—hanging onto their hats with both hands.

I usually rode out on the helicopter with the President, and this time when we landed at the airport I tried to keep close behind him to make sure I wasn't left standing on the ground.

It didn't take long for us to reach this city of warm colors and friendly people. Ambassador and Mrs. Thomas Mann were there to greet the President and Mrs. Kennedy as they came out of the plane. President Lopez Mateos and President Kennedy exchanged greetings, and we started out on a motorcade, which was not only slow but unique. By this time I was a veteran of all kinds of motorcades, but this one I shall always remember.

People pushed and people crowded. They were friendly and seemed extremely pleased to see the Kennedys. The police officers were unable to hold the crowds, and the cars inched along the streets. Then out of the crowded windows what seemed like bushels of shredded paper filled the air. If the weather had been cold I would have thought we were in the biggest blizzard in history. The President was standing up in the back end of his car, covered with paper but obviously thrilled with the reception. The nearer we came to the center of the city, the more the paper storm increased and, if it were possible, the larger the crowd became. Huge pictures of President Mateos and President Kennedy had been placed on one of the buildings. The pictures were so large they almost covered the side of the building, and both were outlined with hundreds of lights, but it was almost impossible to see them through all the confetti.

We almost missed the corner at which we were to break away from the motorcade to go over to the Hotel Maria Isabel, where we were staying during our visit. The President and Mrs. Kennedy proceeded on to Los Pinos, the official residence of the Mexican President, to call on President and Mrs. Mateos.

The hotel was decorated in the true Mexican style. Brilliant colors were everywhere. The carpeting on the floor was deep purple, with draperies in either red or burnt orange. I was delighted with my room; it faced the front, and the view out over the city was beautiful. I was a typical tourist, and always went on an inspection tour of my room before I started to unpack. On my tour I found a wall telephone in the bathroom. Curious, I picked up the receiver. It was answered by one of the signal corps men connected with the White House. It was a pleasant feeling to hear this familiar voice, and once again I thought how very fortunate we were to have men like Colonel McNally, Tony Suglia, and the boys who tirelessly handled the switchboards.

The pleasant voice on the line said that a Mr. Myers, from the American Embassy, had asked that I call him. Mr. Myers told me that an office had been set up for me on the same floor as my room and he would like for me to go down there to see if they had put in all of the supplies I might need. He also offered to do anything he could to make my visit a pleasant one, and asked me to call him if I had any problems. I later learned that all I had to do was to whistle and any number of girls from the Embassy would come over to help me.

I had occasion to go to the American Embassy residence, where the President and Mrs. Kennedy were staying, several times that afternoon. They were both busy attending luncheons and meetings, and I saw them only fleetingly as we passed in the halls.

That evening they were to attend a performance of the Ballet Folklorico at the Bellas Artes Institute as guests of President and Mrs. Mateos. I wasn't sure I wanted to see this performance, but after it started I felt very fortunate to be in the audience. For more than two hours I sat transfixed before a delightful performance of authentic Mexican singing and dancing. I could have watched it for hours longer. Not surprisingly, there were

311

several curtain calls. I felt the dancers were truly inspired by the presence of four dignitaries. I was so enchanted with the performance I hung on the wall of my office in the White House a picture showing the President and Mrs. Kennedy meeting some of the dancers during the intermission.

I had a ringside seat for the wreath-laying ceremony at Independence Monument the next morning. All I had to do was to look out of the window of my hotel room, and I must say it looked mighty impressive from up there.

The rest of the morning we were all busy getting ready for the luncheon President and Mrs. Kennedy were having in honor of President and Mrs. Mateos at the hotel in which I was staying.

No matter how many times I saw the President get up from his chair to make a few remarks, I always had the same great feeling of pride that he was our President. This occasion was no different.

After the luncheon I went on a shopping spree. Again the typical tourist in me came out, and I bought silver jewelry, leather bags, fancy candles, and a colorful Spanish dress I haven't worn to this day.

By the time I got back to the hotel, I had a message from the Ambassador's home telling me the President would like me to come out. When I arrived I found plenty to do, including some dictation to be got out right away.

That night, when I got back to my room, I telephoned Abe to find out how he was getting along. He told me that our good friend Jimmy Roach had died of a heart attack. I was extremely upset and tossed and turned that night, and finally got up early because I couldn't sleep. I was in my room picking at my breakfast when the telephone rang. Once again the President wanted me to come right out to the Embassy.

When I got there, the President said, "Did you bring some envelopes and some money?"

"Yes."

"Put some money in each envelope for each maid and house

man here in the Embassy, and give them to Mrs. Mann, who will distribute them."

I wrote fast, stuffing bills into envelopes, and finished the job while the President and Ambassador Mann talked. I gave the envelopes to Mrs. Mann, and then the President asked all the help to line up out in the hall and he and Mrs. Kennedy went down the line, shaking the hand of each one, thanking them for their fine service.

En route to the airport the President and Mrs. Kennedy went to mass at the Basilica of Guadalupe. I went directly to the airport and was aboard *Air Force One* when they arrived.

It had been a lovely trip. As I always seemed to do when we left a country, I said, "Some day I would like to go back."

On the Fourth of July, the President spoke in front of Independence Hall in Philadelphia. Mrs. Kennedy and the two children had gone to Camp David, in the Catoctin Mountains of Maryland, the night before, and he was going to fly directly there from Philadelphia. He had not spent very much time at Camp David during his year and a half in office, but he was beginning to like it. It is located in a beautiful wooded area, and the cabins were designed to blend in with the trees. The big picture window in the lodge occupied by the President and his family overlooked the valley, and they said on a clear day it was possible to see Washington.

Earlier in the year Morton Downey had offered his home on Squaw Island at Hyannis Port to the President and Mrs. Kennedy for the summer months, and the next weekend Mrs. Kennedy and the children left to spend July and August there. The President joined them on weekends, and I would fly up with him on Friday night and then return to Washington Saturday afternoon.

Even though the Morton Downey house was more secluded than the President's own house in Hyannis Port, he did not want to be completely isolated from the people. Every weekend he drove down to the little store near the Kennedy compound with Caroline, where he would buy her some candy or try to find a magazine he had not read. Such a magazine was infinitely more difficult to locate than the candy.

One evening as the summer neared to an end, he dictated a letter he wanted me to send to Mrs. Kennedy. It was typical of his thoughtfulness and appreciation of others.

"As we will be leaving the Downey house after this weekend, I wonder if you could arrange to have the Presidential flag that has flown out in front of the house put in a frame, with an inscription, similar to the one we left at your stepfather's house in Newport. We could then leave it for the Downeys as a bread-and-butter gift."

After the stay at the Downey house, Mrs. Kennedy and Caroline were going to Italy for a vacation with her sister, Lee. While she was gone, the President planned to take two trips. One was a weekend in Maine, where Gene Tunney had offered the President the use of his home, and the other one was a trip to the Rocky Mountain area.

The press services carried the news that Mrs. Kennedy and Caroline had arrived in Italy for their two-week vacation in an ancient villa overlooking the Mediterranean. She had hoped for privacy, but instead they were greeted by huge crowds and seventy-five photographers. The President was very interested in her activities and kept showing me various pictures that appeared in the newspapers. He found one of Caroline taken by the Associated Press the day they left for Italy and he asked me to get a copy of it. When I did, he wanted me to send it along to Mrs. Kennedy. "I know she'll be pleased to see this picture," he said.

CHAPTER 30

"Ole Miss"

Early in the fall of 1962 President Kennedy went to Wheeling, West Virginia, to speak at the Wheeling Public School Stadium. The motorcade moved down the winding streets, and we passed a group of hospital nurses standing on the sidewalk. As he passed they waved and cheered. He asked his driver, Bill Greer, to stop the car so that he could shake their hands. These nurses were so pleased that the next morning we received a wire from them saying: "Thank you so much for stopping. God bless you. Sincerely, Wheeling Hospital Student Nurses." The President promptly dictated a wire for me to send in return: "If we are ever sick we are coming to the Wheeling General Hospital." With a twinkle he added, "Sign it 'White House staff.'"

But that lightheartedness didn't last long. The next day, Saturday, it gave way to suspense and frustration as a new crisis threatened.

For some time we had known James H. Meredith, a twenty-nine-year-old Negro, was going to attempt to enroll at the University of Mississippi at Oxford and that the Mississippi authorities were pledged to block his registration. The Department of Justice was keeping an eye on the situation and was keeping the White House informed. We hoped Governor Ross Barnett of Mississippi would understand the President had to, and meant to, obey the law of the land, and that Barnett would find some way to withdraw from his extreme position without losing face. But registration was almost upon us, and he had shown no indication of backing away.

On Saturday before the registration on Monday, the President kept his morning appointments and at 1:30 went over to the Mansion.

He was back again in less than five minutes. The Attorney General and his assistant, Burke Marshall, were waiting for him.

There had been word from Mississippi that Meredith's enrollment would be resisted.

The President called Governor Barnett, but received no satisfactory answer. To Barnett, President Kennedy emphasized that the Supreme Court had ordered that Meredith should be allowed to enter the university and that Barnett's oath of office required him to cooperate. He talked to Barnett twice more and still received no cooperation.

Then the President issued a statement that law and order would be maintained in Oxford during the coming week, and that he was federalizing units of the Mississippi National Guard, Army and Air, in case they were needed to enforce the orders of the Supreme Court. He added that telegrams had been dispatched so that these units would be ready for duty on Monday.

The President telephoned Mrs. Kennedy and told her he would not be able to come to Newport this weekend because of the situation in Mississippi. He went over to the Mansion again, but he telephoned me fifteen minutes later to ask what was going on. After several telephone conversations, the President and the Attorney General decided to issue a proclamation that would provide assistance for the removal of unlawful obstructions of justice in the state of Mississippi. The proclamation was ready about midnight and was taken to him in the Oval Room of the family quarters.

I left for home, but returned early the next morning because the situation was still tense. After attending ten o'clock mass the President returned to the White House to welcome his Sunday luncheon guests: Foreign Secretary Lord Home of Great Britain, Secretary of State Dean Rusk, British Ambassador David Ormsby-Gore, Assistant Secretary of State George Ball, and the American Ambassador to the Court of St. James, David K. E. Bruce.

Before the luncheon began, he telephoned me several times.

First, he wanted me to call Senator John Stennis of Mississippi, then Senator William Fulbright of Arkansas, then Ted Sorensen, and then Senator Richard Russell of Georgia. Between these calls the Attorney General talked to him, telling him how things stood in Oxford. And he left word with me to be sure to notify him of any new developments.

It was more of the same in the afternoon. First he talked to the Attorney General, then to Andy Hatcher, his associate press secretary, who was on duty that day, and then to Ted Sorensen. All this time Ted was at home in bed with a bad back, and it was a little difficult for him to get around.

Around six o'clock the President came over to his office. The Attorney General, Burke Marshall, and several others from the Justice Department were in the Cabinet room trying to keep in touch with their associates in Mississippi. The President asked that Kenny O'Donnell and Larry O'Brien be located; he wanted them to be in the office at eight o'clock that evening.

He became nervous and fidgety. He was fearful of violence on the Ole Miss campus. He said he was going on nationwide television at 7:30, and then he changed the time to ten P.M.

At 6:30 P.M., one hundred United States marshals were moved to Oxford to join the state police protecting Meredith. Thirty minutes before the President was to go on the air, the state police were pulled out. It was a touch-and-go proposition. Ten minutes before ten o'clock, the state police returned. Then the President went on the air. In a disturbed and serious tone he said, "The orders of the court in the case of Meredith versus Fair are beginning to be carried out. Mr. James Meredith is now in residence on the campus of the University of Mississippi. This has been accomplished thus far without the use of National Guard or other troops. And it is to be hoped that the law enforcement officers of the state of Mississippi and the federal marshals will continue to be sufficient in the future."

He appealed to the Mississippi officials, to the students on the campus, and to everyone in the state to uphold law and

317

order. He ended by saying, "There is, in short, no reason why the books on this case cannot now be quickly and quietly closed in the manner directed by the court. Let us preserve both the law and the peace and then, healing those wounds that are within, we can turn to the greater crises that are without and stand united as one people in our pledge to man's freedom."

The President had barely finished his speech when the state police left the campus again. Angry, almost hysterical students were gathering outside Meredith's dormitory. They moved from cat calls and jeers to rocks, to acid-filled bottles, to gunfire in an explosion of savagery. Finally the marshals resorted to tear gas. Throughout all this madness the President, worried that innocent people would be harmed, paced the floor and with each call from Mississippi expressed hope that order had been restored. He talked again to Governor Barnett, who was still evasive. At eleven o'clock, the Governor issued a statement that seemed almost a call for violence.

"Some reports interpreting my statement tonight as altering my stand are positively untrue and wholly unfounded. My friends, I repeat to the people of Mississippi now, I will never yield a single inch in my determination to win the fight we are engaged in. I call upon every Mississippian to keep his faith and his courage. We will never surrender."

The President talked to Mrs. Kennedy again and told her about the situation. He said he had asked the Secretary of the Army for more Guard units and had been assured they would arrive in Oxford from Memphis in an hour.

Word now came that the United States marshals were running out of tear gas, and that the students and some outsiders were making a determined assault on the building in which Meredith was located. The marshals asked the President for permission to return the gunfire being directed at them by hidden snipers, but the President wanted to avoid shooting if at all possible.

He ordered reinforcements from other Guard units and kept

walking impatiently from my office to the Cabinet room as the grim news continued to arrive. He sat at my desk, he sat in the rocking chair in my office, he used the other telephone in my office. He would go into the Cabinet room, then come right back into my office. The Attorney General did the same thing. All of the others used the telephone in the Cabinet room. The situation remained critical until the arrival of the additional troops at about 4:15 A.M.

Then the President went over to the Mansion, exhausted. I thought, the sun will soon be coming up. There's no use going home now. Abe had been intensely interested in the situation, and he, too, had stayed up most of the night, checking with me from time to time. The last time he called I told him I would just stay on the job and he agreed that was a good idea.

I washed my face, combed my hair, removed papers from the President's desk and the table in the Cabinet room, and started to straighten my office. But I could not erase from my mind the anguish and the concern on the face of the President as he walked up and down the length of my office during that night.

Before the smoke of the rioting had cleared, two men had died in Mississippi. One was Paul Guihard, a French News Agency reporter, and the other was Roy Guner, an Oxford jukebox repairman. Scores were injured on both sides.

The next morning I ate breakfast brought to me from the Navy Mess. I then learned that, despite everything, James Meredith, escorted by troops and marshals, had enrolled in the University of Mississippi at 8:30 A.M. Minutes later renewed violence began in downtown Oxford. Meredith had a fifty-five-minute session with Registrar Robert Ellis and then emerged smiling.

Now Mississippi authorities were trying to blame the violence on the United States marshals. The Justice Department said no one had been killed or wounded by gunfire from the weapons of federal personnel, pointing out that only four bullets were fired by United States marshals, and these were used to puncture a water hose rioters were using in an attempt to disperse the marshals. The only other shooting by federal personnel was the firing of tear-gas pellets in an attempt to bring the mob under control.

Evidently the President had heard on television the news about Meredith enrolling in the University, for shortly thereafter he made a telephone call to Governor Barnett from the Mansion. During the next forty minutes he made numerous calls. Then he called me and asked, "What time do I leave for the Supreme Court?"

I told him he was due to leave at 9:50.

"I'll be over to the office shortly."

When he arrived at 9:30, he looked completely rested and relaxed. No one would ever guess that just five hours before he had been under tremendous strain.

He left at 9:50 to attend the swearing-in of Arthur Goldberg as an Associate Justice of the Supreme Court. I was told a large detail of Washington police had turned out to provide additional protection because of the tense atmosphere resulting from the Mississippi crisis.

It was a delightful October day, too beautiful to be spoiled by racial hatred. When the Marine Corps band played in the Garden at ceremonies marking the President's presentation of the Distinguished Service Medal to General Lyman L. Lemnitzer, and the swearing-in of General Maxwell Taylor as Chairman of the Joint Chiefs of Staff, it was somehow hard to believe that in another part of these United States people hated the President for his effort to give everyone a fair chance.

CHAPTER 31

Cuba Again

It was October, 1962, and another man was going to be launched into outer space. The President was always extremely interested in these flights, and there was a great deal of excitement around the White House. Commander Walter Schirra was in the space ship early in the morning, waiting for the countdown. I had my television set tuned in for the event. What a relief when he got into orbit. Then the report came that he was having trouble. I rushed in to the President, who was in a meeting, with a little note that read: "They may have to end the space trip at the end of the first orbit—no danger to the life of Schirra—capsule trouble. Andy [Hatcher] is in touch with Cape Canaveral."

The President looked concerned as he read it and said, "Keep me informed."

At 10:35 A.M. I went into his office again, this time with good news. "Schirra completed his second orbit. He is over Africa and all is well." The President read the note and smiled.

Commander Schirra was still in orbit when the President left the office for lunch, and after lunch he stayed in the Mansion and followed the flight on his television set.

After Commander Schirra completed his six orbital flights and had been brought aboard the aircraft carrier *Kearsarge,* the President talked with him. "You did a wonderful job and we are very, very pleased."

Because the midterm elections were to be held in November and the President wanted to help as many Democratic candidates as he could, he scheduled some trips across the country. And he was still welcoming state visitors, who seemed to come one every other week.

The head of state of a Far Eastern country was to call on the

President one day. Mr. Kennedy remembered that the potentate, on an earlier visit, had brought him a little rocking chair. "Mrs. Lincoln," he said, "find out where that little rocking chair is." The chair was much too low for the President, and it had been put away in the Archives, where gifts from foreign countries are stored for safekeeping. It was delivered to my office about half an hour before the visitor arrived. After their meeting, the President pointed it out. "There's your gift," he said. The man was obviously pleased.

"Why don't you try it?" the President said to one of the Cabinet members. Then the President sat down in it, too, followed by the Oriental gentleman. It was so low that I was afraid the President would need a boost to get up again. The one who really enjoyed that rocking chair was John. It was just right for him and he could sit and rock just like his father.

By this time he decided that instead of going out to MATS Terminal to welcome these foreign dignitaries it would be more appropriate if the welcoming ceremonies were held on the south lawn of the White House. One Monday morning he greeted His Excellency Ahmed Ben Bella, Prime Minister and acting chief of state of Algeria. After the ceremonies they walked to the President's office, where they held a conference.

The next morning *The Washington Post* carried a story about Caroline's nursery-school classmates enacting their own welcoming ceremony at the upstairs windows of the White House. It seemed that when the soldiers who participated in the military welcome counted off "One, two, three, four" down on the south lawn, the children in the nursery school mimicked them by marching around and shouting "One, two, three, four."

I learned that the President was very disturbed when he heard those childish voices coming from the White House on this very dignified occasion, but I did not know he had said anything about it. Apparently he had, however, for a day or so later, I found letters from the two teachers in the nursery school. Both had written to the President saying they were sorry if they had caused him any embarrassment.

One day when the Attorney General came to attend a meeting of the National Security Council, he brought his dog Brumus with him. Brumus was a huge black beast that looked more like a bear. When the Attorney General went into the Cabinet room he left Brumus in my office, saying, "You had better shut your doors, or Brumus might go down the hall."

Since it was unusual for my door to be closed, staff members kept peeking in curiously to see what was going on, and they made all sorts of comments. "Who's your friend?" "I guess the Russian Ambassador is here." "Come out from behind that wig, Pierre, we know you." I was almost getting used to the remarks when a girl messenger from the Labor Department opened the door, saw the dog, screamed, threw down the paper she was delivering, and ran.

For several days there had been some discussion concerning a military build-up in Cuba, but we seemed to have problems every day, and I didn't pay much attention to the talk. Then one afternoon the President had a meeting with Andrei Gromyko, the Soviet Foreign Minister, and I began to wonder about the situation in Cuba.

We were off on one of those campaign trips the next day. He went to Cleveland, Ohio, and then to Springfield, Illinois, where he placed a wreath on Lincoln's Tomb, and then to the Illinois Fairgrounds Coliseum to speak.

Our next stop was Chicago, where he spoke at a banquet so well-attended the crowd overflowed into the balcony. Before I went to my room that night to pack my things in readiness for the flight the next morning to Milwaukee, one of the staff members said to me, "Things don't look too good in Cuba. We might have to turn back."

It had been determined that missile bases were under construction in Cuba and that they were a direct threat to the mainland of the United States. Before he left Washington, the President had held a meeting of the executive committee of the National Security Council and discussed what should be done about them.

The next morning after breakfast I stopped by the President's suite and he said, "We are going back to Washington because of things that are happening in Cuba." A few minutes later Pierre Salinger announced the President was cutting his trip short because of a slight cold. The public had not then been told officially about the missile build-up. Back to Washington we flew.

It was Saturday and the government departments were all closed. People were thinking about football, not what was happening in other parts of the world. Washington looked very peaceful as we landed at Andrews Air Force Base just before 1:30 P.M. When we reached the office there was the usual pile of mail, and the usual people. Only a couple of weekends before we had faced the crisis in Mississippi.

The President went into action again and the telephone was ringing constantly. Top men in government intelligence, Defense and State Department officials, and other members of the executive committee of the National Security Council came in the back door for meetings.

I learned that missiles capable of hitting this country were being deployed in Cuba. The Mississippi crisis seemed like a firecracker by comparison.

The situation at the White House was tense all afternoon and evening. I stayed until almost midnight, when the President said, "Why don't you go home and get some sleep, and then come back tomorrow morning."

When I arrived the next morning, I learned that the President had been busy most of the night. At the moment I entered the office, he was talking to Secretary Rusk over the telephone. The President and Mrs. Kennedy went to ten o'clock mass at St. Stephen's Church; by eleven o'clock, they were back at the White House. The rest of the day and far into the night there was a repetition of the day before: an unending series of meetings and telephone calls.

During this very critical time, though the President was impatient for action, his overall mood was one of deep and serious meditation. He didn't want to do anything rash; more than ever before, he wanted to weigh every alternative and argument. Finally, he established three alternatives: (1) do nothing about the offensive missiles; (2) initiate a total or limited blockade; or (3) take military action to destroy the missile sites and invade Cuba.

At noon on Sunday, the President made the decision. It was to be a blockade. Ted Sorensen had been working on a proposed television address in anticipation that the President would make that decision.

The President came over to the office early Monday morning. He immediately held meetings on the crisis. After the first meeting ended he looked out on the south lawn and saw Caroline and her nursery schoolmates playing. He walked out on the portico and clapped his hands, but Caroline didn't come as she usually did. He walked back into the Cabinet room and began another meeting.

In about five minutes Caroline came flying through his office, looked at me, and said, "Where's my Daddy?"

"He's in a meeting in the Cabinet room, but I wouldn't go in there."

"But I *have* to."

With that she opened the door and to the amazement of everyone, blurted out, "Daddy, I would have come sooner, but Miss Grimes wouldn't let me go."

There was laughter and the President said, "That's all right, Caroline."

Caroline was satisfied, and she skipped around my office for a while and then went back out on the south lawn.

The President went to lunch early and returned sooner than usual in the afternoon. He skipped his usual dip in the pool.

His first meeting after lunch was with the National Security Council. Then he met with the Prime Minister of Uganda, A. Milton Obote, as if it were a normal day. Then, before he was to meet with the Cabinet, he summoned the twenty Congressional leaders for a meeting in the afternoon and told them the situation, laid out aerial photographs, and got their views on the decision he had made.

During their meeting, the radio and television men were in my office setting up equipment in preparation for the President's appearance on television at seven o'clock.

He was very serious as he began his address.

"Within the past week, unmistakable evidence has established the fact that a series of offensive missile sites is now in preparation on that imprisoned island. . . . To halt this offensive build-up, a strict quarantine on all offensive military equipment under shipment to Cuba is being initiated. All ships of any kind bound for Cuba from whatever nation or port will, if found to contain cargoes of offensive weapons, be turned back."

He ended by saying, "Our goal is not the victory of might, but the vindication of right; not peace at the expense of freedom, but both peace *and* freedom here in this hemisphere, and, we hope, around the world. God willing, that goal will be achieved."

When he finished he came out of his office, handed the speech to me, and walked straight to the door to the portico and headed toward the Mansion.

The telegrams and telephone calls began pouring in as soon as I reached the office the next morning. People were backing the President one hundred percent. Many of his friends left messages for him. When he came to the office, he seemed not quite so tense now that the decision had been made and the world told. And he was pleased with the messages.

It was a busy morning. He talked with the three living former Presidents—Mr. Eisenhower, Mr. Truman, and Mr. Hoover. He asked me about his schedule and I told him that Sam Harris, his tailor, was in town with a new suit and overcoat and wanted to know if he could see him. He said, "Tell him to come in around six o'clock." And I did.

He had a meeting with the executive committee of the National Security Council again that morning, and then after meeting the newly appointed Ambassador of Jamaica he went to lunch. When he came back from lunch and a rest, he came to my desk and read a new batch of wires and messages. He returned to his office, sat down at his desk, and started to read some memoranda that had come in. I was busy with the mail and telephone and didn't notice that he had gone out on the south lawn.

But soon I discovered that he was out inspecting the grass. What a wonder he is, I thought. The world may soon be in flames, and he knows it, but he goes out to check on the grass.

Soon I had a telephone call for him and stepped to the doorway. When he saw me, he started walking back to his office with increased speed.

Late that afternoon, following another meeting with the executive committee of the National Security Council, he signed the *Proclamation: Interdiction of the Delivery of Offensive Weapons to Cuba.* He sat down at his desk and asked me to tell the photographers to come in and photograph the signing. When he finished, he came out to my desk and handed me a pen he had used in signing the proclamation. I marked the box I put it in and placed it with other treasures he was saving.

All this time Sam Harris, the tailor, had been waiting to see the President. As soon as the photographers cleared out, he went into the office and found that neither the suit nor the overcoat required alterations. The President asked me to send them over to George, his valet, in the Mansion. It was typical of him to go on with the commitments he had made, even while he dealt with a crisis.

The blockade became effective at ten o'clock on Wednesday morning; the first Russian ship heading for Cuba was expected to enter the blockade zone at nightfall. Late in the afternoon, however, some of the vessels altered their course.

The next day, the Navy intercepted the first ship. It was not boarded but allowed to proceed after identification was made. Still there was no backdown by Russia regarding the missiles.

The week wore on and each day became more tense than the preceding one. There were meetings, telephone calls, and a few of the regular appointments. On Friday the White House disclosed that missile-site construction was still underway in Cuba. The meetings that day lasted late into the night—so late I telephoned Abe and told him that instead of coming home for just a few hours I thought I would sleep in the White House. There were some couches in the area adjacent to the situation room. I was glad I made the decision, for just after I hung up, the President called me for a memorandum that he had been reading during the afternoon.

As the hours dragged on, there were more meetings, more telephone calls, and more visits by the President to the situation room to get the latest communications on Cuba. Shortly before midnight, he was told of a message from Chairman Khrushchev, transmitted by the Embassy in Moscow to the State Department, implying an offer to withdraw the missiles under the supervision of the United Nations if the United States would lift the blockade and promise not to invade Cuba.

The President read it with hope and decided to send a reply the following morning.

But hope quickly vanished on Saturday morning, October 27th—a day such as I have never known. Through diplomatic channels another message came from Khrushchev, different in tone and style from the previous one, proposing a trade of missile sites for NATO bases in Turkey.

By now the tension was unbearable—everyone seemed to be listening. What they were listening for, they were afraid to admit, as I was, even to themselves.

The Civil Defense Committee of the Governors' Conference met with the President in order to get the country ready for any emergency.

After lunch I had calls from various security officers briefing me on what to do in case of an attack. They gave me instructions on what to do with my mother and my father-in-law. They said that Abe could be evacuated with the Administrator of the Veterans Administration. I will always be grateful to Ensign George Dalton for the painstaking briefings he gave me on the security of the White House shortly after the Inauguration. Without his foresight I would never have been able to understand the instructions that were given to me that day.

During lunch and later, back in the office, the President scratched out notes for an answer to Chairman Khrushchev's letter of October 26th. He came to my desk and began dictating:

"Dear Mr. Chairman: I have read your letter of October 26th with great care and find in it the indication of a willingness on your part to seek a prompt solution to the problem. I welcome that and assure you that my desire is the same.

"The first thing that needs to be done, however, is for work to cease on offensive missile bases in Cuba and for all weapon systems in Cuba capable of offensive use to be rendered inoperable.

"Assuming this is done promptly I have given my representatives in New York instructions that will permit them this weekend to work out an agreement for a permanent solution to the Cuban problem with the Acting Secretary General and with your representative. If you will give your representative similar instructions there is no reason why we should not be able to complete these arrangements and announce them to the world within a couple of days."

When he finished dictating he said, "Type that up rough draft and bring it to me in the Cabinet room." It formed the basis upon which they were going to work out an answer to Khrushchev.

They worked on it for hours and finally the President emerged from the Cabinet room. He turned to the men who were following him, members of the executive committee of the National Security Council, and said, "That's it, if somebody doesn't foul it up." The letter was released to the press and was soon flashing over the wires to all the world.

Then Roger Hilsman rushed in with news about one of the surveillance planes. It was missing over Cuba and presumed lost. Several of the men moved into the President's office and closed the door. They were still there at midnight.

Once in a while one of them would come out and make a call on one of my telephones, and then rush back into the President's office. Some time later the meeting ended, and the President came out to my desk and said, "Be back here early in the morning."

I thought of the instructions in my bag telling me where to go in case of an emergency, and wondered if I would ever be able to make it back.

While I put the papers away in the files, cleared my desk, and got ready to go home, I kept saying to myself, We are in safe hands. When I got home I tried to be cheerful so Abe would not worry unnecessarily. I figured there would be time enough to tell him if the warning was sounded. Soon we went to bed, but I didn't sleep well. I had the special, tap-proof security telephone beside my bed, and all night long I half expected it to ring.

Sunday morning I got up as usual, dressed, and made breakfast. Abe drove me down Sixteenth Street to the White House. I kept wondering what the day would bring. I had not turned on the radio—I worked right where the news was made and they couldn't know anything I had not already heard. Or maybe I just wanted to shut off the bad news for a little longer.

When we drove through the northwest gate on our way to the west wing of the White House, I thought people looked unusually happy. When I went through the waiting room and down the hall to my office, everyone I met had a glad hello. Finally, someone said to me, "Wasn't it great about the news?"

"It sure was."

I didn't want them to think I didn't know what was going on.

Then I learned by listening to the men who were gathering in my office that Khrushchev had sent a message stating that the USSR had ordered their officers to stop building bases in Cuba, that they agreed to dismantle the equipment, send it back to Russia, and it could all be done under United Nations supervision.

I suddenly felt very lightheaded. I watched the President

330

drive off to mass and thought of that old adage, "God helps those who help themselves."

After church the President came over to the office, and his face reflected his pleasure at the turn of events. He met with the executive committee of the National Security Council for a little over an hour, and then took off by helicopter for Glen Ora to have lunch with his family and Lem Billings, who had flown down from New York for the weekend. I put my things away and was happy to get home to Abe.

The next day the President began to try to think of something to give everyone who had worked with him during the eleven days of the Cuban crisis. At first he considered plastic cigarette boxes like those he had given the entertainers at the Inaugural Ball, but he wanted something on which there would be a calendar showing those eleven days.

He asked Tish Baldrige, the Social Secretary, to check on a silver model of some sort. She suggested a silver cigarette case, but he didn't like that idea either. Then he designed the mementos himself. It was to have the month of October in silver on a wooden base with the eleven days in different lettering, and at the top the initials of the President in one corner and the recipient's initials in the other. He asked me to make a list of everyone who had worked with him during those days. I did, leaving off my own name, and he sent the list to Tish and asked her to handle it from there.

Ten days later the little silver calendars arrived, and he wanted them beside his chair in the Cabinet room so he could give them out at the National Security Council meeting the next morning.

The next morning when he came over from the Mansion I noticed that he had a blue box in his hand, and he walked into my office and handed it to me. He said, "I had one made up for you, too. You went with us all the way."

Words failed me at that moment, but I am sure that he could tell by the look on my face that he could not have pleased me more.

331

The next morning we left the south lawn by helicopter to board *Air Force One* for a trip to Hunter Air Force Base in Georgia. The President wanted to go to some of the bases that were on the alert during the Cuban crisis to show the men who were standing by during the crucial period he appreciated what they did.

From Hunter Field we flew to Hatch Parade Grounds, Fort Stewart, Georgia, then to Homestead Air Force Base in Florida, and then to Key West, Florida.

The Cuban missile crisis was still fresh in his mind a few weeks later when he spoke at the lighting of the nation's Christmas tree on the Ellipse:

"The old year is coming to an end. It has been a long year, a troubled year, a year of anxiety and trial and danger. Yet it is a year which, I deeply believe, has brought the world closer to mankind's abiding vision of peace. . . .

"As we light this tree, as trees are lit across our land and across the earth, let the spirit of Christmas rise freely within ourselves—and, in that divine illumination, let us strive to work in the spirit of the Manger to drive bitterness and hate and cruelty from the souls of men. As Christ knew, this is the hardest, the most unending fight of all—but it was in that fight He found His glory. Our highest hope is to follow humbly in His path. In the words of John Greenleaf Whittier:

"Blow, bugles of battle, the marches of peace;
East, west, north, and south, let the long quarrel cease;
Sing the song of great joy that the angels began,
Sing the glory of God and of good-will to man!"

332

CHAPTER 32

Entering a Third Year

Once again we headed south for the Christmas holidays. And once again the President was to have a preChristmas meeting with British Prime Minister Harold Macmillan in the Bahamas. This time we were staying at Lyford Cay, a truly beautiful place. For four days the two leaders met, discussing, among other things, the United States' plans to cancel the air-to-ground Skybolt Missile.

When we returned to Palm Beach, Mrs. Kennedy, Caroline, and John were at the airport to meet the President, and they all waved to the crowds that lined the way on their drive to the Michael Paul residence, where they were spending the holidays.

I returned to the Palm Beach Towers, thankful that this time the President had completed his autographing of Christmas gifts early. They were giving autographed copies of the *White House Guide Book* bound in red leather to forty-seven close associates, including members of the Cabinet and a few of the White House staff this year. On the cover in the lower right-hand corner were the recipients' initials in gold.

He also personally signed Christmas cards to heads of state and other foreign officials, chiefs of missions in Washington, American Ambassadors abroad, Senators, Representatives, Senators-elect, Representatives-elect, and United States government officials. I often wondered how he had time to do all this and keep his mind on events at home and abroad. And he never complained about doing it. In fact, he considered it a pleasure.

He still had not selected Mrs. Kennedy's Christmas gift, however. The next day, when I went out to the Michael Paul home, I found in my office on the first floor six different drawings he had requested from Wildenstein's of New York. From these six he was to make his selection of a gift for her, and he found it a difficult decision.

He put one up on the desk, stood back, studied it, took it down, and went through the same routine with all six. Then he turned to me and said, "Tell Lee to come down here."

I went in search of Lee Radziwill, Mrs. Kennedy's sister, who was spending the holidays with her, and they looked at the drawings together. One was by Renoir, and the President seemed to give it special consideration.

"There is one in London I know Jackie would like," Lee said.

"That one no doubt is of animals, and I am getting tired of seeing animals," the President said with a twinkle.

"Yes, it is."

Then he said to me, "Get this picture gift-wrapped and placed under the tree and send the others back." He decided to keep the Renoir for Mrs. Kennedy.

That morning he read some startling news in the papers: an announcement of the successful test of the Skybolt, which just two days before he had told Prime Minister Macmillan was being cancelled. He tried to locate Secretary of Defense McNamara, but learned he was on his way to Aspen, Colorado. Then he had me call Secretary Gilpatric, and he read the riot act to him. After he completed the call, he said, "I can't understand them doing this. They must have been tired."

Finally he decided to tell the press that this was only a phase of the Skybolt Missile, and they were still going through with the agreement reached at Nassau.

All this time, British Ambassador David Ormsby-Gore, a house guest of the Kennedys, was outside in the swimming pool with Caroline, John and the Radziwill children.

That afternoon I returned to Washington to spend Christmas with Abe. The next day I had a telephone call from Mrs. Kennedy. She and the President were giving a party in Palm Beach for the Secret Service agents, and planned to present them with cigarette lighters. She asked me where the lighters were, and I promised to find out and let her know. I learned from the

334

social office that they had already distributed the lighters, and relayed this information to the President, since I was unable to reach Mrs. Kennedy. He immediately called the social office for an explanation, but because it was too late to do anything about the lighters, he decided to give the agents copies of the *White House Guide Book* at the party.

When I returned to Palm Beach after Christmas, the President was preparing a speech to be given in Miami. He and Mrs. Kennedy were going to accept the flag of the Cuban Invasion Brigade. Mrs. Kennedy had a brief speech she wanted translated into Spanish. I watched the ceremony on television, and there must have been at least fifty thousand people there.

The President was also making out a list of organizations that would receive his 1962 salary. His 1961 contributions were given to such organizations as Boy Scouts of America, Girl Scouts of America, Boys' Club of America, Girls' Club of America, Services for Crippled Children, National Association for Retarded Children, Federation of Jewish Philanthropies, St. John's Hospital, Santa Monica, California, and Massachusetts General Hospital. His 1962 list consisted of many of the same organizations, but this time he asked me to make sure that the United Negro College Fund and the Cuban Families Committee were included. When I assured him that they had been added, he said, "Fine." Soon the checks were on their way.

There was a flurry of papers to be signed on the last day of the year, before the New Year began, and the President took care of them.

I couldn't forget, however, a news flash that came over one of the press service wires during that last week of 1962: "President Kennedy has just been assassinated while riding in an op—bust, bust. This is not at all true—just kidding ha ha ha ha ha."

What a horrible sense of humor, I thought. How could anyone think that is funny?

Here it was 1963. Soon the President would be entering his third year in office. Things were looking up, and I anticipated having a good year. As I sat in the sun at Palm Beach reading the papers and waiting for the Tournament of Roses television show to begin, I thought how grateful I was we were starting the year without too many earthshaking problems.

Then, only a few days later, the President flew to Oklahoma to attend the funeral of Senator Robert Kerr. The President respected Senator Kerr and was deeply shocked at his passing.

President Kennedy was going to deliver his third State of the Union address on January 14th before a joint session of Congress. Although he wanted to invite some special guests to sit in the Executive Gallery, which was reserved for the President's family and guests, he had trouble finding anyone who could attend.

On Sunday before he was to make the address, he asked me to invite Mrs. Franklin D. Roosevelt, Jr., and Franklin also if he was in town. They were both in Florida, I discovered. The next day he called Mrs. Kennedy from the office and asked her about inviting a couple of women to use the tickets. I couldn't hear what she said, but evidently there was some disagreement because he then said to me in a dejected voice, "Would you like to go?"

"Thank you, Mr. President, I would be delighted."

"You can give the extra tickets to someone else."

I gave them to Tish Baldrige and Pamela Turnure. When we arrived in the Gallery, Mrs. Ted Kennedy was already there, and soon thereafter Mrs. Kennedy arrived with her mother, Mrs. Auchincloss, and her sister, Lee Radziwill.

The President was pleased with the reaction to his speech, and he watched a delayed telecast of it on television from 6:30 to 7:00 P.M.

The President had a warm, close relationship with his mother. One afternoon near the end of a busy day that had included conferences with Prime Minister Fanfani of Italy, a state visitor at that time, his mother, who had been walking out on the south lawn, stopped in to talk to him. She was casually eating an apple. The President buzzed me and asked me if I would get his father on the line, which I did. I went in to tell them the call had been placed, and as I left the room they were discussing with him little pleasantries of the day. Although he was unable to talk back to them, I am sure he was pleased to hear their voices.

Several weeks before Christmas there was an announcement from the White House that the Kennedys were building a new home at Atoka, Virginia, in the hunt country near Middleburg, where they had leased Glen Ora for the past two years.

The idea of living near Middleburg stemmed from Mrs. Kennedy's love for riding. It was for this reason they had leased Glen Ora, but now the lease was expiring and they began looking for a spot to build their own home. Paul Fout, who lived near Middleburg, helped them find about thirty acres of land on Snake Mountain. They liked the site and were soon busy with plans for the house. It was to be used mainly by Mrs. Kennedy, with the President going over there only on weekends, and he left the planning mostly to her.

He knew that she was happy planning the house, and he was very pleased with what she was doing. After it was finished, she spent many hours furnishing it, and they both enjoyed showing it to visitors. Those who saw all agreed "it was a dream house with a view overlooking the valley that was exquisite." Somehow, however, the President never felt at home there, and I think the one thing he missed most was a swimming pool. Many times he begged off going there and suggested instead that they spend the weekend at Camp David. There he could swim and take a walk through the wooded areas.

The President enjoyed walking. One Sunday when he remained in Washington, after returning from mass, he and Charley Bartlett took a short walk on the Ellipse. Then they motored over to and toured the Aeronautics Building at the Smithsonian, then walked along the Reflecting Pool near the Lincoln Memorial. The car picked them up there, and they went over to Arlington National Cemetery, where they went through the Custis-Lee Mansion.

As if that were not enough walking for one day, after Mrs. Kennedy returned that evening he and she walked out of the southwest gate, around the fence that bounds the south lawn, by the east gate entrance, and along the north fence on Pennsylvania Avenue and into the northwest gate before coming back into the White House.

Because of the President's youth and his emphasis on "vigah," people were becoming conscious of the importance of physical fitness. The President himself did daily exercises, which were prescribed by Dr. Hans Kraus of New York City. It was due to Dr. Kraus's persistence that the trouble in the President's back almost vanished. One day when Dr. Kraus was in the office I overheard the President say to him, "I wish I could have known you years ago."

"I appreciate your saying that very much," Dr. Kraus replied.

In one of his speeches, the President observed that he thought people should take hikes, and it wasn't long before the Attorney General went on a 50-mile hike, thereby starting a national epidemic of sore feet.

For several weeks there had been talk among the staff at the White House that Mrs. Kennedy was expecting a baby. I was not surprised to hear the President say one morning to a visitor in his office, "You know my wife will not be able to do a great deal this summer because we are expecting a baby in the fall."

Many times he said, "Mrs. Lincoln, soon you will have three coming over to get candy from your candy dish."

Mrs. Kennedy had had difficulty with child-bearing in the past, and he wanted to make sure that she did not exert herself, risking another miscarriage. On several occasions he substituted for her when she had previously made engagements to attend a public function, and he excluded her from his official travel for that spring and summer.

The first trip was to Costa Rica in March. The President stayed at the American Embassy residence there, which was on a lovely spot, high on a knoll. We were told that the residency had been built from blueprints of Tara, the home in *Gone with the Wind*. My office was on the first floor of this beautiful Embassy.

Whenever the President traveled abroad a large entourage went with him. A chef from the White House always went along to prepare the President's meals, and food and drinking water were transported with him. He insisted that his scales be carried everywhere he went because he kept a daily check on his weight. Sergeant Joe Giordano, who had served many Presidents with pride, checked all of the personal things that were to accompany the President, and it was due to his efficient handling of minute details that everything was always in order when we arrived. The President often remarked that Joe and his assistant, George "Boots" Miller, did a marvelous job.

One other item always accompanied the President: a stereophonic record player and a collection of his favorite records. The collection always included one particular record: a medley of Irish songs, including "When Irish Eyes Are Smiling," and "The Wearing of the Green." After many a hectic day he relaxed by listening to these records.

Shortly after he joined the White House staff, René Verdon, a French chef who could make any food taste delightful, decided to become an American citizen. When the President learned of it, he said, "Mrs. Lincoln, I would like to congratulate him on the day he gets his papers."

When I told this to René, he said, "I don't want to bother the President. He's too busy." But President Kennedy insisted and so, on that all-important day, René appeared in my office wearing his apron and tall white hat. President Kennedy called the White House photographer in, and a proud René had his picture taken standing next to the President. This kind of thoughtful gesture was a basic part of the President's character.

On June 12, 1963, an NAACP field secretary for the state of Mississippi by the name of Medgar Evers was assassinated in Jackson, Mississippi. Not long after the funeral at Arlington Cemetery, the President asked Mrs. Evers and her three children to come by the White House so that he could meet them. Upon their arrival they were brought into the Cabinet room to wait for the time when they could go in to see the President.

As I usually did, I went into the Cabinet room to greet them. I told them all of the historical facts that I knew about the room, and ended by saying, "I am told that if you sit in the President's chair at this table and make a wish, it will come true." One by one they sat in the chair. Finally, it was Darrell Evers' turn. He hesitated, then sat down, folded his hands, and bowed his head. As I was about to leave the room Mrs. Evers' brother-in-law, who was also in the party, came to me and said, "Do you know what Darrell wished?"

"No."

"He hoped and prayed that his father did not die in vain."

CHAPTER 33

Sentimental Journey

The reading papers that went over to the President's bedroom every night had for weeks been about his forthcoming trip to Germany, Ireland, England, and Italy; and staff members were busy working on speeches for him to give in each country.

One morning the papers came back with "Daddy" written on them in red and blue, and on some were the initials CBK. I knew that Caroline had been sitting on his lap while he was reading them and she had initialed them for him.

I kept my office full of pictures. On one wall were Kennedy family pictures. The visits of foreign dignitaries were recorded on another. The third wall held diplomas received by the President during his term of office, and originals of some of his favorite cartoons. On the fourth wall were pictures of important events. Visitors often moved around the room as though they were in a picture gallery, commenting on each one: "There's Caroline on Macaroni"; "Oh, Mother, look at this one of John and the President"; "Where was this taken?"; "Is this the *Honey Fitz?*"

The President liked to show the pictures to his friends. He would lead them around the room, saying, "This was taken when I was in Mexico. . . . This was taken during the visit of Prime Minister Macmillan to the White House."

Mrs. Kennedy often came to look at the pictures, and whenever there was a new one she asked for prints. John-John liked to look, too. He would go from wall to wall looking for pictures in which there was an airplane. When he saw one, he would point and say excitedly, "Aaplane, aaplane!"

At one time I had a rocking horse in my office. Eunice Shriver had brought it into the Cabinet room for a group of mentally retarded children and, when the children left, it was brought to my office. Caroline and John would rock on it, and I heard the President say to a member of the Cabinet, "We keep that rocking horse in here to remind us of the younger generation and what our responsibilities are in making this country a safe place in which to live."

Finally Saturday June 22nd came, our departure date. We left Andrews Air Force Base at 9:35 P.M., and, because we would lose several hours in flight, it would be almost ten o'clock Sunday morning before we arrived at Wahn Airport at Bonn, Germany.

Shortly after we were airborne, the President asked me to come into the cabin for a little dictation. Although he had tentatively planned to visit England, he had not made a public statement to that effect. His dictation began: "In view of the fact that it is now six months since they last met and there are a number of problems they could usefully discuss, the President and the Prime Minister feel that it would be helpful to take advantage of the President's visit to Europe, and the recent change in the President's schedule, to have informal talks together. The Prime Minister has accordingly invited the President to stay at Birch Grove, Sussex. The President has accepted and is expected to arrive late on June 29th and leave on June 30th."

Air Force One glided into the airport at Bonn and, as usual, everyone applauded Captain Swindel's skill as he set the plane down so gently there was hardly a trace of a landing impact. It was a beautiful day and pomp and splendor were everywhere. The highly trained German bands in full regalia stood at attention while Chancellor Konrad Adenauer stepped forward to greet the President. The driver of our car in the motorcade was German and couldn't speak a word of English, but a German standing nearby who could, said, "Never have I seen a crowd like this and the streets all the way the length of the motorcade are just the same."

The speeches at the airport ceremony were short. Toward the end of his remarks the President said, "My stay in this country will be all too brief, but in a larger sense the United States is here on this continent to stay. . . . And so long as our presence is desired and required, our forces and commitments will remain. For your safety is our safety, your liberty is our liberty, and any attack on your soil is an attack upon our own. Out of necessity, as well as sentiment, in our approach to peace as well as war, our fortunes are one."

This was just what the Germans wanted to hear, and their enthusiasm showed it.

The motorcade proceeded to Cologne, where the President signed the Golden Book at the City Hall, made a speech on the plaza, and then went to mass. We returned to Bonn, where the President signed the Golden Book and made another speech. Chancellor Adenauer accompanied him to the residence of Minister Martin J. Hillenbrand, where the President was to stay.

By this time it was well after noon, and I settled myself in one of the rooms of this residence, which was going to be my office during our stay there. When I went out to the kitchen the White House chefs, who had accompanied us on the trip, were busy preparing the President's lunch. I also had a bite to eat.

After lunch I finished wrapping some gifts, and then I asked the President if he would need me any more that day. He said, "If I do I will give you a call." So I left for my hotel. The narrow streets through which we drove to get to this quaint little hotel were very fascinating. Never had I seen such a clean city. The streets seemed scrubbed and polished. And everyone was busy, even the children.

My hotel room overlooked the Rhine. Once again I was impressed with the activity. As I stood on the little balcony outside my room I could see dozens of barges that seemed to be racing up and down the Rhine.

The next day I again worked in my office in the Hillenbrand residence. The following morning we left by helicopter for Hanau, Germany, flying along the Rhine River valley. The scenery was magnificent. It seemed that every piece of land was utilized.

At Fliegerhorst Kaserne I sat in the reviewing stand while the officers and men of the Third Armored Division, Fifth Corps, rendered honors to the President before he spoke. From the base we went to Frankfurt, where the crowds were so immense I could not believe my eyes. The President spoke to a crowd in Roemerberg Square and then walked to Paulskirche, where he made another speech. We arrived in the flower-decked room a little ahead of the President, and took the seats assigned to us.

After the President had finished speaking, he started to leave, and so did we, but so many people crowded after him we were left behind, and suddenly I found myself alone. I rushed out to the street and saw a bus. Thinking it would take me to the helicopter, I got aboard, but when I did not recognize anyone on it, I hopped out and spotted another staff member who was also lost. Fortunately, we ran across an American army officer stationed in Frankfurt, and he offered to drive us to Wiesbaden, where we were to spend the night.

The Hotel General von Steuben looked like heaven to me when we drove up in front of it. The President had asked about me when the helicopters took off without me, but I knew that if I was not there when he was ready to go, I had to shift for myself. Never did I want that to happen again.

The next morning we left for Tegel Airport, Berlin, and the crowds there were even larger. He spoke to the Trade Union Congress of German Construction Workers, and then we went by motorcade to take a look at the Berlin Wall. We passed the Brandenburg Gate, and on the way to "Checkpoint Charlie" stopped at a platform erected to give the President and his party a chance to look into East Berlin.

I arrived ahead of the President and scooted up the steps. I could hardly believe my eyes. On one side of the fence was a bustling society, while on the other side in East Berlin there was no sign of life. Someone snapped my picture as I was looking at the Wall. I heard the excitement that signaled the arrival of the President, and decided I should move on. As I started down the steps, he started up and gave me a little wave as he went by.

Next he spoke outside the City Hall in West Berlin, where the crowd was larger than any I had ever seen before. People were in all the windows, on the tops of buildings—everywhere. After he spoke, the applause lasted a very long time; and when he said, *"Ich bin ein Berliner,"* I thought the cheering would never end.

Late that afternoon we boarded *Air Force One* with cheers still ringing in our ears, and headed for Dublin. The President was eagerly anticipating this visit. His grandfather had emigrated from Ireland to the United States, and now he was going home to the land of his forebears.

For months prior to his visit to Ireland, the relatives of the President had been busily preparing for their illustrious cousin. They had scrubbed the Kennedy homestead, made cakes and pies to serve him when he came, sewed quilts, and bought a knobby cane to give him.

When we landed in Dublin I watched the President meet the President of Ireland, and I could tell he felt he had come

344

home. All the cares of the world had suddenly gone from his shoulders. The more fuss they made over him, the more he beamed. Some members of his staff had thought he should bypass Ireland, that there was nothing to be gained by the visit, but he thought it would be a wonderful experience. The look on his face at this moment proved it.

The President was staying at the American Ambassador's home, and it was quite late when the motorcade took him there. I stopped off at my hotel. The next morning I rode out to the Ambassador's residence, and found that Ireland is really as beautiful as the songs say. The Ambassador's residence was on a large estate surrounded by beautiful wooded areas, and the interior was very tastefully furnished.

My office was an upstairs bedroom next to the bedroom occupied by Eunice Shriver, who had accompanied the President while Mrs. Kennedy remained at home to await the arrival of the new baby in the fall.

I had only one request the next day. I wanted to go with the President when he visited the Kennedy ancestral homestead. We left by helicopter and flew to O'Kennedy Park, New Ross, where the President spoke. From there our motorcade twisted through narrow streets and roads until we arrived at Dugans-town. The President got out of his car and entered the farm-yard, where all of his relatives had gathered. He couldn't possibly have been prouder. They made a fuss over him, laughed at his jokes, offered him cake. They were happy to see him— and he was happy to be there.

I continued with the President while he visited Wexford and laid a wreath at the statue of John Barry. We returned to the Ambassador's residence a little after 3:00 P.M., and I stayed there to finish some work I had to do for the next day.

I stayed behind the next morning to get ready for our visit to England and also to help with the arrangements for the luncheon to be given by the President in honor of AntUachtaran and AnTaoiseach at the Embassy. It was another banner day in his life. He visited Cork and returned only a few minutes before

345

the luncheon. He beamed every time anyone said they thought Ireland was a great country and the Irish a great people.

During the luncheon some Irish girls sang a medley of Irish songs. After lunch he asked these girls to line up out in the reception room so that he could shake their hands.

Later on that afternoon he went to the Dail, the Irish Parliament, where he addressed a joint sitting of both houses of the Oireachtas. From there he motored to St. Patrick's Hall to receive an honorary Doctor of Laws degree from the National University of Ireland.

The weather during our entire visit to Ireland had been cloudy and at times there was a slow drizzle, but it did not seem to dampen the spirits of either the President or the Irish people. I could tell that it was difficult for the President to say goodbye the next morning, but his visit was coming to an end. Just before he boarded the helicopter to go to Galway, he asked me to see if I could find some sweaters for Mrs. Kennedy and the children at the Shannon Airport. I was not going along to Galway but was going to Shannon to await his arrival.

We were all aboard *Air Force One* at the airport when the President arrived from Limerick. I went out to listen to him make his farewell speech. He told that friendly crowd, "I will certainly come back in the springtime."

Then we headed for England. On arrival we took helicopters to Birch Grove House, where the President was to stay. They had arranged for me to stay at Ashdown Forest Hotel, a charming old English inn, but I had an office at Birch Grove House, and Lady Dorothy Macmillan did everything possible to welcome us and make our stay a comfortable one.

On Sunday morning after the President returned from mass, he was steamed up about an article that had appeared in that day's *London Telegraph*. He called for Pierre Salinger immediately to ask him about the article's implication that press arrangements for his trip to Germany had been made to the advantage of the White House correspondents and the disadvantage of European correspondents. He wanted a letter written to the editor of the *Telegraph* telling him the true facts. They worked on the letter for quite some time. First the President would dictate some statements and, after I typed them up, Pierre would dictate revisions. They finally got the letter ironed out, and then the President went to his conference with the Prime Minister.

About four o'clock we left England. It took us only about ninety minutes to get to Italy, and as soon as we were above the clouds the President sent for me to come to his cabin. He was talking to some members of his staff, and he kept right on talking for a while. Then he said to me, "Take this down," and began dictating a statement on the meeting he had had with the British Prime Minister. He ended with this sentence: "The President felt the meeting was most satisfactory."

I typed it up and took it back to him, and, as he always did, he took a pen and made some changes. By this time, we were almost ready to land at the Malpensa airport.

At the airport we transferred to helicopters that took us to the Villa Serbelloni. The grandeur I saw on that trip was unsurpassed. The huge mountains in the background and the lovely lakes below were a sight to behold. We were taken by car up to the Villa, which looked like an ancient castle. The rooms were huge and everywhere there were statues and beautiful paintings. But somehow it gave me a feeling of coldness. It was like going to bed in the rotunda of the Capitol in Washington surrounded by lifesize statues.

I was glad I was not staying there. Instead, I had a room at a hotel perched on the side of a mountain. It was a beautiful place with a patio dining room that overlooked Lake Como.

The next morning we went to Rome. The driver of our bus in the motorcade lost his way and it was some time before we caught up with the President. He went directly to Quirinale Palace, the residence of the President of the Republic of Italy, where he was to have several meetings with President Segni and others. President Kennedy was going to stay at Villa Taverna, the American Ambassador's residence, and he went out there for about an hour following the meetings before he went to Villa Madama for a luncheon in his honor.

I went to my hotel room in the center of Rome before going out to Villa Taverna, where I had an office close by the President's quarters.

The next morning the President was to have an audience with Pope Paul VI, and most of the staff also went to the Vatican. I put on my black dress and a mantilla. When we got there, we went through room after room and finally reached the spot where we were told to wait until it was time to go in to see the Pope.

"But look here," the Monsignor said to me rather severely. "You do not have the proper attire. Your arms can be seen. Can you get something to cover your arms?"

I went out into the large room where many other members of our staff were standing, and where the Pope was going to come out and wave to them, and I asked one of the White House photographers if I could borrow his coat. I put it on and buttoned it so not much of the coat showed in front, but my arms were covered. Then I went back, and soon we were brought into the small throne room where the President and the Pope were conferring. The President asked us to line up, and he introduced each of us to the Pope as we filed by. The Pope shook hands with each of us and gave each of us a medal as a memento of our visit.

That afternoon we left by plane for Naples, where the President spoke, and then we went by motorcade to the Capodichino Airport. A little after seven P.M. we were airborne for home.

When we got back, the President gave cigarette lighters to everyone who accompanied him on the trip. On one side was engraved, "European trip of President Kennedy, June 1963," and on the other side was the Presidential seal.

One bright morning following our European trip, Pierre Salinger was in my office, chomping on his cigar, when Ralph Dungan came in. I looked out of the window and remarked, "The south lawn will look nice with deer on it."

Pierre exploded. "Don't tell me they are going to put deer out there!"

Ralph said, "Deer will never stay in that yard. They'll jump right over the fence."

Just then the President appeared, and caught a little of the conversation. "Why can't we have deer out there?" he demanded. "Call the Zoo. Find out whether it would be safe for them to be there."

I called the Zoo and found out that not only would the deer jump the fence, they would be so frightened by all the noise and activity on the lawn that they might well run head-on through the glass windows and french doors. When I told this to the President he decided against putting deer on the south lawn.

CHAPTER 34

Personal Tragedy

August 7th began just like any other day. The President's first appointment was with a citizens' committee to discuss the test ban treaty. A little later he had an appointment with Dr. Neftali Ponce-Miranda, Foreign Minister of Ecuador. He left at 11:37. I was sitting at my desk looking over the mail when Jerry Behn, the Secret Service agent in charge at the White House, and a very likable man, came through the door. There was a sense of urgency in his expression. He walked to my desk and said in a soft voice, "They called me from up at the Cape and told me that Mrs. Kennedy was on her way to the Otis Air Force Base Hospital." I looked at the clock. It was 11:40 A.M.

"Did she say she wanted the President to know?" I asked.

"No."

I telephoned Mary Gallagher, Mrs. Kennedy's secretary, who was up at the Cape, and one of the boys in the kitchen at the Kennedy house answered. He said Mary had gone with Mrs. Kennedy to Otis.

"Why did she go to Otis?" I asked.

"To have the baby, I guess."

At 11:45 the President came into my office and began to pick up things from my desk to read. I looked at Jerry. Jerry looked at me, and I said to the President, "Jerry tells me that Mrs. Kennedy is on her way to Otis."

"Get Dr. Walsh," he said immediately.

Dr. Walsh was Mrs. Kennedy's obstetrician, and was staying at the Cape to be near her at delivery time.

On second thought, the President said, "No, he will be with her. Call the house. See if she did leave."

I put in a call for Dr. Walsh, and also one to the house. The same boy answered again.

"Dr. Travell is here, maybe you can talk to her."

While she was coming to the phone one of the aides walked into the office and the President asked him to find out if there was a plane available and also whether helicopters were available.

At 11:46 the President talked to Dr. Travell, and she said she would check to see what was taking place. The President hung up and said, "We don't want to tell the press until we know something definite." He walked into his office and told Kenny O'Donnell what was happening. Kenny apparently misunderstood about not telling the press because he called the press office and told them the helicopters would be coming in five minutes. Then Pierre Salinger came in and wanted to know what hospital she was in.

Before I could tell him that the President did not want to give it to the press, Dr. Travell called and told the President that she learned Dr. Walsh was going to operate.

Then there was no doubt in his mind—he was going to Otis.

I asked the President if he wanted me to go along.

350

"Yes, see what happens. If need be, you can come back tomorrow."

I tried to get Abe, but his secretary said he was out to lunch. At 11:52 I dashed out the door to get on the helicopter, and one minute later we took off for Andrews Air Force Base. At 12:03 we arrived at Andrews, boarded a Jet Star, and in seven minutes were airborne.

We all sat in silence as we flew northward. Aboard were the President, Pierre Salinger, Kenny O'Donnell, General McHugh, an Air Force Officer, Jerry Behn, another Secret Service agent, and myself. When we landed at Otis Air Force Base, I looked at the clock—1:25. We went immediately by motorcade to the hospital.

As I walked down the hall, Mary Gallagher came to me and said that a boy, four pounds and ten and a half ounces, had been born. The President came down the hall behind Mrs. Kennedy, who was being brought to her room. I looked at him and said, "Congratulations, Mr. President." He beamed and nodded and went into the room with Mrs. Kennedy.

I went with Mary into a sitting room where they served us lunch. I couldn't understand why everyone was still waiting around. They had said Mrs. Kennedy was doing very well, and the baby, though premature, seemed to be all right. The telephone kept ringing. People wanted to be reassured that Mrs. Kennedy and the baby were all right. At 3:30 P.M. I answered a call from Dr. Hefernan who told me that Dr. Rorbaugh from Children's Hospital in Boston was at the Boston airport. I went out to the main entrance of the hospital, where the President was sitting, and told him about Dr. Rorbaugh.

"When did you get that message?"

"Just now."

Then he asked for Ensign George Dalton, a capable young man who handled all of the communications for the President and Mrs. Kennedy while they were at the Cape or Palm Beach. He could get a message to either one of them at a moment's notice, and I later learned that it was through his alertness that Mrs. Kennedy arrived at the Otis Base Hospital so quickly. The President asked Ensign Dalton to get a helicopter to Logan Airport in Boston to pick up the doctor and bring him to Otis. The President later wrote him a letter thanking him for all he had done.

After the doctor arrived and consulted with Dr. Walsh, they decided that it would be best to take the baby to Children's Hospital in Boston, since he had a respiratory problem. While little Patrick Bouvier Kennedy, named for the President's grandfather, was taken by ambulance to Boston, the President went to the house on Squaw Island.

Later that evening we flew to Boston and went by motorcade to the hospital. We learned the baby had made the trip well and seemed to be getting along all right, but they would not know for sure until morning. That night we stayed at the Ritz-Carlton Hotel and in the morning went to the hospital again. The President stayed for about twenty minutes. The baby's condition seemed the same.

We flew by helicopter back to Otis, and the President went directly to Mrs. Kennedy's room. I spent my time answering the phones in one of the back rooms. We flew to Squaw Island, but before I could even put my briefcase down in my little office near the Kennedy house, the plans were switched suddenly. He was going back to Boston to the hospital, where little Patrick was fighting for his life.

The President stayed at the hospital almost two hours. They moved the baby to a special room where the air pressure could be reduced to see if that would alleviate his breathing problem. The President called Dr. Levine from New York, a noted heart specialist, and General McHugh sent a Jet Star to bring him to Boston.

I was sitting in my room at the hotel that afternoon, just staring into space, when the telephone rang. It was the President.

"Where are you?"

"In my room, down the hall from you."

"Do you have some of my personal paper with you?"

"Yes."

"Will you bring some down here to me?"

When I got to his room I knocked, and George Thomas, his valet, opened the door.

"He's expecting you; go right in."

There sat the President on the bed, without his coat, but otherwise fully dressed. He was staring into space. I thought to myself, this man is really suffering. I waited silently for a full minute, and then he stood up. As I handed the stationery to him, I asked, "How are things with little Patrick?"

"He has a fifty-fifty chance."

"That's all a Kennedy needs. He will make it."

He asked me to wait while he wrote a little note, and then he put it in an envelope, addressed the envelope, and told me to give it to one of the Secret Service agents to deliver. I didn't look at the envelope but handed it to one of the agents and went back to my room.

Weeks later I learned whom he had written to. The New York office telephoned me at the White House and said the bank in which the President kept his money had called and questioned one of the checks. They couldn't make out the signature. It was made out to the "O'Leary Fund." Suddenly I remembered. About the first of August one of the policemen in Boston had been killed defending himself, and a fund was being collected for his family. The policeman's name was O'Leary. I said, "Tell the bank that the check and the signature are authentic."

I don't know whether anyone was able to read the little note the President wrote with the check, but I am sure he didn't care about that. He was concerned only with the welfare of this family—at a time when his own heart was deeply troubled.

We made another trip to the hospital at nine o'clock that night, and I learned then that the Attorney General was on his way to Boston to be with the President. I was relieved to hear this. The President—followed everywhere by a large entourage of newspapermen and surrounded by the silent sympathy of crowds gathered around the hospital and hotel—had seemed completely alone.

I was awakened in the early hours after midnight with word that the President was back at the hospital and little Patrick was not expected to live. Shortly afterward, at 4:04 A.M., he died, and I was called again and told the news.

We drove to Children's Hospital the next morning, and the President thanked the nurses and doctors for everything they had done, and also made final arrangements concerning little Patrick. Then we flew back to Otis, where he visited Mrs. Kennedy for a little while, and then we went by helicopter to Squaw Island.

I had been carrying some important papers sent from the New York office for him to sign, and he silently signed them as I handed them to him one by one.

The funeral was set for Saturday morning, August 10th, at Holyhood Cemetery. Because it was a private funeral and the President no longer needed me, I went back to Washington Saturday afternoon.

Looking back on this incident, I am convinced this was one of the hardest blows the President experienced during the entire time I was with him. I think he looked at this little boy and wished with all his heart there was some way to give him a chance to live. The little fellow didn't have a chance, despite the best medical care in the world. It wasn't so much grief for his own son, but for a potential that would never be realized.

The President's only concern at this time was the welfare of Mrs. Kennedy. He made many visits to the hospital during the weekend, and he remained near her until Monday afternoon. Things had piled up so at the office that on his first day back we didn't finish until after eight o'clock.

During the next couple of weeks, the President flew to the Cape several times each week to be with Mrs. Kennedy. Each time he wanted to take her something that would let her know he had been thinking about her and to share with her something of his life in Washington. Sometimes he would ask that a bouquet of flowers be gathered from those blooming in his garden or on the White House lawn. Then he had another idea.

When the President was in Ireland, several people had offered him gifts—two dogs, a pony, and some deer. He told the children about them, and they kept asking when they would be arriving. Now he thought it would be nice to have one or both of the dogs to take with him on the next visit to Mrs. Kennedy.

The first dog to arrive was a long-eared cocker spaniel. When the President looked at him, he turned to me and said, "Gad, he's sad-looking, don't you think?"

The next day he was on his way to the Cape, and Mrs. Kennedy.

Now that we had four dogs chasing each other around the south lawn, the President decided to get some dog food and feed them himself. For the next few days, whenever he had a free moment and the dogs were near his office, he went out on the portico and clapped his hands. But the dogs didn't know that he was the President, and they paid no attention to him. John-John came out and asked if he could feed them. The President said, "No, I'm going to feed them when they are over here." But the dogs were used to John, and they went to him instead of the President.

After several more tries, President Kennedy finally got three of the dogs into his office, and they began to eat out of his hand. A little later, he walked through my office on his way to the Mansion, the dogs right at his heels. He looked as pleased as a little boy that he had won them over. "And I didn't need to put them on a leash," he said, "to have them follow me."

CHAPTER 35

Caroline and John

The President didn't have to be reminded of his tenth wedding anniversary. When he opened the morning paper there were pictures of him and Mrs. Kennedy taken ten years before, together with recent pictures of them.

As soon as he stepped into the office he wanted me to get Klejman, an art dealer in New York, on the phone. He ordered something for Mrs. Kennedy. I didn't hear what it was, but he asked me to arrange for it to be in Washington in time for him to take with him when he went to her mother's home in Newport that afternoon. "You might also have the gardener fix another bouquet of flowers from the garden."

Then a little later he told me that he had called Wildenstein's Art Gallery and ordered some paintings and he wanted me to arrange for them to be in Newport that evening. The flower room said the bouquet would be ready by 5:30 in time for the President to take with him. Klejman's gift arrived during the afternoon, and the paintings from Wildenstein's were being sent to Newport to be picked up at the airport and delivered to Hammersmith Farm at the time the President arrived.

While Mrs. Kennedy was in Newport, the President took a conservation tour all the way from Pennsylvania to California. It was a wonderful trip, and we saw some gorgeous scenery. But more important to us was the reception the President received everywhere. These trips were like a tonic to the President. He was really a campaigner at heart, and he loved talking to people. Most of all, by getting out among the people he was given the assurance that they approved of what he was trying to do in Washington. He was particularly pleased that the test ban treaty he had worked so hard to achieve was getting a very favorable response.

Shortly thereafter, Mrs. Kennedy and her sister, Lee Radziwill, and Lee's husband, Prince Radziwill, left for a ten-day
cruise in the eastern Mediterranean aboard the yacht *Christina*.

While Mrs. Kennedy was away, Caroline and John came over
a couple of times a day to see their father. Sometimes they
would come around seven o'clock at night, already in their bath-
robes and ready for bed, to romp with their daddy before he
went to the pool. These were happy times for the President.

They would play around in my office until he opened the door
from his office and saw them. He always acted very surprised,
but he couldn't help knowing they were out there with the
squeaks and giggles they let out. He would say to John, "Hello
there, Sam, how are you?"

"I am not Sam, I'm John. Daddy, I'm John."

Sometimes he would say to Caroline, "Hello there, Mary."

"No, my name's Caroline," she would say very seriously. He
would sit in the rocking chair in my office, and they would climb
all over him. Then he would say, "I'll race you over to the pool."
Their little legs would start running before he even moved a
muscle. They always won, and then they went laughing on up
to bed.

For some time the President had been wanting a headstone
placed at the grave site of little Patrick. Richard Cardinal Cushing sent some designs to him, but he didn't care for any one of
them, and one day when he was standing at my desk, he said,
"Mrs. Lincoln, this is the kind of headstone I would like." He
took a piece of paper from my desk and drew the shape of the
stone he wanted. "Send this drawing up to them and tell them
to go ahead with this and I would like to have it on the grave
when I go up to Boston to speak at the Democratic fund-raising
dinner." This meant he wanted it there by October 19th.

To me, October 7th will always stand out as one of the greatest days in the President's administration. On that day he signed
the documents for ratification of the nuclear test ban treaty.
The signing was at ten o'clock in the Treaty Room of the White
House, and I asked him if I could be present when he signed it.

357

I walked along behind him when he went over to sign it. When he had finished and began shaking hands with the Senators and others present, I slipped out and returned to my office.

When he came back to the office he handed me a pen he had used and said, "Will you put this pen away with the other pens we are keeping. And, oh yes, I brought one for you." I knew he appreciated my wanting to see him sign that treaty, and he wanted to show it by giving me a pen that had made a stroke in history.

One morning he asked me to have someone go downtown and buy some little model airplanes to put in his bedroom so that he could give one to John when he came to visit in the mornings. "It doesn't have to be much of an airplane, just a little something because he enjoys receiving them." I gave the assignment to Muggsie, who came back with some fantastic airplanes. They turned, they tumbled, and some looked almost as if they could take off.

The President said they were just fine. "But don't you think I should have something to give Caroline when she comes in with John in the mornings? What about little horses?" So Muggsie went on another shopping spree.

Near the end of October the President went to Massachusetts to receive an honorary degree from Amherst College and speak at the ground-breaking ceremonies for the Robert Frost Memorial Library. When he returned, he flew directly to Atoka, Virginia, where Mrs. Kennedy and he were going to spend the weekend in their new home.

He came back to the office on Monday very anxious over the civil rights legislation. He worked for an hour and a half on it and finally came up with a compromise proposal he thought would pass the House.

Then he went into a meeting on the Algerian question that lasted for about half an hour. While he was in that meeting, Caroline and John came outside my door and tapped on the window. When I looked up, I saw two masks staring at me. I remembered that it would soon be Halloween, and I opened the

358

door and acted as though I were scared stiff. They whooped and hollered and laughed, thinking they had frightened me. Then they wanted to know where their daddy was. I told them he was in a meeting. "Do you think he will know who we are?" Caroline asked.

"He will never recognize you."

They jumped around my office, barely able to wait until he came out and saw them. He, too, acted scared and told them to go away. John pulled off his mask as if to say, "Look who it is," and the President said, "Why, it's Sam." John was so mad he put his mask back on. Then Caroline pulled hers off, and he went through the same thing with her.

Both of them pounced on him then. They wanted him to roll on the floor with them. He went into his office with both of them behind him. He called for the dogs and was going to feed them some dog candy he had asked me to keep in the office, but the dogs must have been penned up over in the flower room because they were nowhere to be found.

As world problems surrounded him, particularly the recent coup in Vietnam, the President seemed to find an antidote for the tension in Caroline's and John's visits.

On Veterans Day, November 11th, the President went to Arlington Cemetery to place a wreath on the Tomb of the Unknowns, and he took John with him. I felt he was going because he thought Abe would appreciate it. I had said to him earlier in the year that Abe was discouraged because some staff members said I was always wanting the President to do things for the Veterans Administration.

While the President placed the wreath on the Tomb, he left John and Agent Bob Foster in the car and told them he would be right back. Then he decided to go up to the speaker's platform and listen to the ceremony, so he sent word to Foster to bring John down in front of the Amphitheater. The next day the papers were full of pictures of little John and his daddy at Arlington Cemetery.

359

While they were riding back to the White House from the Cemetery, the President was in a playful mood, and every once in a while gave John a little nudge. One time John hit him back. The President said, "I'm going to tell Miss Shaw on you," and playfully hit John again. John replied to his father, "I'm going to tell Mrs. Lincoln on you."

CHAPTER 36

I Remember Him Waving

The Presidential election was a year away but already President Kennedy and various members of his staff were working on campaign strategy for the coming months. He decided to go on a southern trip this month, for a number of reasons.

There was increasing restlessness in the South over the civil rights issue, and the President felt the need to visit some of the Southern states and meet with the people, find out first-hand how they felt, and tell them how he felt.

The Republicans had held a meeting in Charleston, South Carolina, and expressed optimism about carrying several Southern states in the next election. He wanted to test the accuracy of this. Finally, the cattle growers were angry about the increase of imports, and he wanted to explain that the real problem was due to their overproduction.

He scheduled a visit to Florida; he was to visit Tampa and then go on to Miami the night of November 18th.

Immediately after the trip to Florida, he scheduled a trip to Texas, where he would speak in Fort Worth, Dallas, and Austin, and Houston, and also visit the LBJ Ranch. Mrs. Kennedy was also going on this trip.

In visiting Texas, the President hoped to win greater support in this state, in which the Kennedy-Johnson ticket was barely victorious in 1960. Also, he hoped to patch a bitter internal dispute among Texas Democrats, who had begun to insult each other. Bitterness developed even over this trip. Some Texas Democrats did not want Senator Ralph Yarborough to sit on the platform with the President, but the President said the Senator had gone down the line with him on legislation and he had earned the right to be with him; he insisted that the Senator ride in the motorcade and be with him on the platform.

As plans progressed for the trips, the President carried on his daily work at the White House. My aunt from Nebraska, Mrs. Nettie Carlson, was visiting us and I arranged for her to attend a performance of The Black Watch (Royal Highland Regiment) on the south lawn one afternoon.

It was a brisk, cool day, but the invited guests, mostly children, began to arrive at 3:30 P.M. When my aunt arrived, I took her to a seat near the front and then rushed back to the office since I had gone out without a coat. Soon I could hear the music and the President's voice. He and Mrs. Kennedy and Caroline and John had watched it from the balcony. Caroline was seated on the arm of her daddy's chair, and she had her arm around him.

That afternoon after everyone had gone from our part of the West Wing of the White House, Miss Shaw brought the children over to the office for another romp with the President before they went to bed. He played with them on the floor and as he was lying there with the two of them pouncing over him I said, "What would the people think if they saw the President down on the floor?" I guess I had the old-fashioned notion that Presidents were not human beings.

He looked at me and said, "After all, Mrs. Lincoln, I am also a father."

"There's no doubt about that."

After they had romped and played a while the President went back into his office, and Miss Shaw, the children, and I went out on the steps leading to the garden. John was running around chasing Shannon, the Irish dog, and Caroline looked up in the sky and saw a star.

"Star light, star bright," she said.

I suddenly felt the President standing beside me. He wasn't saying a thing, just looking up in the sky.

"Star bright, star light," Caroline again.

"First star I've seen tonight," I prompted, and she repeated it after me.

"Up above the world so high," the President said, and she repeated it after him.

Finally he said to Caroline, "Why don't you go over and say that to Mommy?" And then he slowly walked away.

I said goodnight to the children and went into my office. I had the strangest feeling. I couldn't explain it—eerie, like a warning. I shook my head and thought to myself, once you get out in the air and get away from here it will go away. But it stayed with me for quite a while.

The next afternoon he went to Elkton, Maryland, to participate in the dedication of a new turnpike in Delaware and Maryland.

Before we left he had a number of conversations with a friend about getting a fur coverlet for Mrs. Kennedy's Christmas present and arrangements were made for it. In making his selection of the gift, he had had samples of fur in the office. He had looked at them and decided that none of them would do. He had me call various people to find out what they thought, and as a last resort he called a friend of theirs, Mrs. John Kelly, of New York, and left the whole thing in her hands. It was all arranged, and would be delivered in time for Christmas.

It was fortunate the President wore a coat when he took off for Elkton, for it was damp and rainy. We used helicopters to get over there, and it was so cold and muddy I stayed right in the chopper and watched the ceremonies from the window. I noticed that one of the placards someone was carrying read, "We are proud of your work in behalf of retarded children." I knew the President would be glad to see that.

From Elkton we went on to New York, where the President addressed the Fifth Constitutional Convention of the AFL-CIO at the Americana Hotel. He also spoke at the National Convention of the Catholic Youth Organization, and then we left for Palm Beach.

Abe had gone down ahead of me and was already in our suite at the Palm Beach Towers when we arrived. That was a beautiful weekend, and we enjoyed every minute of it. The President called me many times during the weekend, and every time he sounded as though he was really enjoying the sunshine. He had brought his old friend and roommate, Congressman Torby Macdonald, with him.

Monday morning Abe went back to Washington, and I went with the President to Tampa, where he was to make three speeches before going to Miami to speak at an Inter-American Press Association dinner. It was another gorgeous day, and the President had never looked better. He had a sun tan and seemed to be glowing with good health and confidence.

As he stood in the stadium in Tampa, his clear voice coming over the loud speakers, I couldn't help but think, never has he been in such good health and now he has complete grasp of the Presidency.

The dinner in Miami was a huge affair. The ballroom was beautifully decorated with all sorts of fruit, and exotic flowers, and red and gold banners floated in the air above the speaker's table.

We had arranged with the Secret Service that we would step out the side door and get into the motorcade cars when the dinner was just about over. It was fortunate for us we made the arrangements. The President was in such a hurry to leave that Congressman Macdonald never made it to the motorcade and had to get a later plane to Washington.

I was at my desk the next morning, and as usual the President called over and wanted to know when and with whom he had his first appointment.

When he came over to the office he came out to my desk,

went through the mail, read some of the papers, and then turned and went into his office. He rang the buzzer on the other side and his first visitor was ushered in. After his visitor left he came out into my office again and wanted to know where the staff members who went with him on the trip were.

"They are not coming in today," I said. "They are tired."

"Why couldn't they make it? We're here."

Senator Everett Dirksen came that morning with a group to present a Thanksgiving turkey to the President. The presentation was to be made in the garden, and the poor bedraggled turkey was on the table when the President walked out. He felt so sorry for the turkey he said he didn't want to kill it for his Thanksgiving, and he gave it away. But before they took it away he called the nursery school class, down under the trees playing, to come and take a look at the gobbler.

The rest of the day was extremely pleasant. He had very few appointments, and the ones he did have, he took in stride. As I look back on this day, I believe that he was as relaxed as I had ever seen him. He seemed to enjoy thoroughly being "Mr. President." He didn't leave the office until almost eight o'clock.

I sent some memos on ideas for the campaign and the convention to his bedroom for him to read before going to bed.

As I typed up his schedule for the next day, I could see it was going to be a busy one. To top it off, he was having the Judicial reception that night.

I was going to take my aunt to this reception. I wanted her to attend one White House social function, and I wanted her to meet the President.

When she arrived I put her in the Cabinet room until the President came out. I asked him to please wait a minute before going over to the reception because I wanted my aunt to meet him.

"Fine."

When I brought her into my office, he shook hands with her and invited her into his office.

"How about a picture?" he suggested.

364

I had asked a White House photographer to stay around, and called him in. The President stood beside my aunt and then asked me to stand with them so all three of us would be in the picture. Then he decided he wanted to make a telephone call, and my aunt went out in the hall to wait. When I got the party on the telephone, the President came out to my desk to take the call. As he looked out into the hall, he saw my aunt and waved at her.

Finally he went over to the Mansion, and my aunt and I followed soon behind him. While I was there, Mrs. Kennedy, who had been resting at Atoka in preparation for the next day's trip to Texas, came down with the President, much to everyone's delight; there had been some doubt that she would attend.

All during the discussions about the Texas trip, Abe said to me repeatedly, "I think it would be better not to go to Texas."

On November 19th, as we were going over some last-minute reminders for the trip, I told the President about Abe's fear over his Texas trip. The President didn't seem alarmed, he merely said, as I had heard him say many times before, "If they are going to get me, they will get me even in church."

He never had any fear; he had confidence in the American people.

The day before takeoff, the President wanted to find out what the temperature would be in Texas. A note came over to me saying it would be cool down there, and I gave this information to the President.

The next morning the President seemed edgy when he came to the office.

"What is the temperature in Houston?"

I called the Air Force office, and they told me it was going to be warm. When I told this to the President, he became quite angry.

"Now where in heck did we get the report it was going to be cool?"

"Kenny gave me that information."

He was furious—he really raved and ranted. When Kenny

365

said the naval aide's office had given him the information, he picked up the telephone and asked the operator to give him that office. When the man on the other line, who incidentally had just reported for duty in that office that day, answered, the President lit into him.

This was all very unusual—first, his getting so angry and second, bawling out this Navy man.

The President called Provie, and told her about the weather, but it was too late to do much good because all of the bags had been packed and were on the way to the airplane.

After a little while the President calmed down and saw a couple of Ambassadors before the helicopters started to come onto the south lawn to pick us up to go to Andrews Air Force Base. I had all my things packed and ready. A couple of days earlier the usher's office had asked if they could put the new rugs and new draperies in while we were in Texas, and the President and I were looking forward to coming back to newly decorated offices.

Helicopter number three came onto the south lawn, and the ones who were going on that one went out and boarded. Soon it was flying south. Then the other two helicopters came in. That meant it was time for me to get moving. I checked his desk again, checked the safes, and looked around to make sure that I had everything. I remembered to take my Polaroid along.

I was going on the same helicopter as the President. Miss Shaw and John were already aboard when I got there. John was sitting in the big chair opposite the one usually occupied by the President, and Miss Shaw was sitting on a seat along the side. Little John had on a raincoat and rain hat and was very proud to be sitting in a big seat.

Soon his daddy appeared and took a seat opposite John. Mrs. Kennedy hadn't come down yet. The President kicked John's foot, teasing him. John said, "Don't, Daddy." They sat a little longer. The President kicked his foot again and again John said, in a sterner voice, "Don't, Daddy." In about ten minutes Mrs. Kennedy came onto the helicopter and soon we were on our way to the airport. Caroline was still in her school, and didn't make the trip. John and Miss Shaw said goodbye and returned to the White House.

We all entered *Air Force One* and were soon settled down for the flight to Texas. A number of Texas Congressmen were aboard, and every time I went into the cabin with letters for the President, the Congressmen were talking politics with him. Mrs. Kennedy was back in her bedroom.

Everything seemed the same as in every other city we had ever visited when we arrived in Houston and rode along in the motorcade. Everyone appeared happy that the President had come.

I had some work to do that evening, and so I did not go to the Albert Thomas Testimonial dinner, honoring the veteran Congressman from Houston. Mary Gallagher, who had come along to be with Mrs. Kennedy, and I went down to the dining room for dinner.

We spent the night in Fort Worth and in the morning were going to Dallas, where the President was to speak at the Trade Mart.

Before I went to Texas I wrote my sister-in-law's sister, Mrs. Jo Ingram, who lived in Dallas, and asked her to come over to Fort Worth on the morning of the 22nd to have breakfast with me in the hotel room. She replied that she was bringing her cousin and her cousin's daughter with her. I arranged for the dining room to send up three extra breakfasts at a certain time that morning. They arrived, and after we had breakfast I told them the President was just down the hall and would soon be walking by. If we were out in the hall, he would shake hands with them.

I had asked the Secret Service agent to let me know when the President was ready to leave his bedroom, and we rushed out in front of my bedroom to await him. He came down the hall in a dark blue suit, striding along as if he was glad to be alive. When he saw me, he stopped, and I introduced him to the three ladies. He said he was delighted to meet them, then turned to me and said, "Are they some more of your relatives?" I laughed and said, "Relatives of relatives." He turned and walked to the elevator that was waiting to take him down. As he turned into the elevator he waved at us.

We rushed to the window. He was going out in front of the hotel to meet a group waiting for him there. They had been standing for three hours waiting to see him. It was dark and cloudy and looked as if it were going to rain all day.

He looked happy down there in the crowd, and people were pushing around him from all sides. Just then Mary came into the room and said we should be getting out to the airplane. She wanted to make sure she was aboard before Mrs. Kennedy arrived. We said goodbye to the ladies from Dallas and went down to get into a car with Muggsie, Joe Giordano, and "Boots" Miller. They had arranged for a police escort because all of the Kennedys' personal luggage was following us. Once again these responsible men were getting the things to their destination on time.

We were settled on the plane when we heard a commotion and the motorcade with the President and Mrs. Kennedy arrived. People lined up four deep around the fence, and they were shaking hands with everyone they could reach. I noticed that Mrs. Kennedy was wearing a lovely pink suit. I got out my camera and went up front to take pictures of them walking along the fence. When they started toward the airplane, I rushed back to my seat.

It was raining when we left Fort Worth. The flight to Dallas was only fifteen minutes long; it hardly seemed necessary to unfasten our seat belts after takeoff. But I had some memos I had typed the night before that I wanted the President to sign, and I went back into the cabin to see what the prospects were of getting him to sign them.

On the other side of the table from where I was sitting, the girls from the press office were busy getting ready to type the speech the President was going to give in Austin later that afternoon.

The plane was full of Texans wandering up and down the aisle discussing various aspects of the trip.

When I walked into the cabin, several of them were talking to the President. He was sitting in his usual seat, his right hand gripping the arm of the chair as though it were holding him back, and his left hand was on the desk, his fingers flipping through a writing pad lying there.

When I entered I caught some remarks about how enthusiastic the crowds were. "I didn't think I'd get such a fine reception," he said.

When he saw me holding the papers, he reached out to take them without interrupting his conversation, which had now turned to newspaper articles, especially the full-page ad that appeared in one of the Texas papers that morning. That ad had been filled with hate and venom. As they discussed it, I began to wonder about what Abe had said.

I got that strange, unexplainable feeling again. I looked at the President. He was slightly nervous, but then he was always that way when he had work to do. I gave him a pen and he started to sign the memos, but I noticed that he did not read them—he was too engrossed in the conversation.

I tried to look around to see if I could find the article, but he had finished and had laid down the pen. He motioned for me to pick up the memos. As I did, I said to him, "Thank you, Mr. President."

"Fine, Mrs. Lincoln."

I left them talking in the cabin and went out to my seat. I put the memos in my briefcase so I would have them when I got back to Washington.

Mary Gallagher had been in the bedroom compartment helping Mrs. Kennedy during the flight; just before we were to land, she came out and sat down beside me. I looked out the window and said, "Look, Mary, the sun is shining, and it looks like it is going to be warm. I don't believe I'll need my coat."

It occurred to me that the bubble top on the limousine wouldn't be necessary. I knew the President would love that;

he always wanted to get as close to the people as he could. I knew he disliked being cooped up and would much prefer to wave to the crowds in the Dallas streets.

It was time for us to get off the plane and get in our car to go in the motorcade. I turned as we walked along, and I saw that the President and Mrs. Kennedy were shaking hands with the local officials who had come out to greet them, and were slowly moving toward their car. There was a huge crowd at the airport, and it took several minutes for the cars to get moving because of the people pressed up against the President's car. Mrs. Kennedy was carrying a bouquet of red roses that had been presented to her when they arrived. As I got into the car, I looked over to the President's car, which had started to move. There was the President, his right hand in the air, waving at the people as he drove by. I can still see that scene—the President waving as he passed that vast and friendly crowd of people. And I'll always remember him that way because that's the way he really was: a handsome, young, energetic President who had grace and intellect, a man who loved every inch of his country, especially its people.

For many weeks my life resembled that of a sunflower in darkness. The source of energy and direction gone, I could only stand aimless and bewildered.

Gradually, I began to think of him, in the way I believe he would want to be remembered, as someone living in history.

Where was his proper place? And what had we all lost? I remembered a book of poems my husband gave me once. It was called *America Was Promises*. Some of America's promises to the world have long ago been fulfilled. Some are yet to be. John F. Kennedy, too, was promises. He was a promise that all of us might lead a better life in peace. He was a promise that excitement and courage must be kept central in our lives. He was a promise that we could expect more from ourselves, and that we were better than we knew.

I thought, too, of how he worked during all those years traveling no one knows how many millions of miles, often in pain, undiscouraged by religious prejudice and countless enemies who fought against him in the open or struck at him from behind. I thought of his rise from "the kid Congressman" to Senator and President, and his steady growth in character and strength and wisdom. I thought of his hunger for knowledge, and of the way he consumed books by the armload. And all to no end, other than to be struck down on the street by a maniac.

Or was there an end? When friend and foe are reminded through grief of their common humanity, when a nation suddenly recoils in horror and sees the dark side of its nature, when we all suddenly see by its tragic loss that we had possessed a treasure, when we share and know that we share a space empty of a certain smile and flash of wit, a certain drive and determination, a certain boyish, half-shy courage, a certain way of making life yield twice as much fruit, can anyone say there is no greater end?

He said, "Let us begin." He was a man for beginnings. From his mind and heart, I think we will find, has come the beginning of peace and the turning aside from what was sure to lead to war. We are beginning to find the beginnings of making some of America's too-long-delayed promises come true: a land where children are educated as they deserve to be, where the older generation is not forgotten and neglected, where skin color may be no more important than eye color, and where idle hands are seen as the worst kind of waste.

Everyone remembers his rocking chair. But I think of his black briefcase, battered and always full of papers. It is the better symbol for him. It suggests the kind of man who found his happiness through, as he once said, "full use of your powers along lines of excellence."

That's what he did. And, doing so, he reminded us that the greatest of the promises of America is that here all of us should have the right to do the same.